ELEMENTS OF HOTEL ACCOUNTANCY

Neeraj K. Gupta

Post Graduation in Commerce, Ch.C.C University, Meerut

Post Graduation in Economics, Ch.C.C University, Meerut

Post Graduation Diploma in Hospitality Management (Hotel, Catering and Tourism)

Diploma in Hospitality Management from Educational Institute of American Hotel and Motel Association, USA.

Mater of Business Administration in Finance (MBA) from Sardar Vallabh Bhai Patel University, Meerut.

M.Phi. (Managementfrom Vinayak Mission University, Tamil Nadu.

Presently working as a Asst. Prof. in J.P. Institute of Hotel Management and Catering Technology, Meerut.

ELEMENTS
OF
HOTEL ACCOUNTANCY

By

G.S. RAWAT, M.Com, L.T.
Formerly Special Lecturer in Hotel Accountancy
Institute of Hotel Management, Catering & Nutrition
Pusa, New Delhi-110012

J.S.M. NEGI, M.COM., Ph.D., FHCIMA (London)
Senior Faculty Incharge and Head of the Department
Institute of Hotel Management
Pusa, New Delhi-110012

NEERAJ K. GUPTA, M.B.A. (Finance)
Presently Working as a Lecturer in
J.P. Institute of Hotel Management, Catering Technology
Meerut

AMAN PUBLICATIONS
NEW DELHI

Published by
Rajiv Jain for Aman Publications
LG-4A, Ganpati Bhawan,
4675-B/21, Ansari Road,
Darya Ganj, Delhi - 110002
PH: 23255012, 23282127
E-mail: sshjbs@yahoo.com

1st edition 1972
2nd reprint edition 1977
3rd reprint edition 1979
4th reprint edition 1984
5th reprint edition 1994
6th revised edition 2005
7th revised edition 2010
8th revised edition 2012
Reprint 2023

ISBN–81–8204–063-9
978-81-8204-063-2

SOLE DISTRIBUTOR
JINDAL BOOK SERVICES
LG-4A, Ganpati Bhawan,
4675-B/21, Ansari Road,
Darya Ganj, Delhi - 110002

Printed by:
Tarun Offset, Delhi, India

PREFACE TO THE EIGHTEENTH EDITION

It is now 38 years since the publication of the first edition *Element of Hotel Accountancy*. The present eighth revised edition has been considerably enlarged and up-dated in two parts and made relevant to meet the needs of the students of hotel management courses. *Part I* contains Accounting Terminology, Book-Keeping and Accountancy, Accounting Principles, Double Entry System, Journal, Ledger, Cash-book, Subsidiary Books, Trial Balance, Bank Reconciliation Statement, Capital Expenditure, Final Accounts, Depreciation. *Part II* contains 34 chapters on various aspects on hotel accountancy. Chapters XV, XIX, XXI, XX, XXIX, XXXI have been thoroughly revised. An additional topic entitled 'Computer in Hotels' has been included firstly to make the book more competent in terms of its coverage and relevance to the hotel and catering operations, and secondly, in view of the revised syllabus content of various institutes, colleges and universities.

I am happy to put forward the seventh revised and enlarged edition of the book in the hands of my readers both teachers and students. The encouraging response to the previous editions has given confidence and encouragement and opportunity has been taken to make revision in the subject matter wherever necessary.

The present volume contains chapters has enjoyed a great deal of popularity for over three decades. It has been found useful by the students preparing for the examination in Hotel Management.

I am thankful to a large number of readers who have expressed their appreciation of the book and have taken pain to send their suggestions. I am anxious to know the readers' reactions to the work and shall be grateful if they respond constructively.

I express my sincere thanks to Shri Rajiv Jain, M/s Aman Publications, New Delhi, who has taken all the pains to bring out this edition in the present form.

CONTENTS

PART I

CHAPTER I

ACCOUNTING TERMINOLOGY

Accounting Equation The total assets of a business are always equal to the aggregate of its liabilities and capital.

Total Assets = Total Liabilities + Capital

Allowance Journal A journal used to recoped allowance vouchers when a sale is dicounted.

Assets The properties owned by a business firm are called assets. They are tangible or intangible things having value expressible in money, which are owned by business. Assets are that expenditure which results in the acquiring of some property or benefit of a lasting nature. Suppose if a firm pays for land or building or machinery.

Auditing It is that branch of accounting, which examines a firm's financial statement and internal controls for the purpose of expressing opinions regarding the financial statement.

Business Business is an economic activity. It may be defined as "The regular production or purchase and sale of goods undertaken with object of earning profit through the satisfaction of human wants". It also includes the performance of service for others on payment. The person who runs a business is called a businessman.

Capital It is the amount invested by the owner in the business. It includes profits of the business, to the extent they are not withdrawn by the owner.

Capital = Assets – Liabilities.

City Ledger A subsidiary ledger with are prepared at the end of an accounting period to close the temporary proprietorship accounts into permanent

Closing Stock Goods which is lying unsold on a particular date, is called closing stock. Stock may be opening and closing. Goods lying unsold in the beginning of the accounting year is called opening stock. Closing stock includes goods lying unsold at the end of the accounting year.

Creditors A person to whom something owes is called a creditor. 'Cr.' is the abbreviation of creditor.

Current Assets Assets which are meant to convert into cash with in a period of one accounting year or during the normal operating cycle. For example, stock of goods, bank balance, amount due to customers etc.

Current Liabilities Such obligations, which are normally paid with in a period of one accounting year, are called current liabilities. For example, short term loan, bank overdraft bill payables etc.

Debtors A person who owes an amount to somebody is called a debtor. 'Dr.' is the abbreviation of debtor.

Discount When businessman allows any type of concession in the prices of goods to customers is called discount.

Drawings An amount or goods withdrawn by the proprietor for his personal use is called drawings.

Fixed Assets An asset. which is required only for use and not for resale is called fixed assets. These can be tangible assets like land, building, furniture, machinery etc. or intangible assets like goodwill, patents, etc.

Insolvent A person is called insolvent when his liabilities exceeds his assets.

Liabilities They are the amount due by the business firm to others. In other words of Finny and Miller liabilities are debts, they are amount owed to creditors.

Long-term Liabilities Liabilities which do not become due for payment in one year, are called long term liabilities. These are payable after a long term. For example, debentures and long term loans.

Net Worth It is the excess of total assets over total liabilities of a business to outsiders. Net worth is the amount payable from the owners of the business.

Owner One who owns the business is called the owner or the proprietor. He arranges the required capital, attends to business activities, undertakes the risk of running the business and is entitled to get the profit and liable to bear the losses resulting they're from.

Profession It is a practice of intellectual skill by person in a definite field requiring specialized training on the part of the person engaged in it, in that field e.g., an accountant, a doctor etc.

Purchase Return Goods return to the seller being in excess of the quantity or found to be defective or for any other dispute are called purchase return.

Purchases It generally refers to purchase/ acquisition of goods for sale. Goods purchased on cash are called cash purchase and purchase without payment at the time of purchase are called credit purchase.

Sales Return Goods returned by the customer due to some defects.

Sales Sales is the sale of goods to customers if in cash then cash sale and if on credit the credit sale.

Solvent A person is said to be solvent when his assets exceeds Or equal his liabilities.

Voucher It is the written document and evidence of transaction.

CHAPTER II

BOOK-KEEPING AND ACCOUNTANCY

BOOK KEEPING

Book keeping is mainly concerned with recording of financial transactions of a business in a significant and orderly manner, so that information on any point in relation to them may be obtained. It is the science and art of correctly recording in book of account all business transactions that results in transfer of money or money's worth. Book keeping provide the base for the work of accounting. Bookkeeping is mechanical and repetitive. The junior employee of the account section of a business does the work of Bookkeeping.

According to R.N. Carter "Book keeping is the science and art of correctly recording in books of account all those business transactions that result in the transfer of money or money's worth."

According to Northcott "Bookkeeping is an art of recording in books of account the monetary aspect of commercial or financial transactions."

ACCOUNTING

Accounting has often been called the 'language of business', because a firm communicates with the outside world through accounting statement. If a firm does not prepare financial statement, no one can understand the affairs of the firm. Accounting is a disciple which record, classify, summarises and interprets financial information of a business, so that intelligent decisions can be made.

A committee of the *American Institute of Certified Public Accountants* has defined accounting as follows:

> "Accounting is the art of recording, classifying and summarizing in a significant manner and in terms of money, transactions and events, which are, in part at least of financial character and interpreting the results thereof."

According to *American Accounting Association*:

> "The process of identifying measuring and communicating economic information to permit informed judgments and decisions by users of the information".

ATTRIBUTES OF ACCOUNTING

From the above, the following attributes of accounting emerge:

1. ACCOUNTING IS AN ART

Accounting is an art, which helps the user in attaining the objectives of ascertaining the financial result, analysis and interpretation of financial data. The art of accounting requires special knowledge, experience and judgments.

2. IT INVOLVES RECORDING, CLASSIFYING AND SUMMARISING

In accounting, business transactions are recorded by their nature. Recording means systematically writing down the transactions in the books of account. After that, these events and transactions are classified by opening account in the form of ledger. Classification is a process of grouping transactions of one nature at one place. Lastly, all recorded and classified information is summarized by preparation of final account.

3. IT RECORDS TRANSACTIONS AND EVENTS IN MONETARY TERMS

If there are certain events or transactions, which cannot be measured in terms of money, they will not be recorded in the book of account.

4. TRANSACTION AND EVENTS, ONLY OF FINANCIAL NATURE ARE RECORDED

If a transaction has no financial character, it cannot be measured in terms of money and will not be recorded in books of account.

5. INTERPRETING THE RESULT OF ACCOUNTS

Accounting information can be interpreted by the use of various techniques like: ratio analysis, etc.

ACCOUNTING PROCESS

Identifying financial transaction

↓

Measuring them in terms of money

↓

Recording the transactions

↓

Classifying the transactions

↓

Summarizing

↓

Analysis and interpreting the results

OBJECTIVES OF ACCOUNTING

1. Accounting is done to keep a systematic and permanent record of all financial transactions of the business.
2. The chief objective of accounting is to know the result of the activities in a given period usually a year, i.e., to show how much profit has been earned or how much loss has been incurred. This is done by keeping a record of incomes and expenses of a particular time period.
3. It helps in ascertaining the financial position of the business. For this purpose a statement listing assets,

liabilities and owners capital is prepared, which is called balance sheet. Balance sheet shows the value of firms possessions and the amount the firm is owing to others.

4. It helps in seeing to it that there is no unauthorized use of firm's assets and property because proper records are maintained.
5. Accounting helps in making decision concerning the acquisition, use and preservation of scarce resources.
6. It communicates the result of the business or other information to different categories of person as investor, bank, creditors, etc.
7. If accounts are maintained properly, they provide information for meeting various legal requirements as income tax return etc.
8. If accounts are maintained properly and systematically, they can be treated by the court as good evidence.
9. Proper accounting record helps business to compare one years result with those of other year and locate significant factors leading to the changes.

BRANCHES OF ACCOUNTING

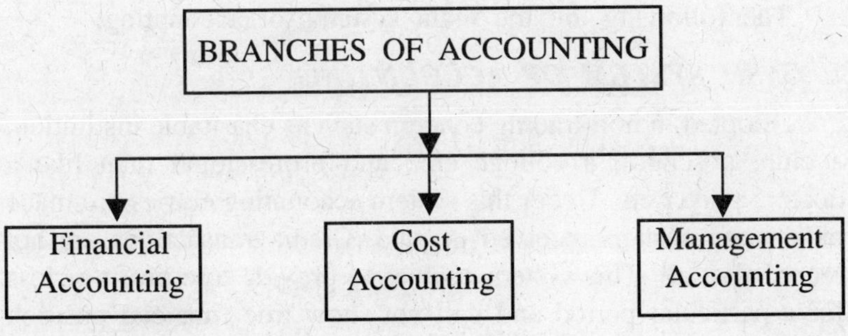

FINANCIAL ACCOUNTING

Financial accounting is concerned with recording and processing all business transaction and events in the book of account, which affect the financial position of the firm. It includes ascertainments of profit earned and loss incurred and position of the business at the end of accounting year. It provides required financial information to the manager. It helps the management to exercise full control over the assets of the business firm and to prepare return and statements concerning taxation.

COST ACCOUNTING

Cost accounting helps in ascertaining the cost of each product produce by the firm. Simply it relates to collection, classification, ascertainment of cost and its accounting. It also helps in cost control relating to various elements of cost. It is basically involved estimating the cost in advance and detailed analysis.

MANAGEMENT ACCOUNTING

It draws both on financial accounting and cost accounting. It is primarily concerned with the supply of the information that is useful to the management in decision making for the successful running of the business. It enables the management to perform its function properly, mainly in respect of forecasting and budgeting, controlling over cost and revenue, both routine and strategic.

SYSTEM OF ACCOUNTING

The following are the main systems of accounting:

1. *CASH SYSTEM OF ACCOUNTING*

Adopted in non-trading concern such as charitable institution, a club, a school, a college etc., and professional man like a doctor, a layer etc. Under this system accounting entries are made only when cash is received or paid. Credit transactions are not recorded at all. This system enables to provide true profit or loss for a particular period and will not show true financial position of the business on a particular day.

2. MERCANTILE/ACCRUAL SYSTEM OF ACCOUNTING

In this system all events and transaction of a business relation of a period are written in the books of account. In addition to the actual receipt and payment of cash, income receivable and expenses payable are also recorded in the books. This system provides a complete picture of the firm. It shows correct profit or loss for the particular period and will also show the true financial position of the business on a particular day.

ACCOUNTING INFORMATION

Users of accounting information: Accounting is called the language of the business as it provides information to different categories of person in time so that appropriate decision may be taken at the right time.

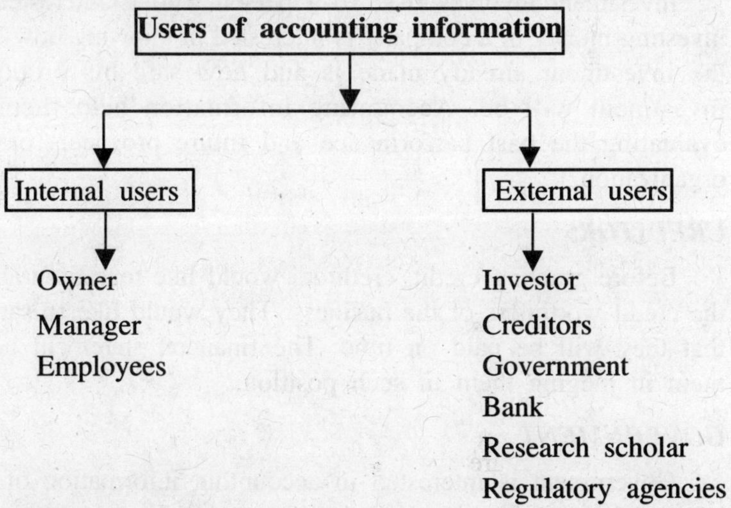

INTERNAL USERS

OWNER

They provide capital to the business. They are interested in knowing the profitability of the business and financial position of the business. For this purpose they needed accounting information.

MANAGER.

The managers of business are concerned with the accounting information because it is they, who are answerable to the owner.

Accounting information helps them in making various business decisions.

EMPLOYEES

They are interested in accounting information on account because their wages increment and payment of bonus depends on the size of the profit earned. They want to know whether their dues like provident funds are being deposited regularly.

EXTERNAL USERS

INVESTORS

Investment involves risk, so a person who is interested in investing money in a company is interested in knowing how safe the investment already made is and how safe his proposed investment will be. Accounting information help them in evaluating the past performance and future prospects of the organization.

CREDITORS

Before granting credit, creditors would like to satisfy about the credit worthness of the business. They would like to satisfy that they will be paid on time. The financial statement helps them in judging them in such position.

GOVERNMENT

Government is interested in accounting information of the business because it want to know earning and sales for a particular time period for the purpose of taxation. It also needs accounting information on account of labour and corporate law.

BANK

Bank and other lending institutions depend upon accounting statement for determining the acceptability of a loan application.

RESEARCH SCHOLAR

Accounting information helps a research scholar who wants to make a study in the financial operation of a firm.

REGULATION AUTHORITY

Various government departments and agencies like company law board, Registrar of Companies use accounting information in evaluating how well various businesses are operating under regulation categories.

CHAPTER III

ACCOUNTING PRINCIPLES

The rules and conventions of accounting are commonly referred to as its principles. Accounting principles are the guidelines to establish standards for sound accounting practices and procedures in reporting status and periodic performance of a business. These *Generally Accepted Accounting Principles* (*GAAP*) provide a uniform basis for preparing financial statements. These are described by term:

— Concepts

— Conventions

ACCOUNTING PRINCIPLES

Accounting Concepts

Business Entity Concept

Money Measurement Concept

Going Concern Concept

Cost Concept

Dual Aspect Concept

Realisation Concept

Accounting Period Concept

Matching Concept

Accrual Concept

Accounting Conventions

Consistency

Conservatism

Disclosure

ACCOUNTING CONCEPTS

The term concept is used to mean necessary accounting assumption upon which accounting is based.

1. **Business Entity Concept:** Accounting assumes that a business is separate and distinct from the person who owns it. All the transactions of the business are recorded in the books from the point of view of the business and not from the point of view of the owner. This concept is based on the sense that proprietors entrust resources to management; the management is expected to use these resources to the best advantage of the firm and to account for the resources placed at its disposal. This concept of a separate entity is applicable to all forms of business organization—sole proprietorship, partnership, joint stock company etc.
2. **Money Measurement Concept:** Accounting records only those transactions and events that can be expressed in terms of money. Events, which cannot be expressed in money, do not find place in the books of account. This concept imposes a severe limitation on the scope of an accounting report. For example, accounting does not record that a competitor has placed a better product in the market, retirement of managing director etc. though those may have financial implication, yet these are not recorded in the books as these can not be expressed in terms of money. Money is a common denominator, which expresses the heterogeneous items of business.
3. **Going Concern Concept:** According to this concept, accounting assumes that the business will continue to operate for an indefinitely long period in the future. It is on this basis that a clear distinction must be made between assets and expenses. On the basis if this concept, fixed assets are recorded at their original cost and depreciated on the basis of their expected life rather than on the basis of their market value. Only on the basis of

this assumption the accounting process remains stable and achieve the objective of correctly recording and reporting on the capital invested. If it is certain that the business will last only for a limited period, the accounting record will keep the expected life in view, probably, treating all expenses, capital and revenue same.

4. **Cost Concept:** According to this concept asset is recorded at its actual cost and this cost is the basis of all subsequent accounting for the assets. For example, a firm purchased a piece of land for Rs. 80,000 and may consider its market value Rs. 90,000 but the entry in the book of account will be made for Rs. 80,000. The market price will not be considered. Cost concept does not mean that assets are always shown year after year for an indefinite period at the cost price. The actual cost figure is systematically reduced over its life by a process called **depreciation.**

5. **Dual Aspect Concept:** According to this concept, every transaction entered into by a firm will have two aspects; if any event occurs, it is bound to have double effect. In a business, the resources earned are called assets and the claims of various parties against these assets are called equities. According to this concept total asset must be equal to the claim of various parties against these assets. This equation is called accounting equation. This fundamental equation will always be right. Thus

   Assets = Equities
   Assets = Capital + liabilities
   Capital = Assets — liabilities

   For example, Sumit starts a business with a capital of Rs. 2,00,000. Business has an asset of Rs. 2,00,000 while on the other hand the business has to pay Rs. 2,00,000 to the owner, which is taken as proprietor's capital. Thus

   Capital (equities) = Cash (assets)

6. **Realisation Concept:** This concept is also called revenue concept. Revenue is earned by sale of goods or by

performance of a service. Revenue is deemed to be realized when the goods have been transferred or the service has been rendered to a customer. It prevents business firms from inflating their profits by recording sales and incomes that are likely to occur i.e. expected incomes or gains are not recorded.

7. **Accounting Period Concept:** According to the going concern concept, a business is intended to continue indefinitely for a long time. But the owner of the business cannot wait for such a long period for the determination of its income. Thus, there is a need to know the amount of profit and loss at regular intervals of time. The accountants generally choose some convenient segment of time generally one year, for determining the profit and loss of the business. Such a time interval is called accounting period. Accounting year may be financial year or calendar year.

8. **Matching Concept:** According to this concept, all expenses that are incurred in an accounting period should be matched with revenue realized in that period. First, revenues should be recognized and then costs associated with these revenues should be recognized. The matching of expenses with revenue is based on accrual system of accounting.

9. **Accrual Concept:** When an event takes place or a transaction is recorded into, its consequences are bound to follow, the amount of assets and liabilities will be affected by the various transactions and events. Even if settlement in cash is at a later period, this must be brought into the accounting. This concept requires that all events and transactions, not yet settled in cash, must be taken into account.

ACCOUNTING CONVENTIONS

The term convention refers to the traditions, which are used as a guide in the preparation of accounting reports and statements

1. **Consistency:** According to this convention various accounting practices should remain unchanged from one period to another. It requires that working rules once chosen should not be changed arbitrarily and without notice of the effect of change to those who use the accounts. For example, if a company has adopted written down method of depreciation, the same should be used in all subsequent years. If frequent changes are made in methods, comparison of accounting figures of one period with that of another period becomes difficult.
2. **Convention of Conservatism:** The essence of this convention is anticipate no profit but provision for all possible losses. All feared losses are considered but all prospective profit left. Valuating stock at cost or market price whichever is less and creating provision for doubtful debts are such examples.
3. **Disclosure:** The full disclosure convention specifies that there must be complete and understandable reporting on the economic affairs of the entity. The purpose of this full disclosure convention is to communicate all material and relevant facts concerning financial position and results of operation to the users.

CHAPTER IV

DOUBLE ENTRY SYSTEM

Double entry system was developed by an Italian merchant **'Luco Pacioli'** who wrote the book ***"De computise et scripturies'*** on double entry system in year 1494. Double entry system is based on scientific principles and is used by most of the business firm. This system is based on the fact that every transaction has two aspects and according to this system both aspects are recorded. Under this system in every transaction an account is debited and some other account is credited. According to his system the account that involves the receiving aspects is debited and the account that involves the giving aspect as credited.

For Example: When we purchase goods for cash we will surrender cash and receive goods in return. Similarly when the business sells good on credit, customer becomes debtors for the amount of goods sold to him. Thus every transaction should always be recorded twice in an accounting system—in two accounts—**One account is given debit other is given credit with an equal amount.** It also provides an automatic check on the arithmetical accuracy of accounting because total of debit is equal to the total of credit.

Double entry system is based on fundamental equation. According to this equation

Assets = Liability + Capital

MERITS OF DOUBLE ENTRY SYSTEM

1. Double entry system provides a complete record of all business transaction.

2. It provides a check on the arithmetic accuracy.
3. The real amount of the profit earned or loss suffered during specified time period can be calculated with the help of detailed profit and loss a/c.
4. This system is a scientific system of recording business transactions.
5. The balance sheet can be prepared at any point of time showing the actual amount of assets, liabilities and capital.

ACCOUNT

An account is an individual record of a person, firm or thing, an item of income and expense. According to Kohler's Dictionary for accounts, an account has been defined as a formal record of a particular type of transaction expressed in money.

If a statement is prepared for customer showing on one side the various credit sales made to him, and on other side, the amount received from him, the statement will be known as an account.

CLASSIFICATION OF ACCOUNT

Basically the accounts are classified in two broad categories.

- Personal accounts
- Impersonal account --

Impersonal account is sub -divided into two

1. Real account
2. Nominal account

Thus all accounts can be classified into personal, real and nominal accounts.

Personal accounts: Those accounts, which are related to persons, firms, companies with whom the business deals is called personal account. This account can be further classified into following forms.

1. **Accounts of natural persons's:** Debtors a/c, creditors a/c, Ramesh's a/c, etc.

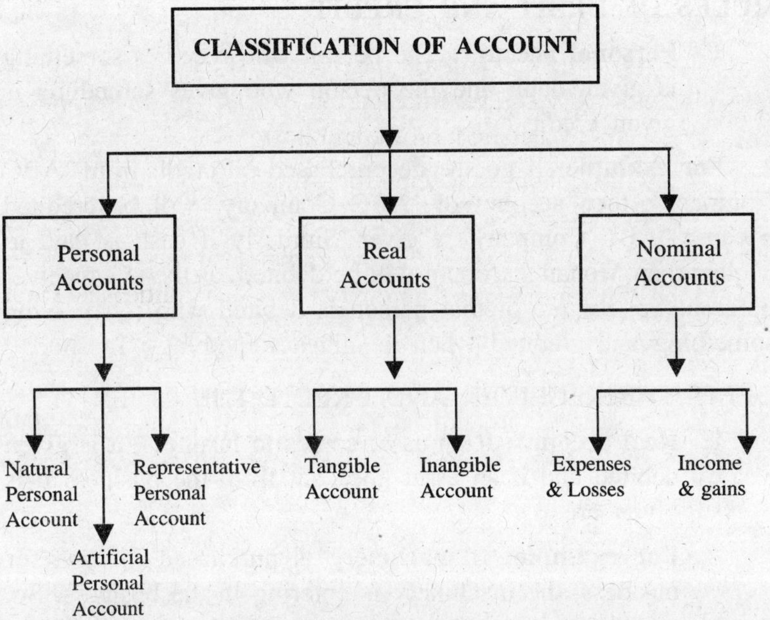

2. **Accounts of ariticial person's and body of persons's:** Partnership firm a/c, company's ac, bank a/c club a/c etc.
3. **Representative Personal account:** Outstanding salary a/c, prepaid rent a/c, these are the accounts of assets.

REAL ACCOUNT

These are the account of assets. Real accounts may be of following types:

1. **Tangible account:** This account represents such things, which can be touched and felt, for example, land, building, stock, cash etc.
2. **Intangible account:** This account represents such things which cannot be touched and felt, for example, goodwill, trademark and patents etc.

NOMINAL ACCOUNT

Accounts which relate to income, expenses, gains and losses are called nominal accounts. interest received, wages, salary, rent and postage etc. are such exmple.

RULES OF DEBIT AND CREDIT

1. **Personal account:** The person who receives something is given debit and the person who gives something is given credit.

For example: If goods are purchased on credit from 'ABC Company', then account of 'ABC Company' will be credited because 'ABC Company' is giver. Similarly if cash is paid to Mohan than Mohan's account will be debited, as the is a receiver of cash. So, the a/c of that person is debited who is receiving something and credited when he gives somethings. In short

DEBIT THE RECEIVER AND CREDIT THE GIVER

1. **Real account:** If an asset comes to business, it is given debited and if an asset goes out from the business it is given credit.

   For example: If machinery is purchased in cash for business, the machinery is entering in the business. So, machinery is debited and cash is going out, so; it should be credited. In short-

DEBIT WHAT COMES IN AND CREDIT WHAT GOES OUT

1. **Nominal accounts:** All the accounts of expenses and losses are debited and all the accounts of income and gains are credited.

   For example: When wages is paid to workers, wages account will be dibited, as it is an expense for the business. Similarly if interest is received, interest account will be credited, as it is an income for the business. In short-

DEBIT ALL EXPENSES AND LOSSES AND CREDIT ALL INCOMES AND GAINS

Thus the are three fundamental rules:

- Debit the receiver and credit the giver.
- Debit what comes in and credit what goes out.
- Debit all expenses and losses and credit all incomes and gains.

SINGNIFICANCE OF DEBIT AND CREDIT

DEBIT

1. Debit shows that the person whose acccount is being debited has become the debtor of the business or due from that persons has increased.
2. Value of assets or the business has accquired more than assets.
3. Firm has incurred so much loss or expenses.

CREDIT:

1. Credit or the due to that person has increased.
2. Value of assets has decreased or the business has disposed off, part or the whole of assets for the amount of the credit.
3. The firm has earned an income.

ACCOUNTING EQUATION

This equation is based on the principle that accounting deals with property and right to property. The sum of the properties owned is equal to the sum of the right of the proprietor. The properties owned by a firm are called assets and the rights to properties are known as equities. The equities are of following types:

— Owner's capital

— Liabilities or amount due to outsiders (creditors)

At any point of time, the total assets of the business will be equal to the total equities of the business. Expressing in an equation, it will be

Assets	=	Equities		
Assets	=	Liabilities +		capital
Capital	=	Assets	–	Liabilities

This equation is known as ***accounting equation.***

Accounting equation can be elaborated as

Capital + Liabilities	=	Assets
↓		↓
Proprietor's capital		Land
+		Machinery
Loans		Building
Bank overdraft		Cash
Creditors		Debtors
Bills payables		Bills receivables

For example: Mukesh started a business with a capital of Rs. 1,00,000; immidiately the business have Rs. 1,00,000 as cash (assets) and at the same time the business will owe to the owner Rs. 1,00,000 which is taken as the proprietor's capital

Capital (1,00,000) = Assets (1,00,000)

CHAPTER V

JOURNAL

Journal is derived from the French word "Jour" which means a day. So journal means a daily record of business transactions. It is a book of original or prime entry because every transaction is the first recorded in it before being posted into the ledger. It provide a chronological (day to day) record of the transactions in which each transaction is recorded in it entirely with relevant supplement information. The process of recording the transaction in the journal is called journalizing.

JOURNAL

Date	Particulars	L.F	Amount (Dr)		Amount (Cr)	
			Rs	P	Rs	P

Journal is kept on a columnar basis. It has the following five columns:

1. **Column 1 (date):** In this column the date of the transaction is recorded. The year is written at the top of the column in each page. In the next line of this column the month and date is recorded

2. **Column 2 (particulars):** In this column the details of the accounts that have to be debited and credited are recorded. First the account to be debited is recorded at the left of this column. The abbreviation "Dr" is written towards the end of the column. In the next line after leaving little space the name of the account to be credited is entered with a prefix "To". In the next line a brief explanation called *narration* for the entry is written. Narration should be as informative and short as possible.
3. **Column 3 (ledger folio):** This column is meant to record the page number on which the various accounts are kept in the ledger.
4. **Column 4 (amount):** This column is used for entering the amount to be debited to the account named.
5. **Column 5 (amount):** This column is used for entering the amount to be credited to the account named.

Some Important Points for Journal Entries

1. All transactions must be recorded in order of dates.
2. The date is entered on the left hand side.
3. The account representing any thing coming into business is debited.
4. The account representing the receiver of anything is debited.
5. The account representing any thing going out of business is credited.
6. The account representing the giver of anything is credited.
7. For every debit there must be a corresponding credit.
8. The abbreviation "Dr" must be written after name of the account to be debited.
9. Narration of every journal entry is necessary.
10. When payment is made on account of any service

rendered, the debit should be given to particular service account and not the personnel a/c of payee.

COMPOUND JOURNAL ENTRY

Transactions that are inter-connected and have taken place simultaneously are recorded by means of combine journal entries. Compound entry is that where more than one accounts are debited or credited in the single entry. For example, receipt of cash from a debtors and discount allowed to him are recorded by means of single journal entry.

Cash a/c	Dr.	450	
Discount a/c	Dr.	50	
To debtors a/c			500

(————————)

If the amount is spent on the same day for salaries, wages, advertisement, repair etc., a combined entry can be passed by debiting all the expenses account with their respective amount and crediting cash account with total amount spent:

Salary a/c	Dr.	500	
Wages a/c	Dr.	400	
Advertisement a/c	Dr.	300	
Repair a/c	Dr.	200	
To cash a/c			1400

(————————)

OPERATING/OPENING ENTRY

When a business house starts the book for the New Year, it has to pass opening entry. It is to debit the respective accounts with the opening balances of various assets and to credit the relevant accounts with the opening amounts due to creditors and to credit capital account with the amount of capital in the beginning.

But if the capital is not given, it can easily find out by deducting liability from assets. Capital account will also be credited.

Cash a/c	Dr	10,000	
Bank a/c	Dr	5000	
Debtors (Customers)	Dr	5000	
Furniture a/c	Dr	5000	
Stock a/c	Dr	8000	
To creditors (Suppliers)			13,000
To capital a/c			20,000

(——————————)

SOME IMPORTANT TRANSACTION

1. ***Outstanding Expenses:*** If liability for an expense is due but not yet paid the relevant expense account will be debit and relevant outstanding expenses a/c will be credited.

   For example: Salary of Rs. 1,000 is due but not yet paid

Salary a/c	Dr	1,000	
To o/s salary a/c			1,000

   (——————————)

   It is a personal account.

2. ***Prepaid Expenses:*** If an amount for an expense is paid in advance, it is prepaid expense.

   For example

   Prepaid expense (————) a/c Dr

   To cash a/c

   (————————)

3. ***Accrued Income:*** If an amount has been earned but not yet received it will be called accrued income.

For example

Interest amounted Rs. 500 has been earned but it is not yet received. The entry will be-

Accrued interest a/c Dr

To interest a/c

(——————)

4. *Income received in advance/unaccrued:* If an income is received in advance, cash account will be debit and relevant income received in advance is credited.

Illustration 1. Journalize the following transactions in the book of Mr. Anil:

1. Sold goods for cash Rs. 400
2. Goods sold to Shyam Rs. 600
3. Goods purchased in cash Rs. 300
4. Salary Paid Rs. 100
5. Rent paid Rs. 50

Solution

In the book of Mr. Anil

JOURNAL ENTRIES

Date	Particulars	L.F	Amount (Dr) Rs	P	Amount (Cr) Rs	P
1.	Cash a/c Dr To goods a/c (Being the goods sold in cash)		400	00	400	00
2	Shyam Dr To goods a/c (Being the goods sold to Shyam)		600	00	600	00
3.	Goods a/c Dr To cash a/c (Being the goods purchased in cash)		300	00	300	00

(contd.)

Date	Particulars	L.F	Amount (Dr) Rs	P	Amount (Cr) Rs	P
4.	Salary a/c Dr		100	00		
	To cash a/c				100	00
	(Being the salary paid in cash)					
5.	Rent a/c Dr		50	00		
	To cash a/c				50	00
	(Being rent paid in cash)					
	GRAND TOTAL		1450	00	1450	00

Illustration 2

Journalize the following transactions:

Year 2005

Jan. 01	Commence business with cash	Rs. 20,000.00
Jan. 02	Paid into bank	Rs. 5,000.00
Jan. 04	Goods purchased in cash	Rs. 1,000.00
Jan. 05	Goods sold to Mohan	Rs. 2,000.00
Jan. 06	Goods purchased from Rakesh	Rs. 3,000.00
Jan. 08	Goods returned to Rakesh	Rs. 500.00
Jan. 10	Cash withdrawl for personal use	Rs. 200.00
Jan. 15	Received from Mohan	Rs. 2,000.00
Jan. 20	Salary paid	Rs. 500.00
Jan. 24	Rent paid	Rs. 400.00
Jan. 26	Final payment made to Rakesh	Rs. 2,400.00
Jan. 28	Paid for stationary	Rs. 300.00

Solution

In the book of..........

JOURNAL ENTRIES

Date	Particulars		L.F	Amount (Dr) Rs	P	Amount (Cr) Rs	P
2005 Jan. 01	Cash a/c	Dr		20,000	00		
	To capital a/c					20,000	00
	(Being the business started with cash)						
02	Bank a/c	Dr		5,000	00		
	To cash a/c					5,000	00
	(Being cash deposited in bank)						
04	Purchase a/c	Dr		1,000	00		
	To cash a/c					1,000	00
	(Being goods purchase in cash)						
05	Mohan	Dr		2,000	00		
	To sales a/c					2,000	00
	(Being goods sold to him)						
06	Purchase a/c	Dr		3,000	00		
	To Rakesh					3,000	00
	(Being goods purchase from him)						
08	Rakesh	Dr		500	00		
	To purchase return a/c					500	00
	(Being goods return to him)						
10	Drawings a/c	Dr		200	00		
	To cash a/c					200	00
	(Being cash withdraw for personal use)						
15	Cash a/c	Dr		2,000	00		
	To Mohan					2,000	00
	(Being cash received from him)						

(contd.)

Date	Particulars	L.F	Amount (Dr) Rs	P	Amount (Cr) Rs	P
20	Salary a/c Dr		500	00		
	To cash a/c				500	00
	(Being salary paid)					
24	Rent a/c Dr		400	00		
	To cash a/c				400	00
	(Being the rent paid)					
26	Rakesh Dr		2,500	00		
	To Cash a/c				2,400	00
	To Discount a/c				100	00
	(Being the payment made and discount received)					
28	Stationary a/c Dr		300	00		
	To cash a/c				300	00
	(Being stationary purchased)					
	GRAND TOTAL		37,400	00	37,400	00

Illustration 3

Journalize the following transactions:

Year 2005

Feb. 01	Commence business with cash	Rs.	30,000.00
Feb. 02	Furniture purchased in cash	Rs.	10,000.00
Feb. 03	Paid into bank	Rs.	5,000.00
Feb. 04	Cash purchase	Rs.	2,000.00
Feb. 06	Paid for stationary	Rs.	300.00
Feb. 07	Goods sold to Rastogi	Rs.	3,000.00
Feb. 08	Goods purchased from Gaurav	Rs.	2,000.00
Feb. 10	Cash withdrawl from bank for personal use	Rs.	200.00
Feb. 14	Electricity bill paid	Rs.	1,000.00
Feb. 16	Machinery purchased from Meerut machinery store	Rs.	5,000.00
Feb. 18	Cash sales	Rs	5,000.00

Feb. 20	Depreciation charged on building	Rs.	1000.00
Feb. 22	Paid to Meerut machinery store	Rs.	2000.00
Feb. 24	Rent paid to Ramesh	Rs.	500.00
Feb. 25	Salary to clerk outstanding	Rs.	1000.00
Feb. 26	Final payment made to Meerut machinery store	Rs.	2,950.00
Feb. 27	Sold to Nayak	Rs.	300.00
Feb. 28	Cash purchase	Rs.	1000.00

Solution

JOURNAL ENTRIES

Date	Particulars	L.F	Amount (Dr) Rs	P	Amount (Cr) Rs	P
2005 Feb. 01	Cash a/c Dr To Capital a/c (Being the business started with cash)		30,000	00	30,000	00
02	Furniture a/c Dr To Cash a/c (Being the furniture purchased)		10,000	00	10,000	00
03	Bank a/c Dr To Cash a/c (Being cash deposited in bank)		5,000	00	5,000	00
04	Purchase a/c Dr To Cash a/c (Being goods purchased in cash)		2,000	00	2,000	00
06	Stationary a/c Dr To Cash a/c (Being stationary purchased)		300	00	300	00
07	Rastogi Dr To Sales a/c (Being goods sold to him)		3,000	00	3,000	00

(contd.)

Date	Particulars		LF	Amount (Dr) Rs	P	Amount (Cr) Rs	P
08	Purchase a/c To Gaurav a/c (Being Goods purchased from him)	Dr		2,000	00	2,000	00
10	Drawings a/c To bank (Being cash withdrawal from bank for personal use)	Dr		200	00	200	00
14	Electricity charges a/c To Cash a/c (Being the electricity charge paid)	Dr		1,000	00	1,000	00
16	Machinery a/c To Meerut machinery store (Being the machinery purchased)	Dr		5,000	00	5,000	00
18	Cash a/c To Sales a/c (Being the goods sold in cash)	Dr		5,000	00	5,000	00
20	Depreciation a/c To Building a/c (Being the dep. charged on building)	Dr		1,000	00	1,000	00
22	Meerut machinery store To Cash a/c (Being the cash paid)	Dr		2,000	00	2,000	00
24	Rent a/c To Cash a/c (Being rent paid in cash)	Dr		500	00	500	00
25	Salary a/c To Outstanding salary a/c (Being salary due but not paid)	Dr		1,000	00	1,000	00

(contd.)

Date	Particulars		LF	Amount (Dr) Rs	P	Amount (Cr) Rs	P
26	Meerut Machinery Store a/c	Dr		3,000	00		
	To Cash a/c					2,950	00
	To Discount a/c					50	00
	(Being final payment made to him)						
27	Nayak	Dr		300	00		
	To Sales a/c					300	00
	(Being goods sold to him)						
28	Purchase a/c	Dr		1,000	00		
	To Cash a/c					1,000	00
	(Being the goods purchased)						
	GRAND TOTAL			72,300	00	72,300	00

PROBLEMS

Q. 1. Journalise the following transactions of Mr. Raman

2005

Jan. 05	Received cash from Rakesh	Rs.	6,000
" 06	Purchased goods in cash	Rs.	3,000
" 07	Sold goods to Hari	Rs.	500
" 15	Paid to Rahim	Rs.	500
" 18	Received from Kishan	Rs.	200
" 20	Purchased Furniture from Ram	Rs.	1,000
" 25	Paid Salary	Rs.	200
" 30	Paid Rent	Rs.	100
" 31	Paid Wages	Rs.	200

Q. 2. Journalise the following transactions:

2005

Feb 2	Rakesh commenced business with cash	Rs. 80,000
" 4	Purchased goods for cash	Rs. 10,000

" 10	Deposit in to bank	Rs. 2,000
" 15	Cash sales	Rs. 4,000
" 18	Sold to Mohan on credit	Rs. 3,000
" 22	Paid Rent	Rs 400
" 25	Paid salaries	Rs. 500
" 28	Paid sundry expenses	Rs 200

Q. 3. Journalise the following transactions:

2004		
Dec.1	Suresh commenced business with cash Rs. 25, 000 and goods worth	Rs. 10,000
" 02	Machinery purchased	Rs. 2,000
" 04	Bought goods from Ram	Rs. 3,000
" 06	Bought furniture from 'Akash Furniture Store' for cash	Rs. 2,000
" 10	Sold goods for cash	Rs. 4,000
" 15	Sold goods on credit to Mohan	Rs. 3,000
" 20	Goods returned to Ram	Rs. 200
" 22	Mohan returned goods	Rs. 50
" 25	Cash sales	Rs. 250
" 30	Paid rent	Rs. 200
" 31	Paid salaries	Rs. 500

Q. 4. Journalise the following transactions of Mr. Rakesh:

2004		
Dec.1	Rakesh commenced business with cash	Rs. 20,000
" 04	Deposit in to bank	Rs. 7,000
" 06	Purchased goods from Dass	Rs. 5,000
" 08	Sold to Shyam on credit	Rs. 6,000
" 10	Cash purchase	Rs. 2,000
" 15	Cash sales	Rs. 4,000
" 20	Received from Shyam	Rs. 5,800

	Allowed him discount	Rs. 200
" 22	Paid to Dass	Rs. 4,850
	Discount received	Rs. 150
" 25	Paid salaries	Rs. 1,000
" 30	Paid rent	Rs. 500

Q. 5. Journalise the following transactions:

2005		
Jan.1	Sohan started business with cash	Rs. 25,000
" 02	Purchased goods for cash	Rs. 2,000
" 04	Sold to Manish on credit	Rs. 4,000
" 06	Cash sales	Rs. 7,000
" 08	Purchased goods from Anju for cash	Rs. 2,000
" 15	Withdrew money from business for private use	Rs. 200
" 20	Furniture purchased	Rs. 3,000
" 25	Deposit in to bank	Rs. 2,000
" 28	Received cheque from Manish in full settlement of amount due by them	Rs. 3,900
" 29	Cheque received from Arun	Rs. 2,500
" 30	Paid for electricity charges	Rs. 500
" 31	Paid salary by cheque	Rs. 300
" 31	Paid rent	Rs. 200

Q. 6. Journalise the following transactions in the book of Mr. Sunil:

2005		
Jan.1	Business started with cash	Rs. 25,000
" 2	Goods sold to Y	Rs. 8,000
" 6	Cash sales	Rs. 15,000
" 7	Paid cartage	Rs. 900
" 8	Furniture purchased for cash	Rs. 12,000
" 9	Goods purchased from Z	Rs. 10,000

" 10	Wages paid	Rs. 2,000
	Paid postage expenses	Rs. 100
" 12	Withdrew money from business for private use	
	Cash	Rs. 2,000
	Goods	Rs. 400
" 15	Deposit in to bank	Rs. 1,000
" 20	Received cash from Y on account	Rs. 6,000
" 25	Paid to Z in full settlement	Rs. 9,500
" 31	Paid salary by cheque	Rs. 800
" 31	Paid rent	Rs. 400

Q. 7. Prem Chand commenced business with Rs. 9,000 cash and goods worth Rs. 6000 on Jan. 1, 2005. Other transactions for the month were as follows: enter these transactions in the journal:

2005		
Jan. 2	Purchased goods for cash	Rs. 4,000
" 3	Stationary purchased	Rs. 500
" 5	Furniture purchased from furniture house	Rs. 3,000
" 6	Cash sold in cash	Rs. 9,000
" 7	Interest received from Mukesh	Rs. 800
" 9	Purchased goods from Mukesh & Co.	Rs. 7,000
" 12	Goods given in charity	Rs. 600
" 15	Paid office expenses	Rs. 500
" 20	Paid in to bank	Rs. 4,000
" 22	Loss of goods by fire	Rs. 300
" 24	Sold to Mani on credit	Rs. 3,000
" 25	Goods purchased on credit	Rs. 9,000
" 26	Withdrew money for private use	Rs. 900
" 28	Deposit in to bank	Rs. 2,000
" 29	Interest received	Rs. 400

" 29	Commission received	Rs. 300
" 30	Salary paid	Rs. 2,000

Q. 8. Journalise the following transactions in the book of Meerut Store:

2004		
Nov. 2	Business started with:	
	Cash	Rs. 30,000
	Goods	Rs. 12,000
" 4	Bought furniture from Gupta & Company	Rs. 7,000
" 5	Goods sold to Amarnath	Rs. 14,000
" 6	Paid for stationary	Rs. 500
" 8	Cash purchase	Rs. 4,000
" 10	Goods purchased from Rajkishor	Rs. 6,000
" 14	Cash sales	Rs. 7,000
" 17	Motorcycle purchased for office use	Rs. 10,000
" 20	Order received from Manoj worth	Rs. 20,000
" 22	Received from Amarnath on account	Rs. 10,000
" 23	Payment made to Gupta and Company	Rs. 6,800
	Discount received	Rs. 200
" 25	Received from Amarnath in full settlement	Rs. 3,500
" 28	Payment made for	
	Salary	Rs. 3,500
	Rent	Rs. 500
	Office Expenses	Rs. 400

Q. 9. Journalise the following transactions:

2004		
Oct. 1	Rajesh started business with cash	Rs. 40,000
" 2	Bought goods for cash	Rs. 10,000
" 4	Sold for cash	Rs. 22,000
" 6	Machinery purchased for cash	Rs. 5,000
" 8	Sold to Amit	Rs. 6,000

" 11	Purchased from Rakesh	Rs. 4,000
" 14	Goods purchased from Rakesh	Rs. 3,000
" 17	Cash sales	Rs. 12,000
" 20	Paid for stationary	Rs. 600
" 22	Goods sold on credit	Rs. 4,000
" 26	Paid for rent	Rs. 600
" 26	Paid for carriage	Rs. 400
" 27	Cash paid to Rakesh	Rs. 2,600
	Discount received from him	Rs. 400
" 28	Salary paid	Rs. 3,000

Q. 10. Journalise the following transactions :

2005		
Jan. 1	Commenced business in cash	Rs. 45,000
" 3	Paid in to bank	Rs. 6,000
" 4	Bought furniture from Shastri & Co.	Rs. 12,000
" 6	Bought goods from Sachin	Rs. 11,000
" 9	Sold to Ghosh	Rs. 16,000
" 15	Sold to Satish for cash	Rs. 13,650
" 18	Rent for one year paid in advance	Rs. 6,000
" 20	Withdrew for house hold expenses	
	Goods	Rs. 600
	Cash	Rs. 850
" 24	Cash withdraw from bank for office	Rs. 5,000
" 27	Repairs to scooter, payment not yet made	Rs. 340
" 28	Bank charges for the month	Rs. 600
" 29	Depreciation charged on furniture	Rs. 1,000
" 30	Cheque received from Ghosh in full settlement	Rs. 15,600

Q. 11. Journalise the following transactions:

2005

Jan. 1	Commenced business with cash	Rs. 50,000
" 2	Deposited in to bank	Rs. 10,000
" 4	Cash sales	Rs. 8,500
" 6	Goods purchased for cash	Rs. 7,800
" 9	Machinery purchased & payment made by cheque	Rs. 12,000
" 13	Goods purchased form Rajan	Rs. 6,400
" 15	Goods sold to Bhuwan	Rs. 7,700
" 16	Goods returned to Rajan	Rs. 1,000
" 18	Paid rent in advance	Rs. 2,500
" 21	Goods returned by Bhuwan	Rs. 2,000
" 24	Final payment made to Rajan	Rs. 5,000
" 26	Wages paid by Cheque	Rs. 950
" 28	Cheque received from Bhuwan in full settlement	Rs. 5,500
" 30	Salary due but not paid	Rs. 1,300

CHAPTER VI

LEDGER

Ledger is a set of accounts. Ledger is a book where all accounts relating to different items are maintained and into which all journal entries must be posted. In fact, ledger is the principle book of entry, which provides complete information about various transactions relating to all parties and all items of assets, incomes and expenses. In this book we open separate accounts for each item and all transactions related to a particular item as recorded in journal are posted in the concerned account. For each and all transactions related to a particular supplier say Mohan, are posted to Mohan's account. Similarly, all cash payment and cash receipts can be posted to cash account.

PERFORMA OF A LEDGER

LEDGER

Dr. **Cr.**

Date	Particulars	Folio	Amount	Date	Particulars	Folio	Amount

POSTING IN TO LEDGER

The process of transferring the debits and credits of the journal to the proper ledger accounts is called posting. Each amount listed in the debit column of the journal is posted by entering it on the debit side of the account in ledger, and each amount listed in the credit column of the journal is posted to the credit side of the ledger account. The following sequence is used for posting to ledger:

1. Locate in the ledger the first account named in the journal entry.
2. Enter in the debit column of the ledger account the amount of the debit as shown in the journal.
3. Enter the data of the transaction in the ledger account.
4. Enter in journal folio column the number of journal page from which the entry is being posted.
5. The recording of the debit in the ledger account is now complete, return to the journal and enter in ledger folio column the number of ledger page to which the debit was posted.
6. Repeat the above five steps for credit side of the journal entry.

BALANCING LEDGER ACCOUNTS

After posting has been completed the difference between the totals of debit and credit sides is ascertained. This is known as balancing accounts. If the total of the debit is more than that of credit side, it is said to have a debit balance and vice-versa if credit side.

Important points to be noted

1. The transactions will be entered in the ledger a/c in order of dates.
2. Every entry must be dated.
3. The date must be shown on the left hand side of the entry.

4. Each entry on the debit side of the account starts with word "to".
5. Each entry on the credit side of the account starts with the word "by".
6. In the folio column, the page of the journal is entered, from which the entries are here posted i.e. transferred.

Illustration 1. Journalize the following transactions in the book of Mr. Anil:

1. Sold goods for cash Rs. 4,000
2. Good sold to Shyam Rs. 6.000
3. Goods purchased in cash Rs. 300
4. Salasry paid Rs. 100
5. Rent paid Rs. 50

Solution:

In the Books of Mr. Anil

JOURNAL ENTRIES

Date	Particulars	L.F	Amount (Dr) Rs	P	Amount (Cr) Rs	P
	Cash a/c Dr To goods a/c (Being goods sold in cash)		4,000	00	4,000	00
	Shyam Dr To goods a/c (Being goods sold to Shyam)		600	00	600	00
	Goods a/c Dr To cash a/c (Being goods purchased in cash)		300	00	300	00
	Salary a/c Dr To cash a/c (Being salary paid in cash)		100	00	100	00

Date	Particulars	L.F	Amount (Dr) Rs	P	Amount (Cr) Rs	P
	Rent a/c Dr		50	00		
	To cash a/c				50	00
	(Being rent paid in cash)					
	GRAND TOTAL		**5,050**	**00**	**5,050**	**00**

LEDGER ACCOUNTS

In the Books of Mr. Anil

CASH ACCOUNT

Dr. Cr.

Date	Particulars	Folio	Amount Rs P	Date	Particulars	Folio	Amount Rs P
	To Goods a/c		4,000.00		By Goods a/c		300.00
					By Salary a/c		100.00
					By Rent a/c		50.00
					By Bal. c/d		3,500.00
	Total		4,000.00		Total		4,000.00
	To Balance b/d		3,550.00				

GOODS ACCOUNT

Dr. Cr.

Date	Particulars	Folio	Amount Rs P	Date	Particulars	Folio	Amount Rs P
	To Cash a/c		300.00				
	To Balance c/d		4,300.00		By Cash a/c		4,000.00
					By Shyam		600.00
	Total		4,600.00		Total		4,600.00
					By Bal. b/d		4,300.00

SHYAM

Dr. **Cr.**

Date	Particulars	Folio	Amount Rs P	Date	Particulars	Folio	Amount Rs P
	To Goods a/c		600.00		By Bal. c/d		600.00
	Total		600.00		Total		600.00
	To Balance b/d		600.00				

RENT ACCOUNT

Dr. **Cr.**

Date	Particulars	Folio	Amount Rs P	Date	Particulars	Folio	Amount Rs P
	By Cash a/c		50.00		By Balance c/d		50.00
	Total		50.00		Total		50.00
	To Balance b/d		50.00				

SALARY ACCOUNT

Dr. **Cr.**

Date	Particulars	Folio	Amount Rs P	Date	Particulars	Folio	Amount Rs P
	To Cash a/c		100.00		By Balance c/d		100.00
	Total		100.00		Total		100.00
	To Balance b/d		100.00				

Illustration 2. Journalize the following transactions and post them to ledger:

Year 2005

Jan. 01	Commence business with cash	Rs.	20,000
Jan. 02	Paid into bank	Rs.	5,000
Jan. 04	Goods purchased in cash	Rs.	1,000
Jan. 05	Goods sold to Mohan	Rs.	2,000
Jan. 06	Goods purchased from Rakesh	Rs.	3,000
Jan. 08	Goods returned to Rakesh	Rs.	500
Jan. 10	Cash withdrawl for personal use	Rs.	200
Jan. 15	Received from Mohan	Rs.	2,000
Jan. 20	Salary paid	Rs.	500
Jan. 24	Rent paid	Rs.	400
Jan. 26	Final payment made to Rakesh	Rs.	2,400
Jan. 28	Paid for stationary	Rs.	300

Solution

In the Book of............

JOURNAL ENTRIES

Date	Particulars	L.F	Amount (Dr) Rs	P	Amount (Cr) Rs	P
2005 Jan 1	Cash a/c Dr To capital a/c (Being the business started with cash)		20,000	00	20,000	00
Jan 2	Bank a/c Dr To cash a/c (Being cash deposited in bank)		5,000	00	5,000	00
Jan 4	Purchase a/c Dr To cash a/c (Being goods purchase in cash)		1,000	00	1,000	00

(contd.)

Date	Particulars	L.F	Amount (Dr) Rs	P	Amount (Cr) Rs	P
2005						
Jan 5	Mohan Dr		2,000	00		
	To sales a/c				2,000	00
	(Being goods sold to him)					
Jan 6	Purchase a/c Dr		3,000	00		
	To Rakesh				3,000	00
	(Being goods purchase from him)					
Jan 8	Rakesh Dr		500	00		
	To purchase return a/c				500	00
	(Being goods return to him)					
Jan 10	Drawings a/c Dr		200	00		
	To cash a/c				200	00
	(Being cash withdraw for personal use)					
Jan 15	Cash a/c Dr		2,000	00		
	To Mohan				2,000	00
	(Being cash received from him)					
Jan 20	Salary a/c Dr		500	00		
	To cash a/c				500	00
	(Being salary paid)					
Jan 24	Rent a/c Dr		400	00		
	To cash a/c				400	00
	(Being the rent paid)					
Jan 26	Rakesh Dr.		2,500	00		
	To cash a/c				2,400	00
	To discount a/c				100	00
	(Being the payment made & discount received)					

(contd.)

Date	Particulars		L.F	Amount (Dr) Rs	P	Amount (Cr) Rs	P
Jan 28	Stationary a/c To cash a/c (Being stationary purchased)	Dr		300	00	300	00
	Grand Total						

LADGER ACCOUNTS

IN THE BOOK OF....................

CASH ACCOUNT

Dr. **Cr.**

Date	Particulars	F	Amount Rs P	Date	Particulars	F	Amount Rs P
2005				2005			
Jan. 1	To Capital a/c		20,000.00	Jan. 2	By bank a/c		5,000.00
Jan. 15	To Mohan		2,400.00	" 4	By purchase a/c		1,000.00
				" 10	By drawings a/c		200.00
				" 20	By salary a/c		500.00
				" 24	By rent a/c		400.00
				" 26	By Rakesh		2,400.00
				" 28	By stationary a/c		300.00
				" 31	By balance c/d		
	Total		22,400.00		Total		12,600
Feb.1	To balance b/d		12,600.00				22,400

CAPITAL ACCOUNT

Dr. **Cr.**

Date	Particulars	F	Amount Rs P	Date	Particulars	F	Amount Rs P
2005				2005			
Jan. 31	To balance c/d		20,000.00	Jan. 1	By cash a/c		20,000.00
	Total		20,000.00		Total		20,000.00
				Feb. 1	To balance b/d		20,000.00

(contd.)

Dr. Cr.

Date	Particulars	F	Amount Rs P	Date	Particulars	F	Amount Rs P
2005				2005			
Jan. 4	To cash a/c		1,000.00	Jan. 31	By balance c/d		4,000.00
Jan 6	To Rakesh		3,000.00				
	Total		4,000.00		Total		4,000.00
Feb. 1	To bal. b/d		4,000.00				

SALES ACCOUNT

Dr. Cr.

Date	Particulars	F	Amount Rs P	Date	Particulars	F	Amount Rs P
2005				2005			
Jan. 31	To balance c/d		2,000.00	Jan. 5	By Mohan		2,000.00
	Total		2,000.00		Total		2,000.00
				Feb. 1	To Balance b/d		2,000.00

BANK ACCOUNT

Dr. Cr.

Date	Particulars	F	Amount Rs P	Date	Particulars	F	Amount Rs P
2005				2005			
Jan. 2	To cash a/c		5,000.00	Jan. 31	By balance c/d		5,000.00
	Total		5,000.00		Total		5,000.00
Feb. 1	To balance b/d		5,000.00				

MOHAN

Dr. **Cr.**

Date	Particulars	F	Amount Rs P	Date	Particulars	F	Amount Rs P
2005 Jan. 5	To Sales a/c		2,000.00	2005 Jan. 31	By cash c/d		2,000.00
	Total		2,000.00		Total		2,000.00

RAKESH

Dr. **Cr.**

Date	Particulars	F	Amount Rs P	Date	Particulars	F	Amount Rs P
2005				2005			
Jan. 8	To P. return a/c		500.00	Jan. 6	By purchases a/c		3,000.00
Jan. 26	To cash a/c		2,400.00				
Jan. 26	To discount a/c		100.00				
	Total		3,000.00		Total		5,000.00

DRAWINGS ACCOUNT

Dr. **Cr.**

Date	Particulars	F	Amount Rs P	Date	Particulars	F	Amount Rs P
2005 Jan. 10	To Cash a/c		200.00	2005 Jan. 31	By Balance c/d		200.00
	Total		200.00		Total		200.00
Feb. 1	To Balance b/d		200.00				

RENT ACCOUNT

Dr. **Cr.**

Date	Particulars	F	Amount Rs. P.	Date	Particulars	F	Amount Rs. P.
2005 Jan. 24	To Cash a/c		400.00	2005 Jan. 31	By Bal. c/d		400.00
	Total		400.00		Total		400.00
Feb. 1	To Balance b/d		400.00				

SALARY ACCOUNT

Dr. **Cr.**

Date	Particulars	F	Amount Rs. P.	Date	Particulars	F	Amount Rs. P.
2005 Jan. 20	To Cash a/c		500.00	2005 Jan. 31	By Balance c/d		500.00
	Total		500.00		Total		500.00
Feb. 1	To Balance b/d		500.00				

DISCOUNT ACCOUNT

Dr. **Cr.**

Date	Particulars	F	Amount Rs. P.	Date	Particulars	F	Amount Rs. P.
2005 Jan. 31	To balance c/d		100.00	2005 Jan. 26	By Rakesh		100.00
	Total		100.00		Total		100.00
				Feb. 1	To balance b/d		100.00

STATIONARY ACCOUNT

Dr. **Cr.**

Date	Particulars	F	Amount Rs. P.	Date	Particulars	F	Amount Rs. P.
2005 Jan. 28	To cash a/c		300.00	2005 Jan. 31	By balance c/d		300.00
	Total		300.00		Total		300.00
Feb. 1	To balance b/d		300.00				

PURCHASE RETURN ACCOUNT

Dr. **Cr.**

Date	Particulars	F	Amount Rs. P.	Date	Particulars	F	Amount Rs. P.
2005 Jan. 28	To balance c/d		500.00	2005 Jan. 31	By Rakesh		500.00
	Total		500.00		Total		500.00
				Feb. 1	To Bal. b/d		500.00

PROBLEMS

Q.1. Journalise the following transactions of Mr. Raman and post them to ledger:

2005	Received cash from Rakesh	Rs.	6,000
Jan. 5	Purchased goods in cash	Rs.	3,000
" 7	Sold goods to Hari	Rs.	500
" 15	Paid to Rahim	Rs.	500
" 18	Received from Kishan	Rs.	200
" 20	Purchased furniture from Ram	Rs.	1,000
" 25	Paid salary	Rs.	200
" 30	Paid rent	Rs.	100
" 31	Paid wages	Rs.	200

Q. 2. Journalise the following transactions and post them to ledger:

2005			
Feb 2	Rakesh commenced business with cash	Rs.	80,000
" 4	Purchased goods for cash	Rs.	10,000
" 10	Deposit in to bank	Rs.	2,000
" 15	Cash sales	Rs.	4,000
" 18	Sold to Rakesh on credit	Rs.	3,000
" 22	Paid rent	Rs.	400
" 25	Paid salaries	Rs.	500
" 28	Paid sundry expenses	Rs.	200

Q. 3. Journalise the following transactions and post them to ledger:

2004			
Dec. 1	Suresh commenced business with cash Rs. 25,000 and goods worth	Rs.	10,000
" 2	Machinery purchased	Rs.	2,000
" 4	Bought goods from Ram	Rs.	3,000
" 6	Bought furniture from Akash furniture store for cash	Rs.	2,000
" 10	Sold goods for cash	Rs.	4,000
" 15	Sold goods on credit to Mohan	Rs.	3,000
" 20	Goods returned to Ram	Rs.	200
" 22	Mohan returned goods	Rs.	50
" 25	Cash sales	Rs.	250
" 30	Paid rent	Rs.	200
" 31	Paid salaries	Rs.	500

Q. 4. Journalise the following transactions of Mr. Rakesh and post them to ledger:

2004			
Dec. 1	Rakesh commenced business with cash	Rs.	20,000
" 4	Deposit in to bank	Rs.	7,000

" 6	Purchased goods from Dass	Rs.	5,000
" 8	Sold to Shyam on credit	Rs.	6,000
" 10	Cash purchase	Rs.	2,000
" 15	Cash sales	Rs.	4,000
" 20	Received from Shyam	Rs.	5,800
	Allowed him discount	Rs.	200
" 22	Paid to Dass	Rs.	4,850
	Discount received	Rs.	150
" 25	Paid salaries	Rs.	1,000
" 30	Paid rent	Rs.	500

Q. 5. Journalise the following transactions and post them to ledger:

2005

Jan. 1	Sohan started business with cash	Rs.	25,000
" 2	Purchased goods for cash	Rs.	2,000
" 4	Sold to Manish on credit	Rs.	4,000
" 6	Cash sales	Rs.	7,000
" 8	Purchased goods from Anju for cash	Rs.	2,000
" 15	Withdrew money from business for private use	Rs	200
" 20	Furniture purchased	Rs.	3,000
" 25	Deposit in to bank	Rs.	2,000
" 28	Received cheque from Manish in full settlement of amount due by them	Rs.	3,900
" 29	Cheque received from Arun	Rs.	2,500
" 30	Paid for electricity charges	Rs.	500
" 31	Paid salary by cheque	Rs.	300
" 31	Paid rent	Rs.	200

Q. 6. Journalise the following transactions and post them to ledger:

2005

Jan. 1	Business started with cash	Rs.	25,000
" 2	Goods sold to Y	Rs.	8,000
" 6	Cash Sales	Rs.	15,000

" 7	Paid cartage	Rs.	900
" 8	Furniture purchased for cash	Rs.	12,000
" 9	Goods purchased from Z	Rs.	10,000
"10	Wages paid	Rs.	2,000
	Paid postage expenses	Rs.	100
"12	Withdrew money from business for private use		
	Cash	Rs.	2,000
	Goods	Rs.	400
"15	Deposit in to bank	Rs.	1,000
"20	Received cash from Y on account	Rs.	6,000
"25	Paid to Z in full settlement	Rs.	9,500
"31	Paid salary by cheque	Rs.	800
"31	Paid rent	Rs.	400

Q. 7. Premchand commenced business with Rs. 9,000 cash and goods worth Rs. 6000 on Jan. 1,2005. Other transactions for the month were as follows; enter these transactions in to journal and post them to ledger:

2005			
Jan. 2	Purchased goods for cash	Rs.	4,000
" 3	Stationary purchased	Rs.	500
	Furniture purchased from furniture house	Rs.	3,000
" 6	Goods sold in cash	Rs.	9,000
" 7	Interest received from Mukesh	Rs.	800
" 9	Purchased goods from Mukesh & Co.	Rs.	7,000
" 12	Goods given in charity	Rs.	600
" 15	Paid office expenses	Rs.	500
" 20	Paid in to bank	Rs.	4,000
" 24	Loss of goods by fire	Rs.	300
" 25	Sold to Mani on credit	Rs.	3,000
" 26	Goods purchased on credit	Rs.	9,000
" 27	Withdrew money for private use	Rs.	900
" 28	Deposit in to bank	Rs.	2,000

" 29	Interest received	Rs.	400
" 29	Commission received	Rs.	300
" 30	Salary paid	Rs.	2,000

Record the above transactions in Premchand's journal and post them to the journal.

Q. 8. Journalise the following transactions in the book of Meerut Store and post to ledger:

2004			
Nov 2	Business started with		
	Cash	Rs.	30,000
	Goods	Rs.	12,000
" 4	Bought furniture from Gupta & Co.	Rs.	7,000
" 5	Goods sold to Amarnath	Rs.	14,000
" 6	Paid for stationary	Rs.	500
" 8	Cash purchase	Rs.	4,000
" 10	Goods purchased from Rajkishor	Rs.	6,000
" 14	Cash Sales	Rs.	7,000
" 17	Motorcycle purchased for office use	Rs.	10,000
" 20	Order received from Manoj worth	Rs.	20,000
" 22	Received from Amarnath on account	Rs.	10,000
" 23	Payment made to Gupta & Co.	Rs.	6,800
	Discount received	Rs.	200
" 25	Received from Amarnath in full settlement	Rs.	3,500
" 28	Payment made for		
	Salary	Rs.	3,500
	Rent	Rs.	500
	Office expenses	Rs.	400

Q. 9. Journalise the following transactions and post them to ledger:

2004			
Oct. 1	Rajesh starts business with cash	Rs.	40,000
" 2	Bought goods for cash	Rs.	10,000

" 4	Sold for cash	Rs.	22,000
" 6	Machinery purchased for cash	Rs.	5,000
" 8	Sold to Amit	Rs.	6,000
" 11	Purchased from Rakesh	Rs.	4,000
" 14	Goods purchased from Rakesh	Rs.	3,000
" 17	Cash sales	Rs.	12,000
" 20	Paid for stationary	Rs.	600
" 22	Goods sold on credit	Rs.	4,000
" 26	Paid for rent	Rs.	600
" 26	Paid for carriage	Rs.	400
" 27	Cash paid to Rakesh	Rs.	2,600
	Discount received from him	Rs.	400
" 28	Salary paid	Rs.	3,000

Q. 10. Journalise the following transactions and post them to ledger:

2005			
Jan 1	Commenced business in cash	Rs.	45,000
" 3	Paid in to bank	Rs.	6,000
" 4	Bought furniture from Shastri & Com.	Rs.	12,000
" 6	Bought goods from Sachin	Rs.	11,000
" 9	Sold to Ghosh	Rs.	16,000
" 15	Sold to Satish for cash	Rs.	13,650
" 18	Rent for one year paid in advance	Rs.	6,000
" 20	Withdrew for house hold expenses		
	Goods	Rs.	600
	Cash	Rs.	850
" 24	Cash withdraw from bank for office	Rs.	5,000
" 27	Repairs to scooter, payment not yet made	Rs.	340
" 28	Bank charges for the month	Rs.	600
" 29	Depreciation charged on furniture	Rs.	1,000
" 30	Cheque received from Ghosh in full settlement	Rs.	15,600

CHAPTER VII

CASHBOOK

In every business house there are numerous transactions relating to cash receipts and payments of it. So it is necessary and useful to the business house to know continuously the balance of cash and bank on hand. For this purpose cashbook is maintained. The object of the cashbook is to keep a daily record of the transactions relating to receipts and payments of cash. Cashbook enables businessman to know the balance of cash in hand or at any point of time. It plays a dual role. It serves the purpose of a book of original entry as well as that of a ledger a/c. If cashbook is maintained there is no need to have a cash account in the ledger.

It has two sides—debit side and credit side. All receipts of cash are recorded on the debit side while on the credit side; all payments of cash are recorded.

TYPES OF CASH BOOK

There are different types of cashbook used by the business. These are

1. Simple cash book
2. Two column cash book
3. Three column cash book
4. Petty cash book

Simple Cashbook

It is like an ordinary cash account. All cash receipts are recorded on the debit side and all payments are recorded on the credit side. In particular column the name of the account, in respect of which the amount is received and paid, is written. The ledger folio column is used for recording the page number of the account where the entry has been posted in the ledger.

Balance the Cashbook

It is like the balancing the cash account. The cashbook is always showing a debit balance because cash payment never exceeds the amount of cash available. So total of the debit side in the cashbook will always be more then the total of the credit side. The different between the two indicates the cash in hand.

SIMPLE CASHBOOK

Dr. **Cr.**

Date	Particulars	LF	Amount Rs. P.	Date	Particulars	LF	Amount Rs. P.

Illustration 1. Enter the following transactions is a simple cashbook:

2005

Jan.	1	Cash balance	Rs. 3,200
”	5	Cash sales	Rs. 4,570
”	8	Rent paid	Rs. 400
”	15	Received from Rakesh	Rs. 2,300
”	18	Commission paid	Rs. 600
”	20	Cash purchase	Rs. 2,600
”	25	Wages paid	Rs. 800
”	28	Deposit in to bank	Rs. 2,500

Solution:

In the books of...............

CASHBOOK

Dr **Cr**

Date	Particulars	F	Amount Rs. P.	Date	Particulars	F	Amount Rs. P
2005				2005			
Jan 1	To balance b/d		3,200.00	Jan. 8	By rent a/c		400.00
Jan 5	To sales a/c		4,570.00	Jan 18	By commission a/c		600.00
Jan 15	To Rakesh		2,300.00	Jan 20	By purchases a/c		2,600.00
				Jan 25	By wages a/c		800.00
				Jan 26	By bank a/c		2,500.00
				Jan 31	By balance c/d		3170.00
			10,070.00				10,070.00
Feb. 1	To balance b/d		3,170.00				

Two-Column Cashbook

In this cashbook an additional amount column for discount is provided on both side of the cashbook. Discount column on the debit side represent cash discount allowed to customer and discount column on the credit side represent cash discount received from creditors. In the cash column on the debit side the actual cash receipt is recorded and in the cash column on the credit side the actual cash paid will be written. So we have two-amount column on each side of the cashbook, one for discount and other for cash. That's why it is called two-column cashbook.

Balancing the cashbook

The discount columns are not balanced. They are simply total. The total of discount column of the receipt side represents the total discount allowed to the customer and debited to discount account. The total of discount column of the payment side shows the total discount received and is credited to the discount account. Only the cash columns are to be balanced.

TWO-COLUMN CASHBOOK

Dr **Cr**

Date	Particulars	F	Dis.	Amount	Date	Particulars	F	Dis.	Amount

Illustration 2. Enter the following transaction in two column cashbook:

2005			
Jan 1	Cash balance	Rs.	4,320
" 5	Cash sales	Rs.	7,800
" 8	Rent paid	Rs.	700
" 15	Received from Rakesh	Rs.	3,460
"	Discount allowed to him	Rs.	40
" 18	Commission paid	Rs.	600
" 20	Cash purchase	Rs.	1,800
" 25	Paid to Shyam	Rs.	980
"	Discount received	Rs.	20
" 28	Deposit into bank	Rs.	2,500
" 29	Cash paid to Rastogi	Rs.	2,380
	Discount received from him	Rs.	120

Solution:

In the book of ....
Two Column Cash Book

Date	Particulars	LF	Dis.	Amount Rs. P.	Date	Particulars	LF	Dis.	Amount Rs. P.
2005					2005				
Jan 1	To balance b/d			4,320.00	Jan 8	By rent a/c			700.00
Jan 5	To sales a/c			7,800.00	Jan 18	by comm. a/c			600.00
Jan 15	To Rakesh		40	3,460.00	Jan 20	By purchase a/c			1,800.00
					Jan 25	By Shyam		20	980.00
					Jan 28	By bank a/c			2,500.00
					Jan 29	By Rastogi		120	2,380.00
					Jan 31	By balance c/d			6,620.00
			40	15,580.00				140	15,580.00
Feb. 1	To balance b/d			6,620.00					

Three-Column Cash Book

In modern business houses transactions with a bank are even more numerous than cash transactions. Hence, the cashbook should have bank column in addition to the cash and discount columns to have a record of bank a/c in the cashbook. This column will record payment in to bank and payments out of bank. Such type of cashbook is known as three-column cashbook.

The following points need consideration in the preparation of three-column cash book:

1. If a new business is started with cash, the amount will be written in the cash column and in bank column if cash is directly put in to bank with explanation to capital a/c.
2. If new cashbook is introduce for a running business, the opening balance will be written with the explanation to balance b/d.
3. If a cheque is received and kept in the cash box, it must be debited in the cash column.
4. If a cheque is received and immediately sent to the bank for collection, the debit should be given in the bank column.
5. When cheque kept in the cashbook is sent to the bank, for collection, contra entry will be recorded in the cashbook.
6. If payments are made through cheque, these should be credited in the bank column.
7. If some cheque sent to bank for collection is dishonored the amount of it will be entered in the bank column on the credit side with the name of responsible party.
8. When cash is deposited in to the bank, it should be debited to bank a/c by entering the amount in the bank column on the debit side of cash book as to cash and credited to cash account by entering the amount in the cash column on the credit side of the cash as by bank a/c in such transaction both account (debit and credit) involves appear

THREE-COLUMN CASH BOOK

Dr. **Cr.**

Date	Particulars	f.	Dis.	Bank	Amount Rs.	P.	Date	Particulars	f.	Dis	Bank	Amount Rs.	P.

in the cash book so letter "c" is written in the ledger folio (l.f.) column on each side of the cash book to indicate that the contra effect of this transaction is recorded on the other side. Such entry of the cashbook is called contra entry.

9. When cash is withdrawn from the bank for office use, the amount will be entered in the bank column on the payment (credit) side and in the cash column on the receipt (debit) side. No posting in the ledger is required for these transactions. In such transactions, both account (debit and credit) involved appear in the cashbook so letter c is written in the l.f. Column on each side of the cashbook to indicate that the contra effect of this transactions on the other side. Such entry of the cashbook is called contra entry.

Illustration 3: Prepare a three-column cashbook from the following transactions:

2005		Rs.
Jan 1	Cash in hand	200
	Bank overdraft	800
" 5	Salary paid in cash	300
" 7	Cash withdrawn for office use	1,000
" 9	Cash paid to Amit	650
" 14	Cash sales	650
" 18	Withdrew for personal use	100
" 21	cheque received from Rakesh and immediately sent to bank for collection	980
	Discount allowed to him	20
" 24	Rent paid by cheque	150
" 27	Cash deposited in bank	600

Petty Cashbook: Generally petty cashbook is maintained in a columnar form. In such type of petty cashbook, a separate column for each head of expenses is provided. This book is also known as analytical petty cash book. The various small cash payment gets automatically analyzed who are recorded in their

Solution

In the book of...........

Three-column cashbook

Date	Particulars	L.F	Dis Rs. P.	Cash Rs. P.	Bank Rs. P.	Date	Particulars	L.F.	Dis Rs. P.	Cash Rs. P.	Bank Rs. P.
2005						2005					
Jan 1	To bal.b/d			200.00		Jan 1	By bal b/d				800.00
Jan 7	To bank a/c	'C'		1000.00		Jan 5	By salary a/c			300.00	
Jan 14	To sales a/c			650.00		Jan 7	By cash a/c	'C'			1000.00
Jan 21	To Rakesh		20.00		980.00	Jan 9	By Amit			650.00	
Jan 27	To cash a/c	'C'			600.00	Jan 18	By drawings			100.00	
Jan 31	To bal. c/d				370.00	Jan 24	By rent a/c				150.00
						Jan 27	By bank a/c	'C'		600.00	
						Jan 31	By bal. c/d			200.00	
			20.00	1850.00	1950.00					1850.00	1950.00
Feb. 1	To bal. b/d			200.00		Feb.1	By bal. b/d				370.00

respective column. The amount received by the petty cashier is written on the debit side of petty cash and all small payments on the credit side.

Every transaction is written twice—one in the total payment column and second in the column of respective expenses head. The total of each column is posted to the respective expenses a/c and the total of payment column helps in finding out the balance of cash with the petty cashier.

Imprest System of Petty Cash Book: In this system, the petty cashier receive a certain sum of money at the beginning of the certain time period, say, one week or a month. The petty cashier makes the small payment for which he is authorized and records them in the petty cashbook. At the end of such period, the chief cashier examines the accounts and pay to the petty cashier the amount spent by him. So that at the beginning of the next period again he has the same amount as he had in the beginning.

For example: On Jan. 1,2005, Rs. 600 are given to the petty cashier and he has spend Rs. 500 during the month, and submit the accounts along with the voucher to the chief cashier, he will be paid Rs. 500 by chief cashier. So that he may again start the next month with Rs. 600.

PROBLEMS

Q. 1. Enter the following transactions in simple cash book:

2005			Rs.
Jan.	1	Cash in hand	5,000
"	4	Bought goods for cash	1,000
"	6	Paid to Rahim	450
"	7	Sold goods for cash	4,500
"	9	Paid for stationary	680
"	14	Office furniture purchased	1,700
"	18	Paid rent	600
"	22	Received from Rastogi	300
"	25	Paid salary	700

Ans.: cash Balance Rs. 4,670

Q. 2. Enter the following transactions in simple cash book of Mr. Ramsudhir:

2004			Rs.
Jan.	1	Cash in hand	1,570
"	8	Sold goods for cash	3,560
"	3	Goods purchased for cash	1,500
"	6	Paid Shyam	1,350
"	9	Paid for stationary	80
"	12	Office furniture purchased	1,380
"	16	Paid rent	600
"	20	Received from R.Gupta	2,790
"	25	Paid salary	900
"	29	Paid for general expenses	340

Ans.: Cash Balance Rs. 1,770

Q. 3. Enter the following transactions in simple cash book:

2005			Rs.
Jan.	1	Cash in hand	5,000
"	9	Paid for advertising	600
"	6	Paid to Sanjeev	3,600
"	4	Cash purchase	2,300
"	7	Cash sales	5,600
"	14	Office furniture purchased	1,700
		Sold goods for cash	3,380
"	18	Paid rent	900
"	22	Received from Amaranth	4,370
"	25	Paid salary	2,700
"	28	Bought goods from Ram on Credit	3,800
		Deposit in to bank	2,000

Ans.: Cash Balance Rs. 4,550

Q. 4. Enter the following transactions in two column cash book:

2005		Rs.
Feb. 1	Cash balance	8,000
" 3	Received cash from Lalsingh	4,300
" 6	Cash purchase	3,600
" 8	Paid to Pankaj	680
	Discount received from him	20
" 12	Sold goods	4,800
" 15	Paid rent	500
" 16	Paid for stationary	640
" 18	Received from Naveen	1,450
	Discount allowed to him	50
" 20	Drew cash for personal use	600
" 25	Paid wages for cash	300

Ans.: Total of Discount (Dr.) Rs. 50 and (Cr.) Rs. 20. Cash Balance Rs. 12,230

Q. 5. Enter the following transactions in cash book:

2005		Rs.
Jan. 1	Business started with cash	8,500
" 2	Cash purchase	6,500
" 5	Cash sales	5,000
" 8	Paid to Raman	860
	Discount received from him	40
" 12	Sold goods to Sumit on credit	6,000
" 16	Paid rent	500
" 16	Paid for advertisement	480
" 18	Received from Amit	1,580
	Discount allowed to him	20
" 19	Paid wages for cash	580
" 22	Sold goods for cash	2,000
" 26	Paid for general expenses	800
" 28	Paid into bank	3,050
" 29	Paid electricity bill	700

Ans.: Total of Discount (Dr.) Rs. 20 and (Cr.) Rs. 40. Cash Balance Rs. 3,610.

Q. 6. Enter the following transactions in cash book:

2005			Rs.
Mar.	1	Cash balance from last month	2,590
"	2	Received cash from Mr. S Agarwal	2,460
"	4	Cash purchase	2,390
"	6	Paid to Pankaj	1,460
		Discount received from him	40
"	7	Sold goods	7,800
"	8	Paid Rajan in full settlement of his account of Rs. 1,000	970
"	11	Purchased office furniture	1,100
"	13	Paid for miscellaneous expenses	450
"	13	Paid rent	680
"	16	Paid for stationery	30
"	17	Received from Naveen	790
		Discount allowed to him	10
"	19	Drew cash for household expenses	570
"	20	Paid wages for cash	470

Ans.: Total of Discount (Dr.) Rs. 10 and (Cr.) Rs. 70. Cash Balance Rs. 5,520

Q. 7. Enter the following transactions in two column cash book:

2005			Rs.
Jan.	1	Cash in hand	16,000
"	4	Purchased good for cash from Suman	4,000
"	6	Received cash from Suresh	2,480
		Discount allowed to him	20
"	8	Paid for petty expenses	700
"	12	Paid into bank	2,600
"	17	Paid for charity	250
"	18	Cash purchase	3,000
"	22	Paid to Satish	400
		Discount received from him	10
"	24	Sold goods for cash	2,600
"	27	Received from Ghosh	870
"	28	Paid for stationary	480

" 28	Paid to Govind	390
	Discount allowed from him	10
" 29	Purchased a cycle for his son	1,233
" 30	Paid for general expenses	470

Ans.: Total of Discount (Dr.) Rs. 20 and (Cr.) Rs. 20. Cash Balance Rs. 8,427

Q. 8. Prepare a three column cash book:

2005		Rs.
Apr. 1	Cash in hand	5,000
" 1	Cash at bank	2,000
" 6	Deposit in bank	2,000
" 8	Cash sales	4,000
" 13	Goods purchased by cheque	500
" 17	wages paid	400
" 19	Rent paid	200
" 22	Salary paid by cheque	400

Ans.: Cash Balance Rs. 6,400 and Bank Balance Rs. 3,100.

Q. 9. Prepare a three column cash book:

2005		Rs.
Mar. 1	Cash in hand	4,000
" 1	Cash at bank	2,000
" 5	Cash purchases	1,000
" 7	Good sold in cash	3,000
" 10	Machinery purchased in cash	2,000
" 15	Cash deposited in bank	3,000
" 18	Paid to Ashit	1,950
"	Discount received	50
" 25	Drew from bank for office use	1,000

Ans.: Total of Discount (Cr.) Rs. 50. Cash Balance Rs. 50 and Bank Balance Rs. 4,000.

Q. 10. Enter the following transactions in the bank column cash book:

2005		Rs.
Jan. 1	Cash in hand	6,000
"	Cash at bank	1,850

" 5	cheque received from Mukesh	900
" 8	Furniture purchased from Ravi Kant	1,000
" 10	Paid into bank	1,500
" 16	Interest allowed by bank	300
" 18	Cash sales	2,000
" 20	Final payment made to Ravi Kant	900
" 23	Cash with drew for office use	1,500
" 25	Paid rent by cheque	200

Ans.: Total of Discount (Cr.) Rs. 100. Cash Balance Rs. 8,000 and Bank Balance Rs. 1,950.

Q. 11. Enter the following transaction in the bank column cash book:

2005		Rs.
Feb. 1	Balance in hand	2,850
	Balance at bank	1,850
" 5	Deposited into bank	2,000
" 10	Interest allowed by bank	400
" 12	Received cheque from Gaurav	500
	Discount allowed to him	10
" 15	Machinery purchased from Mukesh and Co.	800
" 18	Good sold to Raman	1,000
" 20	Cash purchased	200
" 24	Cheque received from Gaurav is Deposited in bank	
" 25	Drew from personal use—Cash	200
	Bank	200
" 27	Withdrew from bank for office use	400
" 30	Payment made (final settelement) to Mohan and company through cheque	780

Ans.: Total of Discount (Dr.) Rs. 10 and (Cr.) Rs. 20. Cash Balance Rs. 850 and Bank Balance Rs. 3,370.

Q. 12. Enter the following transactions in three columns cash book:

2005		Rs.
Mar. 1	Cash in hand	8,000
" 4	Cash at bank	2,000

" 6	Cash sales	6,000
" 8	Purchased goods from Hari on credit	3,600
" 12	Purchased goods for cash	2,000
" 17	Received cheque from Nitin	1,450
	Discount allowed to him	50
" 18	Paid for petty expenses	450
" 22	Paid into bank	2,300
" 24	Paid salary through cheque	1,450
" 27	Cash purchase	2,800
" 28	Paid to Satish by cheque	580
"	Discount received from him	20
" 28	Sold goods for cash and banked the same	600

Ans.: Total of Discount (Dr.) Rs. 50 and (Cr.) Rs. 20. Cash Balance Rs. 7,900 and Bank Balance Rs. 2,870.

Q. 13. Enter the following transactions in three columns cash book:

2005		Rs.
Mar. 1	Cash in hand	5,700
" 3	Bank overdraft	2,000
" 5	Paid wages by cheque	500
" 9	Cash sales	5,300
" 11	Deposited into bank	2,400
" 12	Purchased goods from Ashit on credit	2,800
" 15	Purchased goods for cash	1,740
" 18	Received cheque from Rakesh	3,200
	Discount allowed to him	50
" 22	Paid rent by cheque	470
" 25	Drawn from bank	1,500
" 27	Paid salary in cash	600
" 28	Paid to Ashit in full settlement	2,750
" 29	Deposited Rakesh's cheque into bank	
" 29	Cash purchase	2,100

" 30	Sold goods for cash and banked the same	3700
" 30	Bank charges	300

Ans.: Total of Discount (Dr.) Rs. 50 and (Cr.) Rs. 50. Cash Balance Rs. 2,910 and Bank Balance Rs. 4,530.

Q. 14. Enter the following transactions in Three column cash book:

2005		Rs.
Feb. 1	Started business with cash	40,000
" 5	Opened current account with the bank	15,000
" 7	Cash sales	4,800
" 8	Received a cheque from Ram	4,000
" 9	Bought goods by cheque	2,580
" 12	Paid wages for cheque	500
" 15	Paid cash in to bank	2,000
" 16	Deposited Ram's cheque into bank	
" 18	Ram's cheque returned dishonored	
" 20	Paid taxes	200
" 23	Drew from bank for office use	3,000
" 24	Paid establishment expenses through bank	1,870
" 25	Received from Anand by a cheque and	
"	sent to bank	3000
" 29	Paid to Atul by a cheque Rs. 980 in	
	full settlement of his account of Rs.	1,000

Ans.: Total of Discount (Cr.) Rs. 20. Cash Balance Rs. 30,600 and Bank Balance Rs. 11,070.

Q. 15. Enter the following transactions in three columns cash book:

2005		Rs.
Feb. 1	Cash in hand	5,853
" 2	Bank balance	5,645
" 5	Paid trade expenses	1,222
" 6	Paid into bank	2,300
" 8	Bought goods for cash	3,422

" 9	Paid to HariOm by cheque (Discount allowed Rs. 40)	2,100
" 11	Interest collected by bank	200
" 14	Cash sales	4,377
" 16	Withdrew from bank	2,100
" 18	Withdrew from bank for personal use	322
" 19	Received a cheque for goods sold	2,543
" 22	Received a cheque from Pankaj	1,270
	Allowed him discount	30
" 24	Paid wages	380
" 24	Paid rent by cheque	570
" 27	Bought goods from Gyan on credit	348
" 28	Paid for advertising by cheque	480

Ans.: Total of Discount (Dr.) Rs. 30 and (Cr.) Rs. 40. Cash Balance Rs. 8,819 and Bank Balance Rs. 2,573.

Q. 16. A petty cashier in a firm received Rs. 500, as petty cash impress on 1st March 2005 during the month his expenses here as follows:

2005		
Mar. 4	Taxi charges for managers trip	50
" 6	Cartage	20
" 10	Railway fate on account of books	10
" 12	Wages to casual labour	15
" 15	Repair to typewriter	25
" 20	Stationary purchased	15
" 22	Refreshment to customers	30
" 25	Telegram to head office	10
" 27	Stationery purchased	25
" 30	Sundry expenses	60

Write up the patty cashbook

CHAPTER VIII

SUBSIDIARY BOOKS

All business transactions are first written in the journal and after that posted in to ledger. But in practice, the numbers of business transactions are so large that it is not possible to record all the transactions in journal. It is easy to keep a separate register for each type of transactions, for example, one for credit purchase of goods, one for credit sales of goods, one for cash receipts and payments etc. These types of books are called – books of prime entry. These books of original or prime entry are called subsidiary books. Ledger accounts are prepared on this basis.

SUBSIDIARY BOOKS

The following subsidiary journal/subsidiary books have found their place in modern bookkeeping-

Cash-book

Purchase book

Sales book

Purchase return book

Sales return book

Bills receivable book

Bills payable book

Purchase Book

This book is kept for the purpose of recording all credit purchases of goods. It is also known as bought book, invoice book or purchase journal. Cash purchases will not be entered in this book because all entries of cash purchases must have been made in cashbook. Credit purchases of things, other than goods such as machinery, furniture etc. are journalised, they also will not be entered in the purchase book. Only credit purchases of trading goods and materials will be recorded in purchases book.

FORMAT

PURCHASE BOOK

Date	Particulars	Invoice No.	Ledger Folio	Details		Total	
				Rs	P	Rs	P

The particular column is meant to record the name of suppliers together with details of goods purchased. In 'detail column' the amount in respect of each articles is entered. After totaling the various amounts included in a single purchase, the amount of other charges is added. The amount of trade discount will be deducted. The net amount will be recorded in the 'amount column'.

Posting the purchases book: At the end of each month this book is totaled. The total is posted to the debit of purchase account. A separate account will have to be opened in the ledger for each supplier of goods and the amount of such purchase would be credited to their respective personal account. The double entry will thus be completed.

Illustration 1: The purchases of M/s Pankaj and Co. are as follows:

On 2nd Jan. 2005, from Sunshine and Co. Meerut on credit:

100 electric bulbs of 40 wt. @ Rs. 10 per bulbs

10 fan Usha @ Rs. 600 per fan

Less — 10% trade discounts

On 14th Jan. 2005, from Meerut Electric Company

20 coolers @ Rs. 500 per cooler

10 toasters @ Rs. 100 per toaster

Less — 8% trade discounts

On 20th Jan. 2005, from Prem & Co.

25 fancy light @ Rs. 50 per light

On 25th Jan. 2005, purchased for cash from Raman and Bros.

10 ceiling fan @ Rs. 680 per fan

Prepare a purchase book from the following transactions.

Solution:

In the book of M/S Pankaj and Company

PURCHASE BOOK

Date	Particulars	Invoice No.	L. F.	Details Rs.	P.	Total Rs.	P.
2005							
Jan 2	M/s Sunshine and Co. Meerut						
	100 E. bulbs @ Rs. 10 each			1,000	00		
	10 fan Usha @ Rs. 600 each			6,000	00		
				7,000	00		
	Less: Trade discount 10%			700	00	6,300	00
Jan 14	Meerut Electric Company						
	20 cooler @ Rs. 500 each			10,000			
	10 toaster @ Rs. 100 each			1,000			
				11,000			

(contd.)

Date	Particulars	Invoice No.	L. F.	Details Rs.	P.	Total Rs.	P.
	Less: Trade discount 8%			880	00	10,120	00
Jan. 20	Prem & Company						
	25 fancy light @ Rs. 50			1,250	00	1,250	00
	Total					17,670	00

Sales Book: This book is just opposite to the purchase book. This book is kept for the purpose of recording all credit sales of goods. It is also known as Day book. Cash sales will not be entered in this book because all entries of cash sales must have been made in cash book. Credit sales of any asset will not be entered in the sales book. Only credit sales of trading goods and materials will be recorded in sales book.

FORMAT
SALES BOOK

Date	Particulars	Invoice No.	Ledger Folio	Details Rs	P	Total Rs	P

The particular column is meant to record the name of customers together with details of goods sold. In 'detail column' the amount in respect of each articles is entered. After totaling the various amounts included in single sales, the amount of other charges is added. The amount of trade discount will be deducted. The net amount will be recorded in the 'amount column'.

Posting the Sales Book: At the end of each month this book is totaled. The total is posted to the credit of sales account. A separate account will have to be opened in the ledger for each customer of goods and the amount of such sales would be debited their respective personal account. The double entry will thus be completed.

Illustration 2: From the following write up the sales book of M/s Sunil and Co.

2005

Feb. 1 Sold to Amit & Sons Books Store
10 gross pencils @ Rs. 15 per gross
22 dozen pen @ Rs. 100 per dozen
Less — 10% trade discounts

Feb. 5 Sold to M/s Shubham Stores
5 reams of ruled paper @ Rs. 150 per ream
10 reams of white paper @ Rs. 200 per ream
Less — 10% trade discount

Feb. 15 Sold old office furniture on credit to Sunlight M/s Furnitures for Rs. 5000.

Solution:

IN THE BOOK OF M/S SUNIL AND COMPANY
SALES BOOK

Date	Particulars	Invoice No.	L. F.	Details Rs.	P.	Total Rs.	P.
2005							
Feb. 1	Amit & Sons						
	10 gross pencils @ Rs. 100 per gross			1,000	00		
	22 doz. pen @ Rs. 100 per doz.			2,200	00		
				3,200	00		
	Less: Trade discount 10%			320	00	2,880	00

(contd.)

Date	Particulars	Invoice No.	L. F.	Details Rs.	P.	Total Rs.	P.
Feb. 5	Shubham Stores						
	5 ream ruled paper @ Rs. 150 per ream			750	00		
	10 reams white paper @ Rs. 200 per ream			2,000	00		
				2,750	00		
	Less: Trade discount 10%			275	00	2,475	00
	Total					5,355	00

Purchase Return Book: The goods returned by the trader to the suppliers are called purchase return or return outward. A separate book is used to record such return, which is called 'purchase return book' or 'return outward book'. When goods are returned a debit note is prepared and sent to supplier to whom goods are returned.

FORMAT
PURCHASE RETURN BOOK

Date	Particulars	Debit Note No.	L. F.	Details Rs.	P	Amount Rs.	P

Posting of Purchase Return Book: The account of each individual supplier is debited in the ledger with its respective amount with the words "to purchases return a/c". The total of the purchase return book shows the total of returns made by the organization. This total is credited to purchase return account with the words "By sundries as per purchase return book".

Sales Return Book: The goods returned by the customers to the firm are called sales return or return inward. A separate book is used to record such return, which is called 'sales return book' or 'return inward book'. When the customer returns goods, a credit note is prepared by the firm in the name of customers and sent its original copy to the customer.

FORMAT
SALES RETURN BOOK

Date	Particulars	Credit Note No.	L. F.	Details Rs.	P	Amount Rs.	P

Posting of Purchase Return Book: The account of each individual customer is debited in the ledger with its respective amount with the words "to sales return a/c". The total of the sales return book shows the total of returns made by the customers to the organization. This total is debited to sales return account with the words "By sundries as per sales return book".

Bills Receivable Book: When goods are sold on credit or a loan is advanced, the purchaser or borrower gives a promise in written to pay the respective amount on a specific date. Such written promises are called bills of exchanges or promissory note. For a firm, bills on which it has to collect money are called bills receivable. A separate book is kept to record such bills, which is called bills receivable book.

Bills payable book: For a firm, bills on which it is liable to pay in future are called bills payables. A separate book is kept to record such bills, which is called bills payable book.

Illustration 3: Record the followings transactions in the appropriate books of original entry.

2005

Jan. 2 Purchased on credit from Shubham & Bros.

50 White shirts @ Rs. 150 each

100 Blue shirts @ Rs. 100 each

20 Trousers @ Rs. 200 each

Less — 10% trade discount

Jan. 10 Sold on credit to Amit

40 Black T-shirt @ Rs. 70 each

60 White T-shirt @ Rs. 120 each

12 Cotton shirts @ Rs. 200 each

Jan. 15 Goods return to Shubham and Bros.

5 White shirt @ Rs. 150 each

5 Trousers @ Rs. 200 each

Jan. 20 Sold to Arun on credit

20 Trousers @ Rs. 200 each

5 Neck ties @ Rs. 150 each

Jan. 22 Goods received back from Manoj, a customer

4 Neck-ties @ Rs. 220 each

2 Shirt @ Rs. 50 each

Jan. 28 Purchased from Suman on credit

120 Bush shirts @ Rs. 140 each

20 Neck ties @ Rs. 100 each

25 Shirt @ Rs. 100 each

Less — 10% Trade discounts

Solution

PURCHASE BOOK

Date	Particulars	Invoice No.	L. F.	Details Rs.	P.	Total Rs.	P.
2005							
Jan. 2	Shubham and Bros.						
	50 W. shirts @ Rs. 150 each			7,500	00		
	100 B. shirts @ Rs. 100 each			10,000	00		
	20 Trousers @ Rs. 200 each			4,000	00		
				21,500	00		
	Less: Trade discount 10%			2,150	00	19,350	00
Jan. 28	Suman						
	120 Bush shirts @ Rs. 140 each			16,800	00		
	20 Neck ties @ Rs. 100 each			2,000	00		
	25 Shirts @ Rs. 100 each			2,500	00		
				21,300	00		
	Less: Trade discount 10%			2,130	00	19,170	00
	Total					38,520	00

SALES BOOK

Date	Particulars	Invoice No.	L. F.	Details Rs.	P.	Total Rs.	P.
2005							
Jan. 10	Amit						
	40 Black T-shirts @ Rs. 70 each			2,800	00		
	60 White T-shirts @ Rs. 120 each			7,200	00		
	12 Shirts @ Rs. 200 each			2,400	00		
				12,400	00		
	Less—Trade discount 10%			1,240	00	10,160	00
Jan. 20	Arun						
	20 Trousers @ Rs. 200 each			4,000	00		
	5 Neck-ties @ Rs. 150 each			750	00	4,750	00
	Total					14,910	00

PURCHASE RETURN BOOK

Date	Particulars	Debit Note No.	L. F.	Details Rs.	P	Total Rs.	P
2005							
Jan. 15	Shubham and Bros.						
	5 White shirt @ Rs. 150 each			750	00		
	5 Trousers @ Rs. 200 each			1,000	00	1,750	00
	Total					1,750	00

SALES RETURN BOOK

Date	Particulars	Credit Note No.	L. F.	Details Rs.	P	Total Rs.	P
2005							
Jan. 22	Manoj						
	4 Neck-ties @ Rs. 220 each			880	00		
	2 Shirts @ Rs. 50 each			100	00	980	00
	Total					980	00

PROBLEMS

Q.1. Prepare a purchase book from the following transactions:

2005

Jan 1Bought from M/s Rastogi Traders, Meerut

100 Bags of Rice @ Rs. 690 per bag

80 Bags of Gram @ Rs. 135 per bag

Less—10% trade discounts

Jan. 5Bought from M/s Dubey

35 Bags of Wheat @ Rs. 850 per bag

40 Bags of Oats @ Rs. 300 per bag

Less—7% Trade discount

Q.2. Prepare a purchase book from the following transactions-

2005

Feb. 1 Bought from R.K. Company
30 White shirts @ Rs. 250 each
25 Black shirts @ Rs. 200 each
Less — 10% trade discount

Feb. 7 Bought from M/s Ashit Garments
20 Trousers @ Rs. 235 each
15 Overcoat @ Rs. 190 each
Less — 8% trade discount

Fab. 19 Purchased 20 Shirts from Madan Shirts

Q.3. Prepare a purchase book of M/s Gaurav & Company:

2005

Feb. 1 Purchased 2 typewriters for office use from Radhyshyam Typing Co. for Rs. 800 each

Feb. 8 Purchased from Meerut Stationery Co.
5 Reams of typing paper @ Rs. 25 each ream
15 White paper @ Rs. 70 each ream
Less — 2% trade discounts

Feb. 15 Purchased from Tiwari Books Store for cash
5 Dozen carbon paper @ Rs. 30 per doz.
6 Dozen pencil @ Rs. 30 per doz.

Fed. 20 Purchased from M/s Verma Bros. on credit
4 Dozen exercise book @ Rs. 16 each
3 Dozen file cover @ Rs. 3 each
Less — 5% trade discount

Q.4. Enter the following transactions in the purchase book of Ghosh & Sons:

2005

Mar 1 Purchased from M/s Mukesh Sons, Delhi

200 Shirts @ Rs. 330 each
135 Short shirt @ Rs. 150 each
Less — 8% trade discount

Mar. 5 Purchased from M/s S.N. Dass
70 White T-shirts @ Rs. 100
80 Black T-shirts @ Rs. 150
Less — 5% trade discount

Mar.10 Purchased from B.C. and Company
50 Rain coats @ Rs. 90 each

Q.5. Prepare the sales book from the followings:

Sold to M/s Devi Dayal on credit
115 Chairs @ Rs.88 each
120 Tables @ Rs.110 each
Less — 5% trade discount

Sold to Mohan & Company on credit
20 Computer table @ Rs. 135 each
15 table @ Rs. 165 each
Less — 7% trade discount

Q.6. Prepare a sales book from the following transactions in the book of Radhy Shyam:

2005

Feb. 2 Sold to Dayal Book Corner on credit
10 Dozen Natraj pencil @ Rs. 20 per doz.
15 Dozen Steno pencil @ Rs. 25 per doz.

Feb 5 Sold to Raman Book Store
2 Stapler @ Rs. 45 each
10 Writing pad @ Rs. 15 each
Less — 5% trade discount

Feb. 10 Sold to Sahil Stores

60 Drawing sheets @ Rs. 100 per doz.

5 Ream of white paper @ Rs. 95 per ream

Less — 8% trade discount

Q.7. From the following prepare the sales book of Rajan and Co.

2005

Mar. 1 Sold to Pratap & Sons

50 Cotton shirts @ Rs. 180 each

60 Polyester shirts @ Rs. 110 each

Less — 10% trade discount

Mar. 7 Sold to M/s Rakesh & Company

80 T-shirts @ Rs. 70

75 Short shirts @ Rs. 80

Mar. 9 Sold to Dev & Sons

30 Trousers @ Rs. 135 each

10 Raincoat @ Rs. 145 each

Mar.15 Sold to Bhuwan in cash

30 T-shirts @ Rs. 135

40 Trousers @ Rs. 150

Less — 5% trade discount

Q.8. Prepare a sales book from the following transactions:

2005

Jan. 1 Sold to M/s Heralal Munna Lal, Delhi

75 Bags of Wheat @ Rs. 600 each

50 Bags of Ratna rice @ Rs. 450 each

Less — 10% Trade discount

Jan. 5 Sold to M/s Lakshmi Chand & Sons

40 Tin oil @ Rs. 315 each

50 Begs of Rice @ Rs. 515 each
Less — 7% Trade discount

Jan. 15 Sold to M/s Aggarwal Stores
25 Bags of Gram @ Rs. 312 each
20 Bags of Wheat @ Rs. 525 each
15 Bags of Rice @ Rs. 420 each
Less — 7.5% Trade discount

Q. 9. Enter the following transactions in proper subsidiary book of Kishan for the month of Feb. 2005:

2005

Feb. 1 Purchased from Ram Kishor.
1000 Meters silk @ Rs. 5 per meters
500 Meters velvet @ Rs. 10 per meters
Less — 5% trade discount

Feb. 10 Sold to Sanjeev,
400 Meters silk @ Rs. 7 per meters
100 Meters velvet @ Rs. 120 each
50 Shirts @ Rs. 120 each
Less — 4% trade discount

Feb. 12 Purchased from Neeta
50 T-shirts @ Rs. 120 each
100 Neck-ties @ Rs. 100 each

Feb. 15 Sold to Ayush
500 Meters silk @ Rs. 20 per meters
100 Meters velvet @ Rs. 25 per meters
Less — 5% trade discount

Feb. 20 Goods return to Neeta
5 T-shirts @ Rs. 120 each
10 Neck-ties @ Rs. 100 each

Feb. 22 Goods received back from Neeraj, a customer
10 Meters silk @ Rs. 10 per meters
100 Meters velvet @ Rs. 15 per meters

CHAPTER IX

TRIAL BALANCE

Fundamental principle of double entry system is that for every transaction, one account is debited and some other account is credited with the amount of the transaction. According to this rule the total of debit balance in different account in the ledger must be equal to the total of credit balance in different account. So, the total of both columns should be same. If the two sides differ, it is a signal that there has been some mistake.

TRIAL BALANCE

Trial balance is a statement of debit and credit totals or balances extracted from the various account in the ledger with a view to test the arithmetical accuracy of the books. Trial balance ensures only arithmetic accuracy but not accounting accuracy. In other words a trial balance may be defined as a schedule or list of names and balances of all the account in the order in which they appear in the ledger. The debit balances are listed in the left hand column and the credit balance in the right hand column. The total of the two columns should equal.

OBJECTIVES OF TRIAL BALANCE

The followings are the main objectives of preparing trial balance:

1. To check the arithmetical accuracy of the accounting process. If the trial balance agree it proves that the books are arithmetically accurate.
2. It proves that both the aspect of the transactions have

been correctly recorded in the books of original entry and in the ledger.

3. Trial balance helps one to know the assets, the amount that are one owing to others and the amount due from others.
4. Trial balance facilitates the preparation of profit and loss a/c and balance sheet.
5. It brings to gathers the balances of all the account at one place.

PREPERATION OF THE TRIAL BALANCE

A trial balance can be prepared in the following methods:

1. Total Method

Under this method total of the debit and credit sides of each ledger account are shown in the trial balance. The total of debit and credit column must be equal.

FORMAT

Particulars	L.F.	Dr. Total Amount Rs.	P.	Cr. Total amount Rs.	P.

2. Balance Mathod

Under this method, the balance of each ledger account taken to respective debit credit column of the trial balance and than total is taken out. The total of balance in the debit column must be equal to the total balance in the credit column of the trial balance.

FORMAT

Particulars	L.F.	Dr. Balance Amount Rs.	P.	Cr. Balance Amount Rs.	P.

Agreement of the totals of debit and credit balance in a trial balance is not necessarily a conclusive evidence of the accuracy of books of accounts. Aggrenent of trial balance gives primary evidence that accounts are correct from arithmetic position of view.

ERRORS DISCLOSED BY TRIAL BALANCE

1. Wrong Totalling or Casting of the Subsidiary Books

For example the total of sales book is under cast by Rs. 500. In this case, the debit will exceed the credit by Rs. 500. In the same way the wrong costing of any of the subsidiary books, the total of which is debited or credited in the ledger, will threw the trial balance out.

2. Posting of Wrong Amount from Journal to Ledger

For example, credit sales of Rs. 5,000 to Shyam wrongly posted to his a/c as Rs. 2,000. The effect of this error will be that the amount of debtors will be reduced by Rs. 3,000 and the total of debit side will be less than the total of credit side.

3. Posting an Amount to the Wrong Side

For example, discount Rs. 30 allowed to customer wrongly posted to credit side of the discount a/c. The effect of this error will be that the credit side of the trial balance will be more than the total of debit side.

4. Wrong Additions or Balancing of Ledger a/c

For example, which balancing capital a/c, credit balance of Rs. 700 wrongly taken as Rs. 500. The effect of this error will be that credit side of the trial balance will be less than the total of debit side.

5. Omission of An Amount From Ledger a/c

For example, payments of Rs. 2,000 made to creditor. The entry is made in the cash book on the credit side but by mistake the creditor a/c is not debited by Rs. 2,000 as at should be. The effect of this error will be that debit side of the trial balance will be less than the total of credit.

6. An item in subsidiary book posted twice to a ledger a/c, for example, a payment of Rs. 2,000 to creditors posted twice to his a/c.

UNDISCLOSED BY TRIAL BALANCE

1. Error of Omission

If a transaction has been omitted from being entered in the books of account, it is known as error of omission. For example, if goods worth Rs. 5,000 have been sold to a customer and the entry has not at all been made in the sales books. In that case the customer a/c will not be debited and the sales a/c will not be credited. So, there is no debit and credit and the trial balance will still agree.

2. Error of Commission

If a transaction has been incorrectly recorded in the journal or posted in the ledger, it is an error of commission. For example, wrong entries in the book of primary book, wrong posting etc.

3. Compensatory Error

These errors arise when two or more errors exactly counter balance the effect of each other. In other words, where error are committed in such a way that one error compensates the other so that the net effect of all such error is nil. The trial balance will therefore, remain unaffected.

For example, the overcasting of a sales book by Rs. 200 and then by the excess credit to the sales account, will be arithmetically off set either by over debiting or under crediting a single account or several accounts with a sum of Rs. 200.

4. Error of Principle

These errors arise when some fundamental principal of sound accounting are not properly observed in recording a transaction. Such error arises on account of lack of correct knowledge of the principle governing the preparation of account.

For example, if furniture purchased is debited to purchase account, building sold is credited to sales a/c; commission paid for purchase of land is debited to commission a/c etc., then the error of principle is committed. The trial balance remains unaffected by such error.

Illustration *1*

Journalize the following transactions and post them to ledger and preprae the trial balance:

Year 2005

Jan. 01	Commence business with cash	Rs.	20,000
Jan. 02	Paid into bank	Rs.	5,000
Jan. 04	Goods purchased in cash	Rs.	1,000
Jan. 05	Goods sold to Mohan	Rs.	2,000
Jan. 06	Goods purchased from Rakesh	Rs.	3,000
Jan. 08	Goods returned to Rakesh	Rs.	500
Jan. 10	Cash withdrawl for personal use	Rs.	200
Jan. 15	Received from Mohan	Rs.	2,000
Jan. 20	Salary paid	Rs.	500
Jan. 24	Rent paid	Rs.	400
Jan. 26	Final payment made to Rakesh	Rs.	2,400
Jan. 28	Paid for stationary	Rs.	300

Solution

In the Book of............

JOURNAL ENTRIES

Date	Particulars	L.F	Amount (Dr.) Rs	P	Amount (Cr.) Rs	P
2005 Jan. 1	Cash a/c Dr To capital a/c (Being the business started with cash)		20,000	00	20,000	00
Jan. 2	Bank a/c Dr To cash a/c (Being cash deposited in bank)		5,000	00	5,000	00
Jan. 4	Purchase a/c Dr To cash a/c (Being goods purchase in cash)		1,000	00	1,000	00
Jan. 5	Mohan Dr To sales a/c (Being goods sold to him)		2,000	00	2,000	00
Jan. 6	Purchase a/c Dr To Rakesh (Being goods purchase from him)		3,000	00	3,000	00
Jan. 8	Rakesh Dr To purchase return a/c (Being goods return to him)		500	00	500	00
Jan. 10	Drawings a/c Dr To cash a/c (Being cash withdraw for personal use)		200	00	200	00

(contd.)

Date	Particulars		L.F	Amount (Dr.) Rs	P	Amount (Cr.) Rs	P
Jan. 15	Cash a/c	Dr		2,000	00		
	To Mohan					2,000	00
	(Being cash received from him)						
Jan. 20	Salary a/c	Dr		500	00		
	To cash a/c					500	00
	(Being salary paid)						
Jan. 24	Rent a/c	Dr		400	00		
	To cash a/c					400	00
	(Being the rent paid)						
Jan. 26	Rakesh	Dr.		2,500	00		
	To Cash a/c					2,400	00
	To Discount a/c					100	00
	(Being the payment & discount received)						
Jan. 28	Stationary a/c	Dr		300	00		
	To cash a/c					300	00
	(Being stationary purchased)						
	Grand Total						

LADGER ACCOUNTS

In the book of......................

CASH ACCOUNT

Dr. **Cr.**

Date	Particulars	F.	Amount Rs	P	Date	Particulars	F.	Amount Rs	P
2005					2005				
Jan 1	To Capital a/c		20,000	00	Jan 2	By bank a/c		5,000	00
Jan 15	To Mohan		2,000	00	Jan 4	By purch. a/c		1,000	00
					Jan 10	By draw. a/c		200	00

(contd.)

Date	Particulars	F.	Amount Rs	P	Date	Particulars	F.	Amount Rs	P
					Jan 20	By salary a/c		500	00
					Jan 24	By rent a/c		400	00
					Jan 26	By Rakesh		2,400	00
					Jan 28	By stationary a/c		300	00
					Jan 31	By bal. c/d		12,200	00
	Total		22,000	00		Total		22,000	00
Feb. 1	To Bal. b/d		12,200	00					

CAPITAL ACCOUNT

Dr. Cr.

Date	Particulars	F.	Amount Rs	P	Date	Particulars	F.	Amount Rs	P
2005 Jan. 31	To Bal. c/d		20,000	00	2005 Jan. 1	By cash a/c		20,000	00
			20,000	00				20,000	00
					Feb. 1	To Bal. b/d		20,000	00

PURCHASE ACCOUNT

Dr. Cr.

Date	Particulars	F.	Amount Rs	P	Date	Particulars	F.	Amount Rs	P
2005 Jan 4	To Cash a/c		1,000	00	2005 Jan 31	By Balance c/d		4,000	00
Jan 6	To Rakesh		3,000	00					
			4,000	00				4,000	00
Feb. 1	To Balance b/d		4,000	00					

SALES ACCOUNT

Dr. Cr.

Date	Particulars	F.	Amount Rs	P	Date	Particulars	F.	Amount Rs	P
2005 Jan 31	To Balance c/d		2,000	00	2005 Jan 5	By Mohan		2,000	00
			2,000	00				2,000	00
					Feb 1	To Balance b/d		2,000	00

BANK ACCOUNT

Dr. Cr.

Date	Particulars	F.	Amount Rs	P	Date	Particulars	F.	Amount Rs	P
2005 Jan 2	To Cash a/c		5,000	00	2005 Jan 31	By Balance c/d		5,000	00
			5,000	00				5,000	00
Feb. 1	To Balance b/d		5,000	00					

MOHAN

Dr. Cr.

Date	Particulars	F.	Amount Rs	P	Date	Particulars	F.	Amount Rs	P
2005 Jan 5	To Sales a/c		2,000	00	2005 Jan 31	By Cash a/c		2,000	00
			2,000	00				2,000	00

RAKESH

Dr. **Cr.**

Date	Particulars	F.	Amount Rs	P	Date	Particulars	F.	Amount Rs	P
2005					2005				
Jan 8	To P. Return a/c		500	00	Jan 6	By purchases c/d		3,000	00
Jan 26	To Cash a/c		2,400	00					
Jan 26	To Discount a/c		100	00					
			3,000	00				3,000	00

DRAWINGS ACCOUNT

Dr. **Cr.**

Date	Particulars	F.	Amount Rs	P	Date	Particulars	F.	Amount Rs	P
2005					2005				
Jan 10	To Cash a/c		200	00	Jan. 31	By Balance c/d		200	00
			200	00				200	00
Feb 1	To Bal. b/d		200	00					

RENT ACCOUNT

Dr. **Cr.**

Date	Particulars	F.	Amount Rs	P	Date	Particulars	F.	Amount Rs	P
2005					2005				
Jan 24	To Cash a/c		400	00	Jan. 31	By Balance c/d		400	00
			400	00				400	00
Feb 1	To Bal. b/d		400	00					

SALARY ACCOUNT

Dr. Cr.

Date	Particulars	F.	Amount Rs	P	Date	Particulars	F.	Amount Rs	P
2005 Jan 20	To Cash a/c		500	00	2005 Jan. 31	By Balance c/d		500	00
			500	00				500	00
Feb 1	To Bal. b/d		500	00					

DISCOUNT ACCOUNT

Dr. Cr.

Date	Particulars	F.	Amount Rs	P	Date	Particulars	F.	Amount Rs	P
2005 Jan 31	To Balance b/d		100	00	2005 Jan 26	By Rakesh		100	00
			100	00				100	00
Feb 1	To Bal. b/d		100	00					

STATIONARY ACCOUNT

Dr. Cr.

Date	Particulars	F.	Amount Rs	P	Date	Particulars	F.	Amount Rs	P
2005 Jan 28	To Cash a/c		300	00	2005 Jan 31	By Balance b/d		300	00
			300	00				300	00
Feb. 1	To Ba. b/d		300	00					

PURCHASE RETURN ACCOUNT

Dr. **Cr.**

Date	Particulars	F.	Amount Rs	P	Date	Particulars	F.	Amount Rs	P
2005 Jan 28	To Balance c/d		500	00	2005 Jan. 31	By Rakesh c/d		500	00
			500	00				500	00
Feb. 1	To Bal. b/d		500	00					

Trial Balance as on..............................

Particulars	L.F.	Dr. Balance Amount Rs.	P.	Cr. Balance Amount Rs.	P.
Cash a/c		12,200	00		
Capital a/c				20,000	00
Purchases a/c		4,000	00		
Sales a/c				2,000	00
Bank a/c		5,000	00		
Drawings a/c		200	00		
Rent a/c		400	00		
Salary a/c		500	00		
Discount a/c		100	00		
Stationary a/c		300	00		
Purchase Return a/c				500	00
		22,600	00	22,600	00

PROBLEMS

Q.1 . Journalise the following transactions of Mr. Raman and post them to ledger and prepare the trial balance:

200 5	Received cash from Rakesh	Rs. 6,000
Jan. 5	Purchased goods in cash	Rs. 3,000

Jan. 7	Sold goods to Hari	Rs. 500
Jan. 15	Paid to Rahim	Rs. 500
Jan. 18	Received from Kishan	Rs. 200
Jan. 20	Purchased Furniture from Ram	Rs. 1,000
Jan. 25	Paid Salary	Rs. 200
Jan. 30	Paid Rent	Rs. 100
Jan. 31	Paid Wages	Rs. 200

Q. 2. Journalise the following transactions and post them to ledger and prepare the trial balance:

2005		
Feb.2	Rakesh Commenced business with cash	Rs.80,000
4	Purchased goods for cash	Rs.10,000
10	Deposit in to bank	Rs. 2,000
15	Cash sales	Rs. 4,000
18	Sold to Rakesh on credit	Rs. 3,000
22	Paid rent	Rs. 400
25	Paid salaries	Rs. 500
28	Paid sundry expenses	Rs. 200

Q. 3. Journalise the following transactions and post them to ledger and prepare the trial balance:

2004		
Dec. 1	Suresh commenced business with cash Rs.25,000 and goods worth	Rs.10,000
2	Machinery purchased	Rs. 2,000
4	Bought goods from Ram	Rs. 3,000
6	Bought furniture from Akash furniture store For cash	Rs. 2,000
10	Sold goods for cash	Rs. 4,000
15	Sold goods on credit to Mohan	Rs. 3,000
20	Goods returned to Ram	Rs. 200
22	Mohan returned goods	Rs. 50

25	Cash sales	Rs. 250
30	Paid rent	Rs. 200
31	Paid salaries	Rs. 500

Q. 4. Journalise the following transactions of Mr. Rakesh and post them to ledger and prepare the trial balance:

2004		
Dec. 1	Rakesh commenced business with cash	Rs. 20,000
4	Deposit in to bank	Rs. 7,000
6	Purchased goods from Dass	Rs. 5,000
8	Sold to Shyam on credit	Rs. 6,000
10	Cash purchase	Rs. 2,000
15	Cash sales	Rs. 4,000
20	Received from Shyam	Rs. 5,800
	Allowed him discount	Rs. 200
22	Paid to Dass	Rs. 4,850
	Discount received	Rs. 150
25	Paid salaries	Rs. 1,000
30	Paid Rent	Rs. 500

Q. 5. Journalise the following transactions and post them to ledger and prepare the trial balance:

2005		
Jan 1	Sohan started business with cash	Rs. 25,000
2	Purchased goods for cash	Rs. 2,000
4	Sold to Manish on credit	Rs. 4,000
6	Cash sales	Rs. 7,000
8	Purchased goods from Anju for cash	Rs. 2,000
15	Withdrew money from business for private use	Rs 200
20	Furniture purchased	Rs. 3,000
25	Deposit in to bank	Rs. 2,000
28	Received cheque from Manish in full settlement of amount due by them	Rs. 3,900
29	Cheque received from Arun	Rs. 2,500

30	Paid for electricity charges	Rs. 500
31	Paid salary by cheque	Rs. 300
31	Paid rent	Rs. 200

Q. 6. Journalise the following transactions and post them to ledger and prepare the trial balance:

2005		
Jan. 1	Business started with cash	Rs.25,000
2	Goods sold to Y	Rs. 8,000
6	Cash sales	Rs.15,000
7	Paid cartage	Rs. 900
8	Furniture purchased for cash	Rs.12,000
9	Goods purchased from Z	Rs.10,000
10	Wages paid	Rs. 2,000
	Paid postage expenses	Rs. 100
12	Withdrew money from business for private use	
	Cash	Rs. 2,000
	Goods	Rs. 400
15	Deposit in to bank	Rs. 1,000
20	Received cash from Y on account	Rs. 6,000
25	Paid to Z in full settlement	Rs. 9,500
31	Paid salary by cheque	Rs. 800
31	Paid rent	Rs. 400

Q. 7. Premchand commenced business with Rs. 9,000 cash and goods worth Rs. 6000 on Jan. 1, 2005. Other transactions for the month were as follows: enter these transactions in to journal and post them to ledger and prepare the trial balance:

2005		
Jan. 2	Purchased goods for cash	Rs. 4,000
3	Stationary purchased	Rs. 500
	Furniture purchased from furniture house	Rs. 3,000
6	Goods sold in cash	Rs. 9,000
7	Interest received from Mukesh	Rs. 800

9	Purchased goods from Mukesh & Co.	Rs. 7,000
12	Goods given in charity	Rs. 600
15	Paid office expenses	Rs. 500
20	Paid in to bank	Rs. 4,000
24	Loss of goods by fire	Rs. 300
25	Sold to Mani on credit	Rs. 3,000
26	Goods purchased on credit	Rs. 9,000
27	Withdrew money for private use	Rs. 900
28	Deposit in to bank	Rs. 2,000
29	Interest received	Rs. 400
29	Commission received	Rs. 300
30	Salary paid	Rs. 2,000

Q. 8. Journalise the following transactions in the book of Meerut Store and post them to ledger and prepare the trial balance:

2004		
Nov.2	Business started with	
	Cash	Rs.30,000
	Goods	Rs.12,000
4	Bought furniture from Gupta & Co.	Rs. 7,000
5	Goods sold to Amarnath	Rs.14,000
6	Paid for stationary	Rs. 500
8	Cash purchase	Rs. 4,000
10	Goods purchased from Rajkishor	Rs. 6,000
14	Cash sales	Rs. 7,000
17	Motorcycle purchased for office use	Rs.10,000
20	Order received from Manoj worth	Rs.20,000
22	Received from Amarnath on account	Rs.10,000
23	Payment made to Gupta Company	Rs. 6,800
	Discount received	Rs. 200
25	Received from Amarnath in full settlement	Rs. 3,500
28	Payment made for	
	Salary	Rs. 3,500
	Rent	Rs. 500
	Office expenses	Rs. 400

Q. 9. Journalise the following transactions and post them to ledger and prepare the trial balance:

2004		
Oct.1	Rajesh starts business with cash	Rs. 40,000
2	Bought goods for cash	Rs. 10,000
4	Sold for cash	Rs. 22,000
6	Machinery purchased for cash	Rs. 5,000
8	Sold to Amit	Rs. 6,000
11	Purchased from Rakesh in cash	Rs. 4,000
14	Goods sold to Rakesh	Rs. 3,000
17	Cash sales	Rs. 12,000
20	Paid for stationary	Rs. 600
22	Goods sold on credit	Rs. 4,000
26	Paid for rent	Rs. 600
26	Paid for carriage	Rs. 400
27	Cash paid to Rakesh	Rs. 2,600
	Discount received from him	Rs. 400
28	Salary paid	Rs. 3,000

Q. 10. Journalise the following transactions and post them to ledger and prepare the trial balance:

2005		
Jan. 1	Commenced Business in cash	Rs.45,000
3	Paid in to bank	Rs. 6,000
4	Bought Furniture from Shastri & Co.	Rs.12,000
6	Bought Goods from Sachin	Rs.11,000
9	Sold to Ghosh	Rs.16,000
15	Sold to Satish for cash	Rs.13,650
18	Rent for one year paid in advance	Rs. 6,000
20	Withdrew for house hold expenses	
	Goods	Rs. 600
	Cash	Rs. 850
24	Cash withdraw from bank for office	Rs. 5,000
27	Repairs to scooter, payment not yet made	Rs. 340
28	Bank charges for the month	Rs. 600

29	Depreciation charged on furniture	Rs. 1,000
30	Cheque received from Ghosh in full settlement	Rs. 15,600

Q. 11. The following trial balance has been prepared wrongly. You are required prepare the trial balance:

Particulars	*Amount (Dr.)*	*Amount (Cr.)*
Manufacturing expenses	1,750	
Cash in hand		2,000
Cash at bank		3,000
Wages		500
Freight	600	
Commission received		350
Debtors	8,500	
Creditors	6,000	
Machinery	12,000	
Furniture	8,000	
Sales		40,000
Purchases	15,000	
P. Return	1,000	
Sales Return		500
Capital		13,500
Loan from Kishan		8,000
Land and Building	17,000	
	68,850	68,850

Q. 12. The following trial balance has been prepared wrongly. You are required to prepare the trail balance:

Particulars	*Amount (Dr.)*	*Amount (Cr.)*
Capital		30,000
Cash		2,000

Particulars	*Amount (Dr.)*	*Amount (Cr.)*
Building	12,000	
Furniture	8,500	
Goods	13,450	
Debtors		8,700
Creditors	8,900	
Drawings		2,300
Sundry expenses	1,400	
Wages	1,350	
Discount received		850
Rent paid	750	
Commission paid		450
Interest received	250	
Loan from Rakesh	10,000	
Income from investment		900

Q. 13. The following trail balance has been prepared wrongly. You are required to prepare the trail balance:

Particulars	*Amount (Dr.)*	*Amount (Cr.)*
Commission (Cr)	200	
Stock	5,000	
Creditors		8,750
General expenses		580
Wages and Salary	2,350	
Machinery	15,800	
Loan from Pankaj	7,500	
Interest on loan		300
Rent	400	
Bank overdraft	300	
Sales return		1,000
Purchases and Sales	14,000	18,000

Purchase return	500	
Debtors	13,500	
Bad debts		400
Cash	4,000	
Discount allowed		30
Insurance premium	400	
Capital		19,710
Discount received	100	

CHAPTER X

BANK RECONCILIATION STATEMENT

Generally every businessman open a current a/c in bank and bank issue a pass book, which makes a record of businessmen's transactions with the bank. Entries in pass book are written by bank. Similarly, businessman maintains a three-column cash book to record all the transactions relating to the bank. All deposit in to bank is written on the debit side and withdrawals are written on the credit side in the cash book. In pass book all deposit are written on the credit side and all withdrawals on the debit side. The bank balance as per pass book can be expected to be equal to the bank balance as shown by the cash book. But sometimes these two balances generally differ. If they do not agree, it is necessary to reconcile them. For this purpose a statement is prepared which shows all the cause of differences. This statement is called bank reconciliation statement.

CAUSE OF DIFFERENCE

The followings are the reasons for the difference between these balance shown by the cash book and the pass book:

Cheque issued but not presented for payment

When a cheque is issued by the business in the favors of third party, it is entered on the credit side of the cash book, but the bank will not debit clients account until cheque is actually presented for payments. It means that if cheque is not presented for payment till the date of the preparation of bank reconciliation statement the balance shown in the pass book will be more than the balance shown by the cash book.

Deposit for collection but not yet collected

As soon as a cheque is received it is entered on the debit side of the cash book and sent to the bank for collection. But the bank credit the clients account only when it has collect cash on the cheque so deposited. It results in bank balance as per cash book higher than the balance as per pass book.

Direct payment in the bank by customer

Sometimes customers directly deposit the amount in the bank. If such a payment is received, the bank will record the entry in the pass book. But the accountholder may come to know regarding the amount, when he see the pass book.

Interest allowed by the bank

When bank allow some interest to the customer, it will be recorded in the customer's a/c and later shown in pass book. But the customer is not making the entry in the cash book till he knows the fact. Accountholder will come to know the amount on some later date when he sees the pass book.

Direct collected by bank on behalf of customer

Some times businessman may entrust the task of collection of interest or dividend on investment to the banker. Bank collects the amount and credit the businessman account. But there may be no entry for this income in cash book. Customer will record it in their cash book either on receiving such information from bank or after seeing his pass book.

Direct payment by the bank

Some times bank may be given instructions for certain payments like—insurance premium etc. When bank makes such payments, it immediately records it in the books. Bank debits the account of customer with the amount of payment. But there may be no entry for this payment in cash book. Customer will record it in their cash book either on receiving such information from bank or after seeing his pass book.

Error committed

It is possible that while recording the transaction in the pass book, bank might have committed some mistake. For example, A cheque is collected on behalf of Mr. Gupta but by mistake it is entered in the account of Manish.

Illustration 1

Make the bank reconciliation statement from the following:

1. Debit balance as per cash book Rs.5,000
2. Cheque sent to bank for collection but not cleared Rs.1,500
3. Cheque issued but not presented for payment Rs.1,000
4. Interest allowed by bank Rs. 50
5. Bank charges charged by bank Rs. 100

Solution

BANK RECONCILIATION STATEMENT

Sign	Particulars	Amount plus (+) Rs.	P.	Amount minus (–) Rs.	P.
+	Balance as per cas hbook	5,000	00		
–	Cheque sent to bank for collection but not cleared			1,500	00
+	Cheque issued but not presented for payment	1,000	00		
+	Interest allowed by bank	50	00		
–	Bank charges charged by bank			100	00
		6,050	00	1,600	00
		1,600	00		
+	Balance as per pass book	4,450	00		

Illustration 2

Make the bank reconciliation statement from the following:

1. Debit balance as per pass book — Rs. 4,000
2. Cheque sent to bank for collection but not cleared. — Rs. 2000
3. Cheque issued but not presented for payment. — Rs. 2500
4. Interest allowed by bank — Rs. 150
5. Bank charges charged by bank — Rs. 200
6. A customer directly deposited in bank — Rs. 500

Sulution

BANK RECONCILIATION STATEMENT

Sign	Particulars	Amount plus (+) Rs.	P.	Amount minus (–) Rs.	P.
+	Balance as per pass book	4,000	00		
+	Cheque sent to bank for collection but not cleared	2,000	00		
–	Cheque issued but not presented for payment			2,500	00
–	Interest allowed by bank			150	00
+	Bank charges charged by bank	200	00		
–	A customer directly deposit in bank			500	00
				100	00
		6,200	00	3,150	00
		3,150	00		
+	Balance as per cash book	3,050	00		

Illustration 3

Make the bank reconciliation statement from the following:

1. Cash book shows an overdraft — Rs.4,500
2. Cheque issued but not presented for payment — Rs.1,000

3. Cheque sent to bank for collection but not cleared Rs.1,500
4. Interest allowed by bank Rs. 30
5. Bank charges charged by bank Rs. 120
6. Dividends received by bank on behalf of customer Rs. 500

Solution:

BANK RECONCILIATION STATEMENT

Sign	Particulars	Amount plus (+) Rs.	P.	Amount minus (–) Rs.	P.
–	Overdraft as per cash book			4,500	00
+	Cheque issued but not presented for payment	1,000	00		
–	Cheque sent to bank for collection but not cleared			1,500	00
+	Interest allowed by bank	30	00		
–	Bank charges charged by bank			120	00
+	Dividend received by bank	500	00		
		1,530	00	6,120	00
				1,530	00
-	Overdraft as per pass book			4,590	00

PROBLEMS

Q. 1. Make the bank reconciliation statement from the followings:

(a) Debit balance as per cash book Rs. 2,000
(b) Cheque deposited but not cleared Rs. 1,000
(c) Cheque issued but not presented for payment Rs. 500
(d) Bank charges charged by the bank Rs. 600

Q. 2. Make the bank reconciliation statement from the following:

(a) Balance as per cash book Rs. 1,000

(b)	Cheque deposited in bank but not corrected	Rs. 800
(c)	Bank paid insurance premium	Rs. 200
(d)	Bank charges charged by the bank	Rs. 100

Q. 3. On March 31st 2005 the cash book showed a debit balance of Rs. 2,500 at bank, but the bank pass book made up to the same date showed that cheque for Rs. 800, 500 and Rs. 100 respectively had not been presented for payment, also cheque to the amount of Rs. 500 into the account had not yet been cleared, prepare a bank reconciliation statement.

Q. 4. The cash book shows a balance of Rs. 18,500. On comparing the cash book with the pass-book, the following discrepancies were noted:

1.	Cheque deposited in bank but yet not collected	Rs. 2,500
2.	Cheque issued but not yet presented for payment	Rs. 3,000
3.	Bank paid insurance premium	Rs. 1,000
4.	A customer directly deposited in bank account	Rs. 4,000
5.	Bank charges charged by the bank	Rs. 200

Prepare a bank reconciliation statement.

Q 5. On 31st July 2004 pass book of K.G. Dubey showed credit balance of Rs. 1,500. When compared with the pass book, the following facts were discovered:

1. Three cheques for Rs. 500, Rs. 200 and Rs. 100 issued on July 2004 were presented for payment in the bank in August 2004.
2. Two cheques if Rs. 180 and Rs. 170 were sent to the bank for collection were not entered in the pass-book by July 31st, 2004.
3. The bank charged Rs. 460 for its commission and allowed interest of Rs. 120, which were not mentioned in his bank account. Prepare a BRS.

Q 6. On 31st December 2004 the pass book of Mr. Rastogi's current account show a credit balance of Rs. 20,000. Prepare a BRS with the following information:

1. Rastogi issued a cheque of Rs. 1,300 on 26th December, but this cheque was not presented for payment, whereas this was recorded twice in the cash book.
2. A cheque of Rs. 2,200 drawn on his saving account has been shown as draw on current account.
3. A cheque of Rs. 1,385 issued on December 26, were taken in the cash column.
4. In the pass book a bank charge of Rs. 125 was recorded twice while another bank charges of Rs. 170 was not recorded in the cash book.

Q 7. On December 31, 2004, the pass book of Hari Om showed a credit balanced Rs. 8,300. Cheque of Rs. 1,790 sent to the bank for collection were not collected and credited. Two cheques of Rs. 1,300 and 1,500 respectively were not presented for payment till Jan 31st, 2005.

Bank has paid a bill payable amounting to Rs. 1,000, but it has not been entered in the cash book and a bill receivable of Rs. 500, which was discounted with the bank, was dishonored by the drawee on the due date. Prepare BRS and show the balance as shown by the cash book.

CHAPTER XI

CAPITAL EXPENDITURE

Capital expenditure is the expenditure, which normally yields benefit for a long period. It include acquisition of an asset, which results in an increase in the earning capacity of business firm and not for resale. Plant and machinery, furniture, land and building and commission paid for procuring long-term loans are few examples of such expenditure. Expenditure cannot be said to be a capital expenditure only because the amount is large. An expenditure is treated as capital expenditure in the following circumstances:

1. The expenditure, which results in the acquisition of a permanent asset. For example, machinery, land, building. All money spent for acquiring an asset is capital expenditure.
2. Capital expenditure results in a benefit, which will last for a long time.
3. Capital expenditure results in extra capacity of the firm.
4. All expenditure incurred for making the asset ready for use is capital expenditure.
5. Expenditure incurred in putting an asset in working condition is capital expenditure. For example, over hauling an old machinery or cost of installation of plant machinery.
6. Legal expenses in connection with acquiring or defending suit for protecting fixed assets etc. are treated as capital expenditure.

Examples:

- Purchase of land and building, plant and machinery, other tangible assets.
- Purchase of office, machinery and equipment, computer, furniture etc.
- Interest paid on loan to purchase a fixed asset.
- Cost of shifting factory from one place to another.
- Cost of improvement in the old fixed assets.

REVENUE EXPENDITURE

It consists of expenditure the benefits of which is exhausted in thc accounting period itself or within one year. Revenue expenditure helps in maintaining the earning capacity of a firm. These expenditures are incurred on consumable items or goods and services acquired for resale.

Example:

- Cost of goods, raw material and stores.
- Expenses in connection with production of goods and services.
- Administration, selling and distribution expenses.
- Interest on business loan, depreciation on fixed assets.
- All expenses to maintain fixed assets in working condition.

DIFFERENCE BETWEEN CAPITAL EXPENDITURE AND REVENUE EXPENDITURE

Capital expenditure	Revenue expenditure
1. They are incurred for acquisition of permanent assets.	1. They are incurred for the conduct of business and maintenance of fixed assets in working order.
2. They increase the earning capacity of the business.	2. They do not add to the earning capacity.
3. Their benefit extends to more than one year.	3. Benefits extend to only one year.

Capital expenditure	Revenue expenditure
4. They are shown in balance sheets. 5. They add to the fixed assets.	4. They are transferred to trading account or profit and loss account. 5. They reduce the value of fixed assets.

DIFFERED REVENUE EXPENDITURE

Some times expenditure is of a revenue nature but the benefit of that expenditure is available for more than one year. In such case it is fair to spread the cost of expenditure over number of accounting years.

Suppose: For an advertisement campaign a sum of Rs. 1,00,000 has been spent and the benefit of this campaign does not exhaust in that year, the expenses made should be spread over the estimated years during which the benefit is to be derived. Such expenditures are called deferred revenue expenditure.

Examples:

1. Preliminary expenses
2. Underwriting commission
3. Loss on issues of shares
4. Loss on issue of debentures
5. Discount on issue of shares
6. Discount on issue of debentures
7. Advertisement expenses to introduce a new product.

CAPITAL RECEIPTS

Capital receipts may be said to consist solely of additional capital introduced in the business either by shareholders of a company or by proprietor of a business and receipts from the sale of any fixed assets of a business. Capital receipts do not affect the profit or loss of the business.

REVENUE RECEIPTS

Amount received in the normal course of business are called revenue receipts. Revenue receipts are shown on the credit side of Profit and Loss account, sales of goods, commission and discount received, dividends received on investment are some examples of revenue receipts.

CHAPTER XII

FINAL ACCOUNTS

At the end of every accounting period the owner of the business would like to know about the result of operating business. To ascertain the net profit earned or net loss incurred, final account is prepared.

Final account is a statement that results finally from the preparation of an account showing the profit earned or loss suffered by the firm and financial state of affairs of the firm. The statement showing the profit or loss is known as profit and loss account and the statement showing the financial state of affairs is called the balance sheet.

—Income statement,

—Balance sheet

INCOME STATEMENT

Income statement can be divided into the following:

— Trading account

— Profit and loss account

Trading Account

The trading account is an account, which shows results of the buying and selling of goods. It contains the summarized form all the transactions occurring during an accounting period, which have direct relation to the goods dealt in the business. Finding out the gross profit and gross loss by preparing an account is called trading account. Gross profit is the excess of the selling price over the cost of goods sold. Cost of goods sold can be ascertained by adding net purchaser to the opening stock of goods in trade and detecting the stock of goods at the accounting of the accounting period from the total. It can be computed as follows with assumed data.

Opening stock (Food inventory)	Rs. 5,000
Add: Food purchase	Rs. 20,000
Goods available for sale	Rs. 25,000
Less: Closing stock	Rs. 3,000
Cost of goods used	Rs. 22,000
Less: Cost of employee meals	Rs. 800
Less: Cost of promotional meals	Rs, 500
Less: Transfers to beverage department	Rs. 700
Cost of food sold	Rs. 20,000

The gross profit can be calculated as follows:

Gross profit	= Net. sales – Cost of goods sold
Net sales	= Total sales – Sales returns
Cost of goods sold	= Opening stock + Net purchase + Direct expenses – Closing stock
Net purchase	= Total purchase – Purchase returns

ITEMS OF TRADING ACCOUNT

Posted to debit side

Opening Stock. Generally opening stock is written as the first item on debit side of trading accounting but if new business starts, there will be no opening stock. This is the value of goods in hand at the beginning of the accounting year for which trading account is prepared. Opening stock includes the stock of raw materials, work in progress and finished goods. The amount of opening stock is taken from trial balance.

Purchases. Purchase means goods purchased for resale. It includes both cash and credit purchases of goods. The net amount of purchases is written in trading account. So return and any discount on purchase should deduct from purchase in the inner column. Purchase of any assets like land, machinery is not included in purchase. If some goods are withdrawn by the businessman for his personal use, it should be deducted from the purchases.

Direct Expenses. All the expenses, which have been incurred before the goods become ready for sale are treated as direct expenses. The direct expenses are written on the debit side of trading account.

Wages. If the wages is paid on manufacturing goods, it should be debited to trading account. If nothing is mentioned in the question whether the wages is direct or indirect, it should be treated as direct expense. If any amount of wages is outstanding it should also include in wages account. If wages are clubbed with salaries and the trial balance includes single amount for wages and salaries, then the amount is shown in the trading account.

Carriage or Freight Inward. If these expenses are paid on the purchases of goods, they are shown on the debit side of the trading account. If these expenses are paid in connection with any asset like furniture, it should not be debited to the trading account. Outstanding freight and carriage should also add to these expenses. Outstanding freight and carriage appears as a liability in the balance sheet.

Power and Fuel. All the expenses regarding motive power, coal, gas and fuel are direct expenses and are shown on the debit side of trading account. Outstanding expenses of power and fuel should be added to these expenses.

Factory Lighting. The amount paid for electricity used for the lighting the factory premises will be treated as direct expense and debited to the trading account.

Import Duty and Dock Charges. If goods are purchased from foreign country. The business has to pay import duty and dock charges. These expenses are treated as direct expenses and are shown on the debit side of trading account.

Factory Rent and Rates. All the expenses of factory rent and rates are treated as direct expenses and are shown on the debit side of trading account

Octroi. When goods are bought with in the municipal limits, octroi duty has to be paid. This is a direct expenses and shown on the debit side of trading account.

Royalties. It refers to the payment made for the use of copyright or a patent. If royalty is paid on the basis of production, it is debited to trading account.

CREDIT SIDE

Sales. Sales means selling of those goods which were purchased for resale purpose. It includes both cash and credit sales of goods and refers to the net amount of sales (Sales-Sales return). If a fixed assets is sold it should not be included in sales. Sales of old newspapers etc. are excluded from sales.

Closing Stock. Closing stock means goods in hand at the end of accounting period. It may be of raw material, work in process and finished goods. Generally the amount of closing stock is given outside the trial balance. But sometime when purchase is adjusted, closing stock has a debit balance in trial balance. If closing stock is given outside the trial balance, it will be shown on the credit side of trading account and if it is given in the trial balance, it appears as an assets in the balance sheet. Closing stock is valued at cost or market price whichever is less.

Closing Entries for Trading Acount. The journal entries necessary to transfer the opening stock, purchases, sales and return account to the trading account are called closing entries as they serve to close these account.

For opening stock: Debit the trading account and credit the opening stock

Trading account Dr.

To Opening stock

(Being transfer of opening stock to trading account)

For purchase: Debit the trading account and credit the purchase account

Trading account Dr.

To Purchase account

(Being transfer of purchase account to trading account)

For purchase return: Debit the Purchase return a/c or return outward a/c and credit the purchase account

Purchase return account

To purchase account

(-----------------------------------)

For expenses: Debit the trading account and credit the expense account

Trading account Dr.

To Wages account

To Octroi account

To fuel and gas account

(Being transfer of various expenses account)

For sales: Debit the sales account and credit the trading account

Sales account Dr.

To Trading account (Being transfer of sales a/c to trading account

For closing stock: Debit the closing stock and credit the account

Closing stock account Dr

To Trading account

(Being transfer of account stock to trading account)

TRADING ACCOUNT OF M/S ....
FOR THE YEAR ENDING..............................

Particulars	Amount Rs.	P.	Particulars	Amount Rs.	P.
To opening stock			By sales		
To purchase			Less sales return		
Less purchase returns			By closing stock		
Less drawing (goods)			By gross loss transfer to P/L account		
To wages					
To wages and salary					
To productive wages					
To carriage					
To carriage inward					
To carry and purchase					
To freight					
To octroi					
To dock charges inwards					
To custom duties on imported goods					
To motive power, coal, gas, water, oil grease etc.					
To factory expenses					
To factory rent and insurance					
To royalty based on production					
To gross profit transfer to P/L account					

Illustration 1

Prepare a trading account for the year ending 31st March, 2005 from the following particulars:

Opening stock	2,50,000
Purchases	4,00,000
Sales	9,00,000
Returns to suppliers	20,000

Retruns to customers	10,000
Wages	5,000
Freight inward	7,000
Goods withdrawn by owner for personal use	20,000
Closing stock	5,00,000

(*See Solution on next page.*)

PROFIT AND LOSS ACCOUNT

After ascertaining the gross profit from trading account, the next step is to prepare the profit and loss account —to work out the net profit or net loss. The function of the profit and loss account is to show to business the profit or loss resulting from his transactions during a certain period. There are certain items of income and expenses of the business. These are indirect in nature.

Net profit is the excess of gross profit and other incomes over the indirect expenses and loss. While preparing the profit and loss account, gross profit and other indirect income like commission, rent received, interest received etc. are transferred to the credit of theprofit and loss account. All the indirect expenses are debited to the profit and loss account. Indirect expenses may be administrative, selling and distribution, financial expenses to maintain the assets in to working order. Examples are salary, rent, postage, stationary, depreciation insurance etc. The difference of the two sides of this account is either net profit or net loss. If the total of the credit side is bigger then the total of the debit side, the difference is called net profit and if the debit side total exceed the total of credit side, the difference is called net loss. This account is prepared from nominal account and its balance is transferred to capital account.

IMPORTANT POINTS IN PROFIT AND LOSS ACCOUNT

Salaries: These include salaries paid to clerical staff and godown and warehouse staff and to managers. These salaries are indirect expense and are shown in debit side of profit and loss account. Salaries to partners, or proprietor of the business must be debited separately.

Solution of Illustration 1

Trading account of M/s......................

FOR THE YEAR ENDING MARCH 31, 2005

Particulars	Rs.	P.	Amount Rs.	P.	Particulars	Rs.	P.	Amount Rs.	P.
To opening stock			2,50,000	00	By sales	90,000	00		
To purchase	4,00,000	00			Less sales return	10,000	00	8,90,000	00
Less: Returns	20,000	00			By closing stock			5,00,000	00
Less: Drawings (goods)	20,000	00	3,60,000	00					
To wages			5,000	00					
To freight			7,000	00					
To gross profit transfer to P/L account			7,68,000	00					
			13,90,000	00				13,90,000	00

Rent, Rates and Taxes: These include office and warehouse rent, municipal taxes and taxes. If it is a common item of indirect expenses debited to profit and loss account. It is necessary to see that rent for the full trading period is taken in to account, and if there is any out standing, the same should be duly provided for.

Insurance: Premium paid to insurance company for insurance of assets in to office building, furniture, etc., should be treated as business expenses. It should be charged to profit and loss account.

Interest: Interest receivable and interest payable should be shown separate items. Interest paid on loan, overheads etc. is an indirect expense and is taken to the debit side of profit and loss account. If interest is received on loan advance by the firm, on deposits, should be shown to credit side of profit and loss account.

Commission: Commission received and commission paid should be shown separately. Commission received should be credited to profit and loss account as a gain and commission paid should be debited to profit and loss account.

Repairs: All amount of repairs and renewals related to the existing assets such as plant and machinery, fixture and fitting etc. should be treated as expenses and debited to profit and loss account.

Stable Expenses: These are the expense for the fodder of the house and wages paid to person looking of the stable. It is indirect expense and should be debited to profit and loss account.

Trade Expenses: Trade expenses represent various small expenses, which incurred in a business. They are amalgamated under trade or general of petty expenses, sundry expense or miscellaneous expenses. These are debited to profit and loss account.

Advertisement: All amount spent under this head and relating to the period under review must be written off to the profit and loss account, if a large amount is paid under a contract covering two or three years, proportionate part should be charged to profit and loss account and the balancing amount should be written in balance sheet as assets. .

Samples: The business firm to increase sales distributes samples of the goods free. These expenses are indirect expense and therefore, should be debited to profit and loss account.

Apprentice Premium: It is an amount taken from the person who gets training in the business. It is indirect income and should be credited to profit and loss account.

Packing: Packing charges or cost of packing materials is a distribution expenses and so it should be debited to profit and loss account.

Legal Charges: If any amount is paid as legal expense in connection with the business during any accounting period, it should be debited to profit and loss account.

EXPENSES THAT ARE NOT SHOWN IN PROFIT AND LOSS ACCOUNT

Income tax: Income tax is paid by the owner on his income and in such a way it is his private expenses and it should not be shown in profit and loss account. It should be added to drawings or directly deducted from capital.

Drawings: These expenses are not the expense of business firm, therefore, these should not be written in profit and loss account. It should be treated as personal expenses and added to drawings. Drawings are debited to the capital account.

Life insurance premium: If premium is paid on the life policy of proprietor, it should not be shown in profit and loss account.

PROFIT AND LOSS ACCOUNT

For the Year Ending ....

Particulars	Amount Rs.	P.	Particulars	Amount Rs.	P.
To gross iost transfer from trading account			By gross profit transfer from trading account		
To salaries			By rent from tenants		
To rent rates and salaries			By discount received		
To stationary and printing			By commission received		
To postage and telegrams			By interest receive		
To audit fees			By bed debt recovered		
To legal charges			By apprenticeship premium		
To telephone expenses					
To insurance premium			By income from investment		
To entertainment expenses					
To repair and renewal			By dividends on shares		
To depreciation of assets			By misc. revenue and gains		
To interest			By income from other sources		
To sundry trade expenses					
To conveyance			By net loss transferred to capital account		
To charity					
To bank charges					
To office expenses					
To establishment expenses					
To general expenses					
To stable expenses					
To licenses fee					
To brokerage					
To upkeep of cart and vans					
To office lighting					
To loss by fire, theft					
To commission					
To advertisement					
To freight and carriage outwards					

(*contd.*)

Particulars	Amount Rs.	P.	Particulars	Amount Rs.	P.
To export duty To discount To packing expenses To bad debt or bed debt write off To traveling expenses To distributors expenses To net profit transferred to capital account					

Illustraion 2

From the following balance extracted on 31st March 2005 prepare profit and loss account.

Gross profit	50,000
Salaries	2,000
Rent	500
Fire insurance premium	600
Bad debts	300
Commission (Cr.)	1,000
Interest (Cr.)	500
Legal charges	600
Telephone expenses	800
Repair expenses	700
Interest on capital	800
Income from investment	400
Sundry expenses	800
Discount (Cr.)	100
Discount (Dr.)	300
Printing & stationary	800
Rates & Taxes	250

PROFIT AND LOSS ACCOUNT
For the Year Ending........................

Particulars	Amount Rs.	P.	Particulars	Amount Rs.	P.
To salaries	2,000	00	By gross profit transfer		
To Rent	500	00	from trading account	50,000	00
To Fire ins. premium	600	00	By commission received	1,000	00
To bed debt	300	00	By interest receive	500	00
To legal charges	600	00	By discount received	100	00
To telephone expenses	800	00	By income from invest	400	00
To repair	700	00			
To interest on capital	800	00			
To sundry expenses	800	00			
To discount	300	00			
To printing & stationary	800	00			
To rates & tax	250	00			
To net profit transferred to capital account	43,550	00			
	52,000	00		52,000	00

BALANCE SHEET

After ascertaining the net profit or net loss by preparing the trading and profit and loss account, the next step is to prepare the balance sheet. The purpose of balance sheet is to ascertain the financial position of a business i.e., to know what the business owes and what it owns on a certain date. Hence it shows all assets and liabilities of the business as at the end of the accounting year. A balance sheet is a statement prepared with a view to measure the exact financial position of a business on a specified date. This includes what the business owns and what the business owes. All the assets and liabilities are recorded in the balance sheet in a classified form. All properties assets and other rights owned by the business are shown on the right hand side, the liabilities to outsiders and amount invested by owners as capital on the left hand side. The excess of assets over liabilities represents the capital of the owner. The total of the both side of the balance sheet must tally because of the equation viz.

Assets = Liabilities + Capital

CLASSIFICATION OF ASSETS AND LIABILITIES

Assets

Assets denote the economic resources and possession of a business. Land, machinery, furniture, building, books, debts, cash, and bill receivables are some examples of assets.

The classification of assets depends on their nature assets may be divided in to following class:

Fixed Assets

Those assets, which are acquired for, continued use in the business over a long period and are used for the purpose of earning profits. These are permanent in nature and with the help of these assets business is carried on. Land, buildings, machinery furniture and fixtures are some example of these assets.

Current Assest

Assets, which kept temporary for subsequent conversion in to money, are called current assets. They are likely to be realized with in a period of one year or during the normal operating cycle. Current assets include—cash balance, bank balance, closing stock, debtors, bill receivable, short-term loan etc. they are also called floating or circulating assets.

Tangible Assets

These are definite assets, which can be seen, touched and have some volume such as building, furniture, machinery, stock etc.

Fictitious Assets

These assets are fictitious in nature i.e., they are not really assets. These are either the past accumulated losses or expenses which are incurred once in the life of a business and are capitalized for the time being, for example, profit and loss account (debit balance), loss by fire, discounted on issue of shares or debentures, preliminary expenses etc.

Intangible Assets

Those assets which cannot be seen or felt, or touched and have no volume but values are treated as intangible assets. For example, goodwill, patents and trade-marks etc. Intangible assets are not necessarily useless.

Wasting Assets

Wasting assets are those assets, which have a fixed, content, for example, mines, quarries etc. they become exhausted or reduce in value as they work.

Liquid Assets

Cash and other marketable securities, which can be converted in to cash quickly, are called liquid assets.

Liabilities

A liability is an amount, which a business is legally bound to pay. It denotes the claim by an outsider on the property of the business. Liabilities may be divided into following classes:

Fixed Liabilities: Those liabilities which are payable only on the termination of the business are called fixed liabilities such as capital.

Long-term Liabilities: Long-term liabilities are those liabilities which are not payable by the business with in the next accounting period but will be payable after a long period of time (five to ten years). For example, debentures, long term loans.

Current Liabilities: Those liabilities, which have to be redeemed by the business with in next accounting year. For example, bills payables, short-term loans, sundry creditors, bank overdraft etc.

Contingent Liabilities: These liabilities are not actual liabilities but their becoming actual liabilities.

IN ORDER OF PRESENCE

Balance Sheet of ....

As On........................

Liabilities	Amount Rs.	P.	Assets	Amount Rs.	P.
Fixed liabilities			**Intangible assets**		
Capital			Goodwill		
Long-term liabilities			Patents		
Loan from bank			Copyright		
Debentures			**Fictitious assets**		
Current liabilities			Advertisement		
Bills payable			Misc. expenses		
Sundry creditors			Profit & loss a/c		
Bank overdraft			**Fixed assets**		
Outstanding expenses			Machinery		
Short term loan			Building		
			Furniture & fixtures		
			Motor car		
			Floating assets		
			Sundry debtor		
			Investments		
			Bill receivable		
			Stock in trade		
			Prepaid expenses		
			Liquid assets		
			Cash in hand		
			Cash in bank		

IN ORDER TO LIQUIDITY

Balance Sheet of......................

As On...................

Liabilities	Amount Rs.	P.	Assets	Amount Rs.	P.
Current liabilities			**Liquid assets**		
Bills payable			Cash in hand		
Sundry creditors			**Cash in bank**		
Bank overdraft			**Floating assets**		
Outstanding expenses			Sundry debtors		
Short term loan			Investments		
Long-term liabilities			Bill receivable		
Loan from bank			Stock in trade		
Debentures			Prepaid expenses		
Fixed liabilities			**Fixed assets**		
Capital			Machinery		
			Building		
			Furniture & fixtures		
			Motor car		
			Fictitious assets		
			Advertisement		
			Misc. expenses		
			Profit & loss a/c		
			Intangible assets		
			Goodwill		
			Patents		
			Copyright		

DIFFERENCE BETWEEN TRADING A/C AND PROFIT &N LOSS A/C

Trading account	Profit & loss account
1. Trading account is the first part of income statement	Profit and loss account is the second part of income statement.
2. Trading account is prepared to ascertain the gross profit or gross loss of the business	Profit and loss account is prepared to ascertain the net profit or net loss of the business

(*contd.*)

Trading account	Profit & loss account
3. All direct expenses are shown in trading account	Indirect expenses are shown in profit loss account, for example, sales & distribution expenses, financial expenses, administration expenses etc.
4. The balancing figure (gross profit) of trading account is transferred to profit and loss account	The balancing figure (Net profit) of Profit & loss account is transferred to the capital account of the owner.

DIFFERENCE BETWEEN TRIAL BALANCE AND BALANCE SHEET

Trial balance	Balance sheet
1. It is prepared to check the arithmetical accuracy of the books of account	It is prepared to measure the financial position of the business on a certain fixed date
2. It is not possible to get the information regarding profit from the trial balance	Balance sheet also shows the profit of the business
3. Preparation of trial balance is desirable	Preparation of balance sheet is essential
4. The two sides of trial balance are headed as debit and credit	The two sides of balance sheet are headed as liabilities and assets
5. All three acounts—personal, real, and nominal are written in trial balance	Only personal and real accounts are written in balance sheet. Nominal accounts are not shown in balance sheet
6. It can be prepared every month and whenever desired	It is prepared only at the end of accounting year
7. It is prepared without any	All adjustment entreis are shown in adjustment shown in balance sheet

ADJUSTMENTS

While preparing the trading and profit and loss account for a particular period, one point that must be kept in mind is that all expenses, losses, incomes and gains relating to that particular period are to be considered. If an expense has been incurred but yet not paid during that particular period, liability for the unpaid amount should be created before calculating the profit or loss. All such expenses and incomes should properly be adjusted through entries. These entries are passed at the end of the accounting year. These entries are called adjusting entries.

SOME IMPORTANT ADJUSTMENTS

Closing Stock: The unsold goods lying in stock at the end of accounting year are referring to closing stock. Stock is to be valued at cost price or market price whichever is less. Closing stock is not included in trial balance. It is given in the form of additional information after the trial balance. The following entry will be passed for closing stock at the end of the year.

Closing stock a/c Dr.

To trading a/c

(——————————)

The closing stock is treated in the final a/c as

1. It will be shown of the credit side of trading a/c as a separate item.
2. It will be shown on the asset side of balance sheet as a separate item under current assets.

TRADING ACCOUNT

Particulars	Amount Rs.	P.	Particulars	Amount Rs.	P.
			By closing stock	——	——

BALANCE SHEET

Particulars	Amount Rs.	P.	Assets	Amount Rs.	P.
			Closing stock		

Adjusted purchase and closing stock: If the closing stock is given in the trial balance, it means that both the opening and closing stock have been adjusted in the purchases. In such a case, there will be no opening stock in the trial balance. Adjusted purchase and closing stock will be shown in the trial balance. Adjusted purchases will be shown on the debit side of the trading account. Closing stock will be shown on the asset side of the balance sheet.

Outstanding Expenses: Those expenses, which have been incurred during the accounting year and are due for payment, i.e., have not been paid as yet are called outstanding expenses. At the end of accounting year, all such expenses must be considered otherwise the profit and loss account will not show the actual picture. The common examples of such expenses are: salary, rent for the last month of the year, which are paid in the first month of next year. In order to bring these expenses in to the book of accounting, the following adjusted entry will be passed.

Concerned exp. account Dr.

To Outstanding expenses account

(————————————————)

The outstanding expenses will be treated in the final a/c as

1. It will be added to the concerned expenses in trading and profit and loss account.

2. It will be shown on the liabilities side of balance sheet as a separate item under current liability.

BALANCE SHEET

Particulars	Amount Rs.	P.	Assets	Amount Rs.	P.
Outstanding expenses (—)				——	

Prepaid Expenses: Expenses, which have been paid in advance means whose benefit will be available in future, are called prepared expenses. Interest paid in advance, unexpired insurance etc. are some examples of prepaid expenses. In order to bring these expenses in to the book of accounting, the following adjusted entry will be passed

Prepaid expenses account Dr.

To concerned expenses account

(——————————————————)

The prepaid expenses will be treated in the final account as:

1. It will be subtracted from the concerned expenses in trading and profit and loss account.
2. It will be shown on the assets side of balance sheet as a separate item under current assets.

BALANCE SHEET

Particulars	Amount Rs.	P.	Assets	Amount Rs.	P.
			Prepaid expenses (—)	——	

Depreciation: Depreciation is the decrease in the value of fixed asset due to its use, wear and tear or obsolescence. Fixed assets are used for earning purpose, therefore, the reduction in their value should be considered as expenses or loss and must be charged to the profit and loss account. Depreciation is generally charged at the end of accounting year. In order to bring these expenses in to the book of accounting, the following adjusted entry will be passed

Depreciation account Dr.

To Concerned asset account

(————————————)

The depreciation is treated in the final a/c as

3. It will be shown of the debit side of profit and loss account as a separate item giving details of depreciation
4. It will be deducted from the value of concerned asset in the assets side of balance sheet

PROFIT & LOSS A/C

Particulars	Amount Rs.	P.	Assets	Amount Rs.	P.
To Depreciation on (---) (concerned asset)					

BALANCE SHEET

Liabilities	Amount Rs.	P.	Assets	Amount Rs.	P.
			Concerned asset — *Less*: Depreciation —	——	

Illustration 3

From the following trial balance, prepare a trading and profit and loss account for the year ending December 31, 2004 and balance sheet as on that date:

Opening stock	700	Cash in bank	3,375
Bill receivable	2,250	Commission paid	500
Purchases	19,300	Interest on capital	350
Wages	1,600	Stationary	100
Insurance	500	Sundry expenses	125
Debtors	14,000	Returns inward	650
Carriage inwards	200	Rent & rates	575
commission (cr.)	200	Carriage outward	750
Return outwards	250	Sales	25,000
Office fixture	400	Bills payable	1,500
Creditors	9,825	Capital	8,950
Cash in hand	350		

The closing stock was valued at Rs. 12,500.

Solution

TRADING AND PROFIT AND LOSS ACCOUNT OF M/S

....

For the year ending Dec.31, 2004

Particulars	Amount Rs.	P.	Particulars	Amount Rs	P.
To opening stock	700	00	By sales 25,000		
To purchase 19,300			Less: Sales return 650	24,350	00
Less: Purchase returns 250	19,050	00	By closing stock	12,500	00
To wages	1600	00			
To carriage inward	200	00			
To gross profit transfer to P/L account	15,300	00			
	36,850	00		36,850	00

(contd.)

Particulars	Amount Rs.	P.	Particulars	Amount Rs	P.
To insurance	500	00	By gross profit transfer		
To commission	500	00	from trading account	15,300	00
To interest on capital	350	00	By commission	200	00
To stationary and printing	100	00			
To sundry expenses	125	00			
To rent rates	575	00			
To carriage outward	750	00			
To net profit transferred to capical account	12,600	00			
	15,500	00		15,500	00

Balance sheet of ....
As on Dec 31, 2004

Liabilities		Amount Rs.	P.	Assets	Amount Rs	P.
Capital	8,950			Fixture	400	00
Add net profit	12,600	21,550	00	Sundry debtors	14,000	00
Sundry creditors		9,825	00	Bill receivable	2,250	00
Bills payable		1,500	00	Closing stock	12,500	00
				Cash in hand	350	00
				Cash in bank	3,375	00
		32,875	00		32,875	00

Illustration 4

From the following trial balance, prepare a trading and profit abd loss account for the year ending December 31, 2004, and balance sheet as on that date:

	Amount (debit)	*Amount (credit)*
Bank overdraft		5,900
Capital		10,000
Traveling expenses	1,300	
Opening stock	3,000	

(*contd.*)

	Amount (debit)	*Amount (credit)*
Purchases	18,000	
Sales	52,000	
Wages	6,000	
Freight	3,000	
Salaries	5,000	
Rent	4,000	
Sales return		2,000
Discount received		500
Furniture	3,500	
Machinery	8,000	
Repair expenses	2,300	
Sundry expenses	6,000	
Debtors	7,000	
Creditors		4,000
Cash in hand	1,300	
Cash in bank	1,000	
Octroi	1,000	

The closing stock was valued at Rs. 5,000 on Dec 31, 2004.

Solution

TRADING AND PROFIT AND LOSS ACCOUNT OF M/s...............

For the Year Ending Dec 31, 2004

Particulars	Amount Rs.	P.	Particulars	Amount Rs	P.
To opening stock	3,000	00	By sales	52,000	00
To purchase	18,000	00	Less: Sales return 2,000	50,000	00
To wages	6,000	00	By closing stock	5,000	00
To freight	3,000	00			
To Octroi	1,000	00			
To gross profit transfer to P/L account	24,000	00			
	55,000	00		55,000	00

(contd.)

Particulars	Amount Rs.	P.	Particulars	Amount Rs	P.
To Traveling expenses	1,300	00	By gross profit transfer from trading account	24,000	00
To Salaries	5,000	00	By Disçount	500	00
To Rent rates	4,000	00			
To Repair	2,300	00			
To Sundry expenses	6,000	00			
To Net profit transferred to capital account	5,900	00			
	24,500	00		24,500	00

BALANCE SHEET OF ....

As On...............

Liabilities		Amount Rs.	P.	Assets	Amount Rs	P.
Capital	10,000			Machinery	8,000	00
Add net profit	5,900	15,900	00	Furniture	3,500	00
Creditors		4,000	00	Debtors	7,000	00
Bank overdraft		5,900	00	Closing stock	5,000	00
				Cash in hand	1,300	00
				Cash in bank	1,000	00
		25,800	00		25,800	00

***Illustration* 5**

From the following balances from the books of Raman on 31st March 2005 prepare trading and profit and loss account and balance sheet.

Debit		*Credit*	
Cash in hand	1,170	Sales	98,200
Cash in bank	2,000	Return outwards	100
Purchases	40,275	Capical	65,000
Return inwards	100	Creditors	3,300

(contd.)

Debit		*Credit*	
Fuel & power	5,000	Commission	9,000
Carriage on sales	4,200		
Wages	5,250		
Carriage on purchase	5,000		
Stock (1st April 2004)	5,760		
Machinery	20,000		
Building	7,500		
Land	25,000		
Salaries	10,000		
Patents	17,000		
Sundry expenses	4,000		
Rent	3,600		
Drawings	5,245		
Debtors	14,500		

Taking in to account the following adjustments prepare the trading and profit and loss and balance sheet as on 31st March 2005.

1. Stock was valued at Rs. 6,800 as on March 31, 2005.
2. Machinery is to be depreciated at the rate of 10%.
3. Building is to be depreciated at the rate of 20%.
4. Outstanding salary is Rs. 1,500.
5. Commission accrued Rs. 1,000.
6. Prepared rent Rs. 85.

Solution

TRADING AND PROFIT AND LOSS ACCOUNT OF M/s RAMAN

For the Year Ending March 31, 2005

Particulars		Amount Rs.	P.	Particulars		Amount Rs	P.
To opening stock		5,760	00	By sales	98,200		
To purchase	40,275			Less: Sales return	100	98,100	00
Less: Returns	100	40,175	00	By closing stock		6,800	00
To fuel & power		5,000	00				
To wages		5,250	00				
To carriage on purchases		5,000	00				
To gross profit transfer to P/L account		43,715	00				
		10,4,900	00			10,4,900	00
To carriage on sales		4,200	00	By gross profit transfer from trading account		43,715	00
To salaries	10,000			By commission	9,000		
Add: Outstanding	1,500	11,500	00	Add: Accrued	1,000	10,000	00
To sundry expenses		4,000	00				
To rent	3,600						
Less: Prepaid	85	3,515	00				
To Dep. on machinery		2,000	00				
To Dep. on building		1,500	00				
To net profit transferred to capital account		27,000	00				
		53,715	00			53,715	00

BALANCE SHEET OF M/S RAMAN

As On March 31, 2005

Liabilities		Amount Rs.	P.	Liabilities		Amount Rs	P.
Capital	65,000			Building	7,500		
Less: Drawings	5,245			Less: Dep.	1,500	6,000	00
	59,755			Machinery	20,000		
Add: Net profit	27,000	86,755	00	Less: Dep.	2,000	18,000	00

(contd.)

Liabilities	Amount Rs.	P.	Liabilities	Amount Rs	P.
Creditors	3,300	00	Patents	17,000	00
Outstanding salary	1,500	00	Land	25,000	00
			Debtors	14,500	00
			Closing stock	6,800	00
			Cash in hand	1,170	00
			Cash in bank	2,000	00
			Accrued commission	1,000	00
			Prepaid rent	85	00
	91,555	00		91,555	0 0

PROBLEMS

Q. 1. From the following balance, prepare trading and profit and loss account and balance sheet.

Cash at bank	1,500	Return outwards	650
Opening stock	70,000	Capital	14,000
Debtors	20,000	Sales	1,28,000
Purchases	65,000	Creditors	18,000
Freight inward	275	Interest received	250
Carriage outward	100	Bank overdraft	2,500
Advertisement	200		
Rent	400		
Bad debts	1,000		
Return inwards	3,900		
Discount allowed	25		
Bank balance	1,000		

Closing stock was valued at Rs. 55,000 as on March 31, 2005.

Ans.: G.P. 44,475, N.P. 43,000, B/S 77,500

Q. 2. From the following balance, prepare trading and profit and loss account and balance sheet.

Debit balance		**Credit balance**	
Machinery	25,000	Discount	50
Opening stock	10,000	Commission	2,000

Debtors	5,000	Capital	20,000
Purchase	28,000	Creditors	8,000
Wages	3,500	Sales	50,000
Bank	8,000	Bank loan	5,000
Freight	2,350		
Rent	350		
Salaries	2,350		
General expenses	300		
Repair	200		

Closing stock was valued at Rs. 10,000.

Ans.: G.P. 16,150, N.P. 15,000, B/S 48,000

Q. 3. The following are the balances as at 31st December, 2004 extracted from the books of Gaurav Sharma. You are required to prepare the trading and profit and loss account and balance shee.

	(Amount Dr.)	(Amount Cr.)
Capital a/c	-	10,440
Purchases	12,000	-
Purchases return	-	600
Sales	-	15,000
S. return	200	-
Cash in hand	300	-
Cash at bank	1,920	-
Opening stock	2,000	-
Freight & carriage	340	-
Salaries	600	-
Discount	10	-
Sundry expenses	900	-
Rent	500	-
Commission	-	500
Discount	-	50
Interest received	-	160

Rent received	-	150
Bad debts	300	-
Debtors	2,500	-
Furniture	1,320	-
Building	3,000	-
Drawings	460	-
Bills receivable	-	900
Bills payable	350	-

Closing stock was valued at Rs. 3,600 on Dec 31, 2004.

Ans.: G.P. 4,660, N.P. 3,210, B/S 13540

Q. 4. The following are the balances as at 31st December 2004 extracted from the books of Anand Gupta. You are required to prepare the trading and profit and loss account and balance sheet.

Capital	18,000	Furniture	2,300
Opening stock	2,720	Machinery	5,000
Bills payable	2,608	Building	10,000
Creditors	10,000	Commission (Cr.)	400
Debtors	5,300	Insurance	132
B/R	3,091	Rent	400
Sales	13,439	Postage	300
Purchases	10,692	Discount (Cr.)	617
Sales return	2,000	Salaries	1,000
Purchase return	1,400	Freight	410
Cash in hand	1,000	Wages	1,500
Depreciation	600		
Discount (Dr.)	19		

Closing stock was valued at Rs. 7,929 as on December 31, 2004

Ans.: G.P. 5,446, N.P. 4,012, B/S 34,620

Q. 5. The following trail balance is etracted from the books of a merchant on 31st December 2004.

Debit Balance		Credit Balance	
Furniture	12,500	Capital	16,430
Motor vehicles	8,500	Bills payable	12,500

Building23,700	Creditors	23,000	
Bad debts	670	Sales	40,000
Sundry debtors	12,400	Bank o/d	2,000
Opening stock	3,650	Purchase return	430
Purchases	22,560	Commission	550
Sales return	430		
Advertisement	2,300		
Interest	600		
Cash in hand	800		
Sundry expenses	3,500		
Salaries	3,300		

Closing stock was valued at Rs. 8,800. From the abovc prcparc trading and profit and loss account for the year ended December 31, 2004.

Ans.: G.P. 22,590, N.P. 12,770, B/S 66,700

Q. 6. The following trial balance is extracted from the books of M/s Bhagwan Dass on 31st March 2005

	Debit amount	*Credit amount*
Capital		60,065
Drawings	2,300	
General expenses	5,600	
Building	32,000	
Machinery	12,500	
Stock	5,600	
Power	3,000	
Rent & Tax	950	
Wages	8,600	
Debtors	9,800	
Creditors		12,450
Bad debts	650	
Loan		15,000
Sales		34,600
Purchases	22,650	

	Debit amount	*Credit amount*
Motor Car	12,800	
Commission received		600
Sundry expenses	675	
Bills payable	6,780	
Cash	5,690	
Bank overdraft	6,700	
Charity	670	
Interest received		850

Stock on 31st March 2005 was valued at Rs. 6,500. You are required to prepare the trading and profit and loss account and balance sheet.

Q. 7. The following trial balance is extracted from the books of a mechant on 31st March 2005

Debit balance		**Credit balacne**	
Plant & machinery	75,000	Capital	57,985
Purchases	57,000	Sales	96,000
Sales return	4,500	Purchases return	2,300
Opening stock	32,000	Discount received	600
Discount allowed	450	Creditors	24,600
Wages	4,800	Commission received	675
Salaries	6,800	Interest received	1,200
Freight inward	2,460	Loan	23,000
Freight outward	1,350	Bank overdraft	5,400
Rent & rates	760		
Advrtisement	2,670		
Bad debts	500		
Cash in hand	5,680		
Cash at bank	4,530		
Bank charges	760		
Debtors	12,500		

Stock on 31st March 2005 valued at Rs. 34,000. From the following balance, prepare trading and profit and loss account and balance sheet.

Ans.: G.P. 31,540, N.P. 20,725, B/S 1,31710

Q. 8. The following are the balance as at 31st March 2005 extracted from the books of M/s Jagat Shah & Sons. You are required to prepare the trading and profit and loss account and balance sheet.

Plant & machinery	25,000	Capital	42,945
Purchases	37,000	Sales	56,800
Return outward	1,800	Return inward	1,200
Opening stock	15,600	Discount received	600
Discount allowed	250	Creditors	12,400
Wages & Salaries	4,800	Commission received	675
Salaries & Wages	3,560	Bank overdraft	3,400
Freight inward	1,560	Bills payable	10,000
Rent & rates	460		
Insurance premium	2,100		
Furniture & fitting	15,600		
Cash in hand	7,690		
Cash at bank	4,340		
Debtors	6,700		
Interest on capital	1,560		

Stock on 31st March 2005 was valued at Rs. 14,700.

Ans.: G.P. 11,940, N.P. 5,285, B/S 74,030

Q. 9. The following trial balance is extracted from the books of a merchant on 31st December 2004

Debit balance		**Credit balance**	
Opening stock	15,600	Capital	1,06,730
Plant & machinery	25,000	Sales	1,12,000

Debit balance		Credit balance	
Purchases	79,600	Return inward	3,200
Return outward	1,800	Discount received	960
Land & building	30,000	Creditors	22,750
Discount allowed	1,200	Commission received	600
Wages	24,800	Bank overdraft	4,400
Salaries	31,560	Bills payable	12,460
Freight on purchase	2,800	Loan from Arjun	22,670
Rent & rates	2,000		
Insurance premium	2,100		
Furniture & fitting	24,380		
Cash in hand	7,090		
Cash at bank	5,400		
Debtors	18,700		
Interest on capital	2,260		
Stationary	3,480		
Trade expenses	1,560		
Traveling expenses	3,890		
Postage	350		
General expenses	2,200		

The following further information was given:

1. Salaries amounting to Rs. 1,300 were unpaid.
2. Prepaid rent Rs. 300.
3. Depreciation on plant & machinery is to be charged @ 10%
4. Depreciation on furniture & fitting is to be charged @ 15%
5. The value of closing stock was Rs. 8,000.

You are required to prepare the trading and profit and loss account and balance sheet.

Ans.: G.Loss 1,400, Net Loss 57,597, B/S 1,12,713

Q. 10. The following is the trail balance of Mr. Rakesh on 31st March 2005.

	Amount (Debit)	Amount (Credit)
Capital		1,58,230
Drawings	2,600	
Purchases & Sales	76,000	99,900
Debtors & Creditors	14,300	17,650
Returns	2,100	1,200
Opening stock	21,000	
Discount	1,200	760
Commission	600	590
Rent & Taxes	8,700	-
Telephone charges	780	-
Freight on purchases	3,400	-
Printing & stationary	8,400	
Postage and telegram	950	
Land & building	89,000	
Furniture	40,000	
Bank over draft		6,000
Cash in hand	8,000	
Cash at bank	4,500	
Insurance premium	2,800	

The following further information was given:

1. Outstanding Salaries amounting to Rs. 1,490.
2. Prepaid rent Rs. 900 and insurance premium Rs. 500.
3. Depreciation on land and building is to be charged @ 10%.
4. Depreciation on furniture is to be charged @ 12%.
5. The value of closing stock was Rs. 28,000.

You are required to prepare the trading and profit and loss account and balance sheet.

Ans.: G.P. 26,600, N.Loss 9,270, B/S 1,71,500

Q. 11. The following trial balance has been extracted from the book of Messrs Radhy Shyam & sons on 31 March, 2005.

	Debit	*Credit*
Capital		15,914
Cash in hand	3,570	-
Cash at bank	5,300	-
Purchases & sales	23,000	33,400
Fixtures & fittings	4,500	-
B/R & B/P	8,750	9,860
Wages	6,784	-
Salaries	4,390	-
Rent	870	-
Discount	400	250
Commission	-	1,340
Debtors & Creditors	8,650	12,450
Printing & Stationary	2,480	-
General expenses	1,240	-
Advertisement	680	-
Carriage outward	1,300	
Carriage inward	2,300	
Loan		24,500
Machinery	23,500	

The following further information was given:

1. Outstanding Rent amounting to Rs. 320
2. Salaries oustanding Rs. 600
3. Commission accrued Rs. 450
4. Depreciation on Machinery is to be charged @ 8%
5. The value of closing stock was Rs. 7,000

Ans.: G.P. 8,316, Net Loss 3,804, B/S 56,840

Q. 12. From the following trial balance and other information, prepare trading and profit and loss account for the year ending 31st December, 2004 balance sheet as on that date:

Stock (1st Jan, 2004)	22,000	-
Debtors	33,000	-
Creditors		14,000
Cash in hand	4,000	-
Cash at bank	4,760	-
Plant & machinery	23,000	-
Sundry expenses	3,560	-
Sales		1,56,800
Salaries	4,660	-
Wages & salaries	8,500	-
Carriage inwards	560	
Carriage outwards	890	
Rent	5,400	
Discount	570	360
Factory lighting	2,000	-
Purchases	78,000	-
Insurance premium	2,000	-
Income from investment		21,000
Furniture	12,500	-
Capital	-	13,240

The stock on 31st December 2004 was Rs. 14,300. Rent was unpaid to the extent of Rs. 100 and Rs. 350 were outsanding for wages; Rs. 400 are to be written off as bad debts out of the above debtors. Depreciate plant and machinery by 10% and furniture by 15%.

Ans.: Gross Profit 59,690, Net Profit 59,295, B/S 86,985

CHAPTER XIII

DEPRECIATION

Meaning of Depreciation

In simple words, depreciation refers to a fall in the value of an asset. Due to depreciation, sooner or later the asset will become useless. Depreciation is charged on every fixed asset.

According to Spicer and Pegler

Depreciation may be defined as a measure of the exhaustion of the effective life of an asset from any cause during a given period.

Pickles defined Depreciation as

The permanent and continuing diminution in the quality, quantity or value of an asset .

According to Chartered Institute of Management Accountant (CIMA) Landon

"Depreciation is the diminution in intrinsic value of the asset due to use and lapse of time".

So depreciation refers to that part of the cast of fixed asset which has expired on account of its usage and the passage of time. In other words it is, thus, reduction in the value of a fixed asset.

Characteristics of Depreciation

There are some salient characteristics of depreciation:

1. Depreciation is a reduction in the book value of fixed

assets except land.

2. It refers the decrease in the book value of the asset but not its market value.
3. Depreciation on assets is permanent, gradual and has continuing nature.
4. Depreciation is a continuing process.
5. It takes place gradually unless there is a quick physical detraction.
6. Depreciation is not the process of valuation of asset. It is a process of allocation of cost of the asset to the period of its estimated working life.
7. The depreciation is used only for tangible fixed asset.
8. Depreciation is charge against profit.
9. Depreciation is different from maintenance.
10. Depreciation is charge for those assets, which are expected to be used during more than one accounting year.

CAUSES OF DEPRECIATION

(i) **Wear and Tear:** Wearing out of the assets due to its constant use is called wear and tear. It is an important cause of depreciation in the case of tangible.

(ii) **Efflux of Time:** Some assets have a fixed period of life like a lease, patents etc. On the expiry of the life the asset will cease to exist machinery

(iii) **Obsole Scence:** New invention or changed fashion may be the cause of replacement of assets by new model. Suppose new machinery performs the same operation more quickly and economically, than old machine is said to have become out of date.

(iv) **Accidents:** Meeting of an accident may reduce the value of an asset. Such loss may be permanent but it is not continuing and gradual.

(v) **Depletion:** Some assets are of a wasting character. Natural resources like quarries, mines, oil well etc. come under this heading. These assets get exhausted through working. Depreciation in case of these assets is computed on the basis of actual depletion.

DEPRECIATION AND OTHER RELATED CONCEPTS

Depreciation and depletion: The term depletion is used in respect of the exhausted of natural recourses. Examples are quarries, coal mines etc. Depletion reduces the availability of quantity of the material or assets. In fact it is a method of depreciation which is used, for wasting assets.

Depreciation and Obsolescence: Obsolescence refers to decrease in usefulness caused on account of the external factors like change in technology etc. Depreciation is a loss in value of an asset generally arising on account of wear and tear. Obsolescence is regarded as one of the cause of depreciation.

Depreciation and Amortisation: Amortisation refers to cost allocation of intangible assets like goodwill; copyright etc. Depreciation is the writing off the expired cost of the tangible assets like machinery, building etc.

OBJECTIVES OF PROVIDING DEPRECIATION:

Ascertaining the True Profits: Depreciation refers to the expired cost of a fixed asset due to its usage in business. This expired cost is a part of the total expenses so depreciation becomes an important element of the cost of product. Depreciation must be debited to profit and loss acount before profit is ascertained. If depreciation is not charge, the profit and loss acount will not show the true amount of profit.

Ascertaining the true cost of Production: Depreciation on fixed asset in the factory is an important component of the cost of production. So if there is no provision for depreciation, the cost calculation will be incorrect.

Presentation of True Financial Position: True financial position of the firm can be studied from the balance sheet. The value of fixed assets reduces by depreciation year after year an account of their usage and passing of time. For the purpose of presenting true financial position it is necessary that depreciation must be deducted from the assets and reduce value of assets must be shown in the balance sheet. So depreciation must be taken in to account.

Funds for Replacement of Assets: Charging depreciation reduces the profit available for distribution to shareholders. It enable the firm to retain a part of its profit and thus accumulate funds for replacement of the fixed assets as and when required.

Factors Influencing Depreciation: The amount of depreciation is affected by following factors:

Original Cost of the Asset: Cost of asset will include all expenses incurred to bring the asset to usable condition. The example of such expenses are transportation cost, eraction cost etc.

Estimated Life of Asset: The use full or working life of the asset can be stated in following ways:

In terms of time—years, months, hours etc.

In terms of quantity — number of units produce etc.

In any other operating measure — kilometers in the case of lorries, etc.

Estimated Scrap Value: Scrape value refers to estimated sale value of the asset at the end of its economic life to the firm. Suppose a machine is purchased at a cost of Rs. 70,000. The expected life of this machine is 10 years. At the end of this period it will have a scrap value of Rs. 15,000. We must provide a total depreciation of Rs. 55,000 in 10 years.

Methods of Providing Depreciation: The following are the principal method for providing depreciation:

1. Fixed Instalment Method or Straight Line Method
2. Diminishing Balance Method or Written Down Value Method
3. Annuity Method

4. Depreciation Fund Method
5. Insurance Policy Method
6. Revaluation Method
7. Depletion Method
8. Machine Hour Rate Method

Fixed Instalment Method or Straight Line Method: In this method a fixed percentage of the original cost of the asset is written off every year. So that, the asset account will be nil or to it's scrap value at the end of the estimated life of the asset. The amount of depreciation is same for every year. To calculate the amount of depreciation under this method the original value of the asset is divided by the number of years of its estimated life.

$$\text{Depreciation} = \frac{\text{Original cost of asset} - \text{Estimated scrape value}}{\text{Estimated life of asset}}$$

$$\text{Percentage of depreciation} = \frac{\text{Depreciation}}{\text{Original cost of asset}} \times 100$$

For example: An asset costing Rs. 21,000 is estimated to have a life of 10 years and the scrape value is estimated Rs. 1,000 at the end of its life, the amount of depreciation would be

= (21,000 – 1,000)/10

= 20, 000/10

Rs. 2,000

The amount of depreciation charged during each period of the assets life is uniform. When the amount of depreciation is presented on a graph paper and the points joined together, then the graph will reveal a straight line, that is why it is also called as straight line method.

If the depreciation is charged some percentage per annum and asset is purchased during the accounting year, suppose on

July 1, in such condition the depreciation for six month to be charged if the accounting year closed on Dec. 31.

MERITS OF STRAIGHT LINE METHOD

1. It is simple and easy method of calculating depreciation.
2. The value of asset can be reduced up to the estimated scrap value or zero value.
3. This method is suitable for those assets which have a fixed life e.g. machinery, furniture, fixture etc.
4. Every year, some amount of depreciation is debited to profit & loss. So there is some effect on profit and loss acount every year.

DEMERITS OF STRAIGHT LINE METHOD

1. It does not take in to account the interest on capital invested in assets.
2. It does not consider the effect of utilization of assets.
3. Under this method it is difficult to calculate the depreciation on additions made during a year.
5. Sometimes under this method, book value of an asset becomes zero but yet the assets are used in the business.
6. This method tends to report an increasing rate of interest since the net balance of the asset is taken.
7. It doesn't recognize the fact that as an asset become older, the amount spent for repair and renewal goes on increasing. So the combined charges on a/c of depreciation and maintenances will not be uniform throughout the working life of asset.

Illustration 1

A company purchased machinery on 1st Jan. 2001 at a cost of Rs. 68,000. The estimated working life of the machinery is 10 years with scrap value of Rs. 8,000. Find out the amount of depreciation and show the machinery account and depreciation account for three year.

Solution:

Calculation of depreciation

$$\text{Depreciation} = \frac{\text{Cost of machinery} - \text{Scrap}}{\text{Estimated working life}}$$

$$= \frac{\text{Rs. } 68{,}000 - \text{Rs. } 8{,}000}{10 \text{ Years}}$$

$$= \frac{\text{Rs. } 60{,}000}{10 \text{ Years}}$$

= Rs. 6,000 every year

IN THE BOOK OF
MACHINERY ACCOUNT

Dr **Cr**

Date	Particulars	F	Amount Rs.	P.	Date	Particulars	F	Amount Rs.	P.
2001 Jan 1	To Bank a/c		68,000	00	2001 Dec. 31	By Deprecia-tion a/c		6,000	00
					Dec. 31	By Bal. c/d		62,000	00
			68,000	00				68,000	00
2002 Jan 1	To Balance b/d		62,000	00	2002 Dec 31	By Deprecia-tion a/c		6,000	00
					Dec. 31	By Bal. c/d		56,000	00
			62,000	00				62,000	00
2003 Jan 1	To Balance b/d		56,000	00	2003 Dec. 31	By Deprecia-tion a/c		6,000	00
					Dec. 31	By Bal. c.d		50,000	00
			56,000	00				56,000	00
2004 Jan 1	To Balance b/d		50,000	00					

DEPRECIATION ACCOUNT

Dr **Cr**

Date	Particulars	F	Amount Rs.	P.	Date	Particulars	F	Amount Rs.	P.
2001 Dec 31	To Machinery a/c		6,000	00	2001 Dec 31	By P & L a/c		6,000	00
			6,000	00				6,000	00
2002 Dec 31	To Machinery a/c		6,000	00	2002 Dec 31	By P & L a/c		6,000	00
			6,000	00				6,000	00
2003 Dec 31	To Machinery a/c		6,000	00	Dec 31	By P& L a/c		6,000	00
			6,000	00				6,000	00

Illustration 2

A Company purchased machinery for Rs. 50,000 on 31st Jan 2001. The machinery is depreciated at 10% per annum on the original cost. The machinery was sold for Rs. 15,000 on 31st Dec, 2004.

Show the machinery a/c, assuming the books are closed on 31st Dec each year.

MACHINERY ACCOUNT

Dr **Cr**

Date	Particulars	F	Amount Rs.	P.	Date	Particulars	F	Amount Rs.	P.
2001 Jan 1	To Bank a/c		50,000	00	2001 Dec 31	By Depreciation a/c		5,000	00
					Dec 31	By Bal. c/d		45,000	00
			50,000	00				50,000	
2002 Jan 1	To Balance b/d		45,000	00	2002 Dec 31	By Depreciation a/c		5,000	00
					Dec 31	By Bal. c/d		40,000	00
			45,000	00				45,000	00

Date	Particulars	F	Amount Rs.	P.	Date	Particulars	F	Amount Rs.	P.
2003					2003				
Jan 1	To Balance b/d		40,000	00	Dec 31	By Depreciation a/c		5,000	00
					Dec 31	By Balance c/d		35,000	00
			40,000	00				40,000	00
2004					2004				
Jan 1	To Balance b/d		35,000	00	Dec 31	By Depreciation a/c		5,000	00
					Dec. 31	By Bank a/c		15,000	00
					Dec. 31	By P & L a/c (loss)		15,000	00
			35,000	00				35,000	00

DIMINISHING BALANCE METHOD OR WRITTEN DOWN VALUE METHOD

In this method, depreciation is calculated at fixed percentage each year on the balance of the asset, which is brought forward from the last year. The amount of depreciation is not fixed in each period. The amount of depreciation to be charged goes on reducing from year to year. The amount of depreciation is higher in initial period than those in the later period.

MERITS OF DIMINISHING BALANCE METHOD

1. It ensures fairly even charges of depreciation against revenue each year.
2. It ensures a fairly even charge of depreciation and repair to profit and loss acount.
3. This method is easy to follow.
4. On the addition to the assets, the depreciation can be computed easily in this method.
5. The income tax authorities in India certify this method.

DEMERITS OF DIMINISHING BALANCE METHOD

1. Under this method, value of assets cannot be brought down to zero.
2. It is a difficult task to ascertain the proper rate of depreciation.
3. Under this method, interest on capital invested is not taken in to consideration.

Illustration 3

A Company purchased machinery for Rs. 50,000 on 1st Jan 2001. The machinery is depreciated at 10% per annum on the diminishing balance.

Show the machinery a/c for three years assuming that the books are closed on 31st Dec each year.

In the book of

MACHINERY ACCOUNT

Dr **Cr**

Date	Particulars	F	Amount Rs.	P.	Date	Particulars	F	Amount Rs.	P.
2001					2001				
Jan 1	To Bank a/c		50,000	00	Dec 31	By Depreciation a/c		5,000	00
					Dec 31	By Bal. c/d		45,000	00
			50,000	00				50,000	00
2002					2002				
Jan 1	To Balance b/d		45,000	00	Dec 31	By Depreciation a/c		4,500	00
					Dec. 31	By Bal. c/d		40,500	00
			45,000	00				45,000	00
2003						2003			
Jan 1	To Balance b/d		40,500	00	Dec 31	By Depreciation a/c		4,050	00
					Dec. 31	By Bal. c/d		36,450	00
			40,500	00				40,500	00
2004									
Jan 1	To Bal. b/d		36,450	00					

Illustration 4

Gupta and Company purchased machinery for Rs. 38,000 on 1st Jan 2001 and spent Rs. 2,000 on its installation. On 31st Dec 2004 the machinery was sold for Rs. 15,000. Assuming the books are closed on 31st December each year and the rate of depreciation is 10% per annum on the diminishing balance, show the machinery account.

Solution

In the book of ....

MACHINERY ACCOUNT

DR **CR**

Date	Particulars	F	Amount Rs.	P.	Date	Particulars	F	Amount Rs.	P.
2001					2001				
Jan 1	To Bank a/c		38,000	00	Dec 31	By Depreciation a/c		4,000	00
Jan 1	To Bank a/c (Installation exp.)		2,000	00	Dec 31	By Balance c/d		36,000	00
			40,000	00				40,000	00
2002					2002				
Jan 1	To Balalance b/d		36,000	00	Dec 31	By Depreciation a/c		3,600	00
					Dec. 31	By Bal. c/d		32,400	00
			36,000	00				36,000	00
2003					2003				
Jan 1	To Balance b/d		32,400	00	Dec 31	By Depreciation a/c		3,240	00
					Dec 31	By Bal .c/d		29,160	00
			32,400	00				32,400	00
2004					2004				
Jan 1	To Balance b/d		29,160	00	Dec 31	By Depreciation a/c		2,916	00
					Dec. 31	By Bank a/c		15,000	00
					Dec. 31	By P & L a/c (loss)		11,244	00
			29,160	00				29,160	00

DIFFERENCE BETWEEN STRAIGHT LINE AND WRITTEN DOWN VALUE METHOD

Straight Line Method	Written Down Value Method
1. Depreciation is calculated on the original cost.	Depreciation is calculate on the diminishing balance or written down value of fixed asset
2. The amount of depreciation is same in every year.	The amount of depreciation goes on decreasing in every year.
3. The amount of balance in the asset a/c will reduce to zero at the expiry of the working life the asset	The balance in the assets account will never reduced to zero.
4. Calculation of depreciation is easy under this method	Calculation of depreciation is difficult under this method
5. The combine cost of depreciation and repair lower during the initial years and higher during the later years.	The combine cost depreciation and repair is more or less equal throughout the period
6. This method is suitable for assets, which gets depreciated on a/c of expiry of time.	This method is suitable for asset, which requires heavy repairs in later years of their working life.

ANNUITY METHOD

In this method, amount spent on the purchase of an asset is taken as an investment, which is assumed to earn interest at a certain rate. Interest is calculated on the opening balance of an asset. Asset account is debited with the amount of interest and credited with the amount of depreciation. The amount of depreciation is calculated from the annuity table. This method is refers to as scientific method as it treats the purchase of an asset as an investment in the business itself. The chief demerit is that the amount of depreciation and repair put together does not remain fairly same from year to year. This method is mainly used for lease in respect of which a lump some payment is made in advance.

DEPRECIATION FUND METHOD

This method says that the amount of depreciation should be kept aside and invested outside the business in sellable securities. The security accumulates and when the lives of asset expire the securities are sold and with the amount released new asset is purchased. As the securities always earned interest, it is not necessary to written off the full amount of cost of depreciation. How much amount should be invested every year so that a given sum is available at the end of a given period depends on the rate of interest, which can be calculated from sinking fund table. Depreciation charged under this method will be lower as compare to various other method. This method is also known as sinking fund method.

INSURANCE POLICY METHOD

In this method, some arrangement is made with an insurance company. The business takes an insurance policy for the required amount to replacement the asset. A fixed amount of premium is paid to the insurance company at the beginning of each year. At the end of the certain period the insurance company pays the agreed amount with which new asset can be purchased.

This method can be adopted where:

1. The repair and maintenance cost are reducing over the life of the asset, and
2. The revenue and operating efficiency are uniform or increasing over the life of the asset.

REVALUATION METHOD

This method is also known as inventory method. In this method, the asset is revalued at the end of the each accounting year. At the end of accounting year the value is compared with the value of the asset at the beginning of the year. The difference in the two figures is treated as depreciation. This method is used in the case of assets which are large in quantity but have small value like—bottle, corks, loose tools etc.

DEPLETION METHOD

This method is used for wasting assets like—mines, quarries, etc. In this method the amount of depreciation is calculated on the output during the year. The amount of depreciation is related to the quantity taken out and not the passage of time. Under this method the amount of depreciation is varies from year to year depending upon the actual output.

MACHINE HOUR RATE METHOD

This method is also known as service hour method. This method is useful in case of machines. Under this method the life of the machinery is estimated in terms of hours. The amount of depreciation is calculated by dividing the cost of the machine by the total number of hours for which the machine is expected to be used. Depreciation to be written off in a year will be calculated by multiplying the hourly rate of depreciation with the number of hours that the machine actually runs in the accounting year.

PROVISION

Provision represent an estimated amount to meet a loss or expenses in future whose amount as yet in not certain. If the amount of such liability is ascertained, it will be treated liability and not a provision. For example, provision for outstanding rent, salary cannot be called provision.

The Indian Companies act has defined it as—'any amount written off or retained by way of providing for depreciation, renewals or diminution in value of assets, or retained by providing for any known liability of which the amount cannot be determined with substantial accuracy.'

Provision for taxation, provision for depreciation, provision for doubtful debts, provision for discount on debtors, provision for repairs and renewal and provision for contingencies are some examples of provision. It is a charge to profit and loss acount. The provision are created by debiting the profit and loss acount and either shown on the liability side of balance sheet or reduced from the related asset.

RESERVE

Reserve represent an amounts set aside out of profit. It is an appropriation out of profits to strengthen the financial position of the firm. It is not a charge against profits. Reserves are not meant to cover up liabilities, contingency or reduction in the value of assets. General reserves reserve for expansion, reserve for equalization of dividends, reserve for increased costs of replacement etc. are some examples of reserve.

The chief objective of creating reserve is to provide for unexpected losses in future and also retain profits with in the business to provide such fund for expansion of the business.

RESERVE FUND

If the amount of reserve has been invested in outside securities, the reserve will called reserve fund. Employees welfare fund, pension fund, gratuity fund, debenture redemption fund etc. are some example of it. If the amount of reserve is being utilized by the business it self and not invested in outside the business, it cannot be called reserve fund but merely a reserve.

IMPORTANCE OF RESERVE

Reserves are very important in business to strengthen the financial position of the firm. The purpose of reserve may be:

1. It helps in expansion of the business.
2. It helps in better financial position of the business.
3. It helps in redemption of liabilities.
4. It is useful in meeting unforeseen contingencies.
5. It helps in making dividends uniform from year to year.
6. Meeting legal requirement such as investment reserve required by the income tax.

TYPES OF RESERVES

Revenue Reserves: Revenue reserve is generally created out of business profit, which is available for distribution of dividends. General reserve, Staff welfare Debenture redemption reserve, Dividend equalization reserve, Investment fluctuation reserve Contingency reserve etc. are some examples of revenue General reserve.

Capital Reserve: Any reserve, which is created, out of Capital profits and normally are not available for distribution as cash dividend. Profit made prior to incorporation Premium received on issue of share or debentures Profits on redemption of debentures, Profits on forfeiture of share, Profit on resale of fixed assets Capital redemption reserve and Profit on revaluation of fixed asset and liabilities, etc. are examples of Capital reserve.

DISTINCTION BETWEEN REVENUE RESERVE AND CAPITAL RESERVE

Revenue Reserve	Capital Reserve
1. It is created out of business profit.	1. It is created from the capital profits.
2. It can be utilize for distribution of dividends without any prescribed by the Indian Companies Act	2. It can be utilize for distribution of dividends only if the company satisfies certain conditions prescribed by the Indian Companies Act.
3. It is credited for strengthen the financial position, and meeting the unforeseen contingencies or some specific purpose.	3. It is created for meeting capital losses or to be used for any purpose which is specified by Indian company act.

General Reserve: General reserve is that amount set asides out of profits which is not created for any specific purpose. It is available for any unforeseen contingency or expansion of the business. These are created to provide additional working capital and strengthening the financial position of the business.

Specific Reserve: Specific reserve is that reserve which is created for specific purpose and can be utilized only for that purpose. Workmen's compensation, debenture redemption fund, dividend equalization reserve are the example of specific reserve.

Secret Reserve: A secret reserve is a reserve the existence and the amount of which does not appear on the face of the balance sheet. Secret reserve are created in those concern where more public confidence is required for its working. Showing the assets at a lower value and liabilities at a higher value creates such reserves. The chief objective of secret reserve is to reduce the disclosed profit so that during bad period. This hidden profit may be merged into the earning and these help in equalizing the dividends.

WAYS OF CREATING SECRET RESERVE

1. By writing off excessive depreciation.
2. By under valuing of closing stock in trade.
3. By under valuing of goodwill.
4. By writing off capital expenditure to profit and loss account.
5. By suppressing the sales.
6. By showing a contingent liability as an actual liability.
7. By grouping free reserve as creditors.
8. Showing an asset as a contingent asset.
9. By making excessive provision for bad and doubtful debtors.

ADVANTAGES OF SECRET RESERVE

1. It increases the working capital of the business and strengthens it's financial position without disclosing this fact to the shareholders or the public.
2. It discourages competition through not disclosing the actual profit made by a concern in a particular line of business and industry.

3. It enables the directors to tide over unfavorable times.

DISADVANTAGES OF SECRET RESERVE

1. The balance sheet will not show a true and fair view of the state of affairs of the business.
2. The companies worst position can be concealed by the director for some time by making the use of secret reserve.
3. When secret reserves are created the assets are shown at lower value in the balance sheet. The concern will not get full claim for loss by fire of the assets as and when such assets are destroyed by fire.

DIFFERENCE BETWEEN RESERVE AND PROVISION:

Reserve	Provision
1. It is an appropriation of profit.	It is a charge against the profit.
2. It is debited to profit and loss appropriation account.	It is written on the debit side of profit and loss account.
3. It can be invested ouside the business.	It cannot be invested outside the business.
4. The purpose of reserve is to strengthen the financial position of the firm and to meet the unforeseen liabilities and losses.	The purpose of provision is to meet the specific expenses or losses.
5. It is written on the liabilities side of the balance sheet.	It is deducted from the related items.
6. It reduces only divisible profits.	It reduces net profit.

PROBLEMS

Q. 1. Mohan purchased machinery for Rs. 43,000 on 1st Jan. 2001. The estimated working life of the machinery is 10 years. Its scrap value at the end of the period was Rs. 3,000. The books are closed on 31st December every year. Show the machinery and depreciation account for first three years according to fixed installment method.

Q. 2. Amit purchased machinery on 1st Jan. 2001 costing Rs.

50,000 and spent Rs. 2,000 on its erection. The estimated working life of the machinery is 10 years. Its scrap value at the end of the period was Rs. 12,000. The books are closed on 31st December every year. Calculate depreciation on the stright-line method and show machinery account of first three years.

Q. 3. Ashok and Sons purchased machinery on Jan. 1, 2000 for Rs. 32,000 and spent Rs. 3,000 on its eraction. The estimated working life of machinery is 5 years. Scrap value is estimated to Rs. 5,000. Find out the amount of depreciation to be charged every year and show the machinery account.

Q. 4. On 1st Jan. 2000 Suman purchased a machinery costing Rs. 61,000 and spent Rs. 4,000 on its eraction. The estimated working life of the machinery is 10 years with scrap value of Rs. 5,000. Calculate depreciation on the straight-line method and show machinery account for first 4 years.

Q. 5. On 1st Jan. 1998 Ram Kumar and Co. purchased machinery worth Rs. 50,000. On 1st July 2000, it buys additional machinery worth Rs. 10,000 and spent Rs. 1,000 on its eraction. The books are closed on 31st Dec. every year. Machinery was depreciated by fixed installment method at 10% per annum. Show the machinery account for first 5 years.

Q. 6. A Company purchased machinery on 1st April 2002 worth Rs. 30,000. It purchased additional machinery on 1st Oct 2002 costing Rs. 20,000 and on 1st July 2003 costing Rs. 10,000. On 1st Jan 2004 one third of the machinery installed on 1st April 2002 became obsolete and was sold for Rs. 3,000. Machinery was depreciated by fixed installment method at 10% per annum the company follow calendar year as accounting year. Show the machinery account for first three years.

Q. 7. On 1st April 2002, Atul and Sons purchased machinery-costing Rs. 60,000. Additional machinery was purchased on 1st Oct. 2002 for Rs. 40,000 and on 1st July 2003 for Rs. 20,000. On 1st Jan. 2004, one third of the machinery purchsased on 1st April 2002 was found to have become obsolete and was sold for Rs. 6,000.

Prepare machinery account for the first three years assuming depreciation @ 10% per annum of fixed installement method. Accounts are closed on 31st Dec. each year.

Q. 8. On 1st Jan. 2002, Brown and Co. purchased machinery costing Rs. 2,40,000 and additional machinery costing Rs. 1,00,000 was purchased. On 1st Jan. 2004, the machinery purchased on 1st Jan 2002, was found to have become obsolete and was sold for Rs. 1,43,000 and on the same date, a new machinery was purchased at a cost of Rs. 2,00,000. Prepare machinery account for the first four-year. Depreciation is charged at 5% by fixed installment method. The company observes calendar year as its accounting year.

Q. 9. On 1st Jan. 1998, Meheta and Sons purchased a machinery costing Rs. 1,00,000. Its estimated working life is 10 years. Depreciation is to be allowed at the rate of 10% per annum on Diminishing balance method. The Company observes calendar year as its accounting year. Show the machinery account for first four years.

Q. 10. On 1st July 2002 Shubham Bros. purchased machinery costing Rs. 25,000. Rs. 1,000 was spent on its eraction. Depreciation is to be charged @ 10% per annum on diminishing balance method. The Company observes calendar year as its accounting year. Show the machinery account for first three years.

Q. 11. On 1st July 2001 Shukla and Sons purchased machinery for Rs. 18,000 and spent Rs. 2,000 on its eraction. On 30th June 2004 the machinery was disposed of for a sum of Rs. 13,600. Rate of Depreciation is 10% per annum on diminishing balance method. The company observes calender year as its accounting year. Show the machinery account for first four years.

Q. 12. On 1st April 2002, a company purchased furniture for Rs. 8,000. On 1st July 2004 a part of furniture valued in the book of the firm at Rs. 1,600 on 1st April 2002 was sold for Rs. 1,000. Depreciation is to be provided @ 10% per annum on the written down value mehtod. Show the machinery account for first three years.

PART II

CHAPTER XIV

INTRODUCTION

In ancient times people travelled for various reasons. They had either a desire to know the unknown or to gain knowledge of religion, culture, civilisation and trade conditions of other places. In India, in the ancient period, travel within the country was mainly for the purpose of trade and religion. It is on record that almost all the religious places had *'Dharamshalas'* which used to provide free lodging to the travellers.

As we had *'Dharamshalas'* in India, there were 'Caravan *Sarais*' in the middle east, 'Taverns' in America, 'Inns' in England and European countries. All these places were self service institutions, unhygienic and without proper security. They provided only shelter for the travellers and their animals.

With the coming up of railways, steamships and aircrafts the travellers' radius of movement widened and need for lodging became acute. Travel created the demand for home away from home. Travellers, who left their homes, required accommodation either at destination or on the way on long journey. On account of this, these 'inns', 'taverns' etc. were converted into profitable trade which is known as hotel. By the year 1820 the term 'Hotel' was accepted by almost all countries for the place where people could stay and lake their meals on payment.

Today hotels provide lodging, food, entertainment and protection of luggage. Besides this, some hotels give many other comforts and luxuries to their guests. The word hotel is derived from the term 'host' or 'hospitality' and this, even in the rush of trading, is never forgotten in this hotel business.

In India the hotel industry was neglected till the Independence of the country, so far as incentives and facilities for development were concerned. The Britishers had started a few hotels in India either for their own use or for their foreign guests. Only a few large and some small hotels were opened by Indians. Till Independence, the number of foreign tourists was also very low but after that the tourist traffic suddenly increased. This increase posed a big problem for the hotel industry. At that time a few small hotels were in existence which were started by private enterprisers.

They were not better than Dak Bangalows, Hostels or Rest houses. It was not an easy job for hoteliers to bring them up to the international standard by investing their own money and without government's aid and incentives. It is worth appreciating that the hoteliers, however, tried to raise the standard of hotels and they got the success.

After Independence, the Government also realised the acute shortage of hotel accommodation and the need to build more hotels to accommodate tourists in the country.

In 1956 the first Government hotel was opened in New Delhi to accommodate UNESCO delegates. Later on the Government constituted the Hotel and Restaurant Classification Committee to classify the hotels according to their standard norms. Gradually a number of private sector and public sector hotels were opened by private enterprisers and Government in different parts of the country. India Tourism Development Corporation was constituted by Government of India in October 1966. This Corporation also opened many small and large hotels in various cities of the country.

In 1967 the Government of India announced various incentives for the first time for approved hotels to attract investment in hotel industry. The incentives are revised from time to time.

CATEGORISATION OF HOTELS

The hotels cater to the needs of various types of tourists who came from different parts of the country and the world to a particular place either for some business or for entertainment or for recovery of health or for some other work. They like comfortable stay in a hotel according to their requirements.

For different types of tourists there are a number of hotels in different parts of our country. Though there is no particular rule for categorisation of these hotels but from the point of view of their size, length of guests' stay, location etc. the hotels may be categorised as under:—

(1) Size

Hotels may be categorised according to the size or number of guest rooms. Though there is no particular formula or criteria for this categorisation but generally according to size the hotels can be of following types :—

(a) *Small hotels*— A hotel having 25 rooms or less may be called small hotel.

(b) *Average or medium hotels*—A hotel having 26 to 100 rooms come under this category.

(c) *Above average hotels*—A hotel having 101 to 300 rooms may be called above average hotel.

(d) *Large hotels*—A hotel having 301 and more rooms may be know as large hotel. Generally they are International hotels with modern amenities and facilities.

International hotels—They are of the western style hotels with are amenities and facilities. Generally they are the units of International hotel chains or group of hotels. They are opened in metropolitan cities, large towns, and tourist centres. They meet the needs of rich national or international tourists. They provide many types of comforts and luxuries to the guests.

(2) Length of Guest Stop over

There are three categories of hotels based on length of guest stay.

(a) Transient Hotels

Such hotels are meant for the guests who are *en route* and stay for a very short period say one day or two days. Such hotels are situated near bus terminals, railway stations, airport etc.

(b) Residential Hotels

They are a sort of apartment houses with complete hotel services. The rooms are sold to guests for a longer period say for three months, six months or one year. They are charged for furnished or unfurnished accommodation.

The guest has to sign the lease deed that describes the terms and conditions of both the lessor and lessee. Generally they are operated on European plan i.e., in quoted rates, the guest is given only accommodation. For meals he has to pay extra.

(c) Semi-residential Hotels

Such hotels provide the facility of short-term stay as well as long-term stay (one month or more).

(3) Location

The hotels based on location can be classified as under—

(a) City Hotels

Such hotels are situated in the heart of the city or in important business and industrial centres. If they are in the business or commercial centres then they can be called Commercial hotels also. These city and commercial hotels primarily cater to the needs of high officials or people of business community or industrialists. Generally such people want comfortable stay, so these hotels provide all possible comforts and luxuries to their guests.

(b) Resort Hotels

These hotels are generally located either in hills or beaches or places of natural beauty. They cater to the needs of the people who come to these hotels either for the change of atmosphere or for the rest or recovery of their health or entrainment. These hotels provide some additional facilities besides normal services.

Generally they operate a number of departments which provide necessary facilities according to the requirement of the guests. They have provisions of swimming pool, golf course, tennis court, boating, indoor games etc. on the basis of their location. They are generally seasonal hotels and can also be called winter resort, health resort or summer resort etc.

(c) Highway Hotels

Such hotels or motels are located on highways. In these hotels generally guests stay for a night and continue their journey on the next morning. Guests are charged for apartment at fixed rate. They have to pay extra for food.

(4) Plan

Hotels may be categorised according to type of plans as under-

(a) European Plan

If a hotel is operated on European plan system then in the quoted rates the guest is given only room (accommodation). He has to pay extra money for food and other services.

(b) Continental Plan

If a hotel is operated on Continental plan then in the quoted rates, the guest is given accommodation and continental breakfast (which is very light).

(c) American Plan

In American plan hotel a guest is given room (accommodation) and three meals (Breakfast, lunch and dinner) in the quoted rates.

(d) Modified American Plan

Some hotels are operated on this plan also. According to this plan in quoted rates a customer is given room (accommodation), breakfast and one major meal (lunch or dinner).

APPROVAL AND STAR CLASSIFICATION

Hotels of the above categories can apply for approval and/or classification according to star grading system.

Approved Hotels

They are the hotels which are approved at the planning stage and/or as functioning units by the Department of Tourism, Government of India from the point of view of their suitability for tourists. A new hotel which is to be started can apply for approval at a planning stage, keeping in view the star category at the functioning stage on its completion. Old unapproved hotels can also apply for approval at functioning stage. Approved hotels become eligible to various fiscal reliefs and benefits. Approved hotels get world-wide publicity through Tourists literature, published by Department of Tourism and distributed by Tourist offices of Government of India in the country and abroad. They are for eligible to spend certain percentage of foreign exchange earned by them for import of their essential equipment under hotel incentive quota scheme.

A hotel which seeks approval of the Department of Tourism must fulfil necessary conditions laid down by them in their annexure. It must have at least 10 rooms and bathrooms of adequate size. The management must agree to abide by the regulatory conditions prescribed by Department of Tourism. The hotel, seeking approval, has to fill up the prescribed form containing necessary information and send it along with the application for approval. A committee inspects the hotel. If basic requirements are found according to their norms and the hotel is found suitable for tourists then it is approved by the Department of Tourism, approved Government of India.

Classification of Hotel According to Star Categories

The Department of Tourism classifies approved hotels at functioning stage under the star system into seven categories:

1. ONE STAR HOTELS	*
2. TWO STAR HOTELS	* *
3. THREE STAR HOTELS	* * *
4. FOUR STAR HOTELS	* * * *
5. FIVE STAR HOTELS	* * * * *
6. FIVE STAR DELUXE HOTELS	* * * * * Deluxe
7. HERITAGE HOTELS	
8. APPROVED HOTELS	Unclassified Hotels

For this purpose the Government of India has set up a committee known as Hotel & Restaurant Approval and Classification Committee (H.R.A.C.C.). This Committee has under it 4 Sub-Committees for inspection of Hotels and Restaurants in the Eastern, Western, Northern and Southern Regions.

The Central Committee consists of the following members—

1. Chairman—Appointed by Deptt. of Tourism.
2. Member Secretary—Appointed by the Deptt. of Tourism.
3. One member from Federation of Hotel and Restaurant Association of India.
4. One member from Travel Agents Association of India (T.A.A.I.)

The Regional Committee consists of the following members—

1. Chairman— The Secretary (Tourism) of the concerned State/UT Government.
2. Convener—Regional Director, Government of India, Department of Tourism.
3. Member—The Principal, Institute of Hotel Management in the Stale/UT.
4. Member—Representative of Federation of Hotel & Restaurant Association of India.
5. Member—Representative of Travel Agent Association of India.

6. Member—Representative of Indian Association of Tour Operators.
7. Co-opted Member—Representative of Heritage Hotel Association.

Approved hotel which likes to be categorised according to star system has to apply in a prescribed form to the Director General, Tourism, Government of India. The hotel has to furnish the details of the hotel also in a prescribed form. It has to pay the necessary fee for classification along with application form.

The classification fee is payable by means of a demand draft drawn in favour of Pay and Accounts Officer, Department of Tourism, New Delhi.

On receipt of the application and prescribed fee the Regional Classification Committee of that Region visits the hotel and inspects the general feature of the hotel, facilities available in the hotel, services provided by the hotel, distance from the important places of the city and many other things according to their norms. The Regional Classification Committee awards marks for each point mentioned in their format. On the basis of total marks scored by a hotel as also subject to their having qualified in all individual items of the format the Regional Committee recommends appropriate star classification or rejection as the case may be. The recommendation of the H.R.A.C.C. is further examined in the Department of Tourism, Government of India and after the approval of the Minister of Tourism the applicant hotel is either placed in the appropriate star category or rejected.

CHAPTER XV

REVENUE PRODUCING DEPARTMENTS OF HOTEL

The hotel is a modified form of an 'inn'. Primarily it provides lodging, food and protection of luggage. Besides this most of the hotels toady provide many types of comforts, luxuries, professional services and other facilities to their guests under one roof. To provide above facilities the hotel has to open different departments. The number of departments depend upon the policy of management. Some hotels run a few departments but others run more departments.

ORGANISATION OF A HOTEL

The increase in tourism, the changing demand for accommodation and growth of large hotel chain has led to the construction of many hotels. Today's hotels are highly organised commercial units. For our present study, the organisation of a large hotel consists of two major groups of department:

(1) *Operational Department.* These departments are necessary for the business activities of the hotel and for dealing with all the needs and requirements of the guests.

(2) *Support Department.* These departments contain the additional specialist expertise which is an essential 'back up' to a tourist class hotel.

The departmentalization of a hotel will basically depend on its size. In small hotels, the manager or proprietor, attends to the administration and control of whole operation. He may be assisted by a receptionist, a housekeeper, a cook and a waiter. These are assisted by part time or casual staff. As regards to the administrative organisation it also vary from hotel to hotel.

Each hotel produces its own organisational structure to meet its basic and special needs. The tasks have to be sub-divided into separate areas of work and supervised by sectional heads.

ORGANISATIONAL CHART

OF A

MEDIUM-SIZED HOTEL

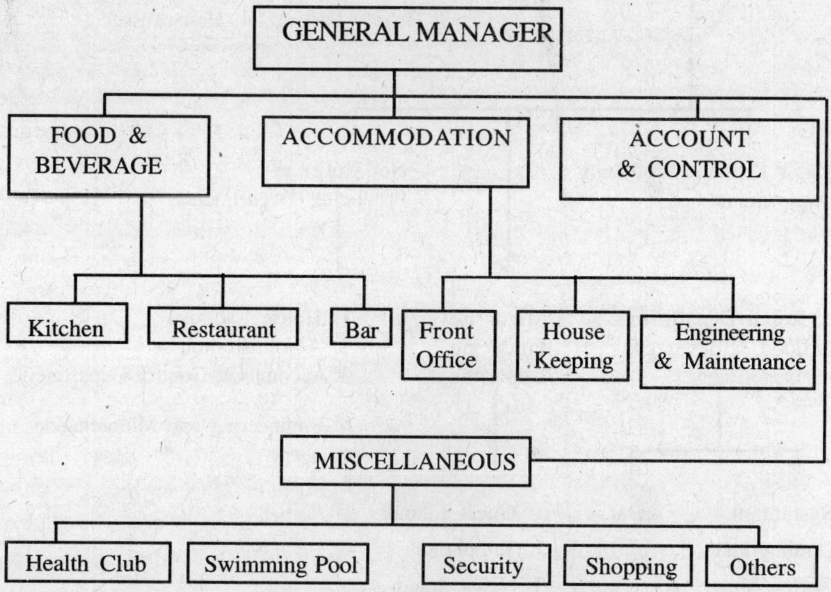

Fig. 1. Organisation of a Hotel

In general the departments of a hotel can be divided into two groups from the point of view of earning revenue—

1. Departments operated by the management of the hotel
2. Departments which are not operated by the management of the hotel but operated by outsiders who arc experts in their fields.

1. DEPARTMENTS OPERATED BY THE MANAGEMENT OF HOTEL

These departments are run by the management by employing its own persons. The whole expenditure is borne by the hotel and the whole profit, whatsoever is earned, goes to the hotel. These departments are further divided into three groups from the revenue point of view—

REVENUE PRODUCING DEPARTMENTS OF A HOTEL

Departments operated by the management of Hotel

- Major Revenue Producing Departments
  1. Room Departments
  2. Food & Beverage Department
     - Restaurant
     - Dinning Hall
     - Coffee Shop
     - Room Service
     - Banquet Deptt.
     - Bar
- Minor Revenue Producing Department
  1. Guest Laundry
  2. Telephone
  3. News Stand
  4. Swimming pool
  5. ....
  6. ....
- Non-Revenue Producing Departments
  1. House Laundry
  2. Administration
  3. Accounts & Control Department
  4. Engineering and Maintenance Deptt
  5. .... 6. ....

Departments which are not operated by the management of Hotel but run by outsiders. They produce Revenue:

1. Chemist Shop 2. Handicraft

3. Beauty Parlour 4. Hair dresser

5. .... 6. ....

Fig. 2. Revenue Producing Departments of a Hotel

(a) Major Revenue Producing Departments.

(b) Minor Revenue Producing Departments.

(c) Non-Revenue Producing Departments.

(a) Major Revenue Producing Departments

Under this category such departments are kept from where the hotel earns more revenue in comparison to other departments. There is no hard and fast rule that a particular department will fall under this head. It differs from hotel to hotel. If a particular department is operated by the hotel itself and earns more revenue then only it comes under this head. If that particular department is operated by outsiders then it will fall under the category of departments operated by outsiders.

Generally following departments produce more revenue for a hotel:—

(i) Room Department

(ii) Food and Beverage Department.

(i) Room Department. The main function of a hotel is to provide accommodation or lodging to the guests. The rooms are sold by the front office to the guests according to their requirements. From the sale of rooms, a hotel earns more revenue in comparison to many other departments.

Generally a hotel sells following types of rooms to the guests according to their requirements to earn revenue .—

Single room—Room with single bed.

Double room—Room with double bed.

Twin bedroom—Room with two separate single beds.

Studio room—Room with one single bed and one sofa cum bed.

Single suite—Single room with one living room.

Double suite—Double room with one living room.

It is an admitted fact that a hotel earns high revenue from the sale of rooms.

(ii) Food and Beverage Department. This department sells food and drinks. From the sale of food items, soft and alcoholic beverages a hotel earns more revenue.

Food Sale. The second important function of a hotel is to sell food to the guests. From the sale of food a hotel earns more revenue. Generally the food items are sold by the following departments food items are a hotel may have one or more restaurants where food items are sold to 3 types of guests—Residents, Credit Card holders and guests from the general public for cash or on credit according to the type of guests.

Dining hall. Here the food is sold to residents of a hotel.

Coffee shop. Generally it remains open for 24 hours. The sale of coffee, tea and snacks take place here.

Room service department. This department sells food to the residents and make supplies in the respective rooms of the guests.

Banquet department. This department organises banquets. Only large hotels operate this department. This department earns more revenue of a Besides the above departments, the food items are sold at lobby and Swimming Pool also to earn revenue.

Sale of soft drink. Soft drinks are sold at Restaurant, Coffee shops, Lobby and Bar. No licence in required for the sale of soft drinks.

Sale of Alcoholic beverages. For the sale of alcoholic beverages a hotel has to obtain licence. Without licence it cannot be sold. It may be sold either at Bar or Floor Bar or Dispensing Bar or in the room depending upon the type of licence obtained by a hotel. It is true that hotel earns more revenue from the sale of alcoholic beverages.

(b) Minor Revenue Producing Departments

They are the departments from where hotel earns less revenue in comparison to Room, Restaurant and Bar. As they produce less income therefore, they are known as Minor Revenue Producing Departments. Guest Laundry, Telephone, News Stand etc. are the examples of it. Here by Laundry we mean, Guests Laundry which is meant for guests only and from where Yearns revenue. It is different from House Laundry.

(c) Non-Revenue Producing Departments

As the name shows 'Non-Revenue Producing Departments' mean departments which do not produce directly any revenue. It is true that they help in Producing revenue indirectly. The departments which are busy in maintenance of building and equipment, in maintaining the accounts and in affairs for smooth running of the Hotel and House Laundry etc. fall under this category.

India is famous for its hospitality and courtesies to its guests. Its image can be seen in our hotels which provide certain facilities without additional charge. Thus the departments which are either busy for the smooth running of the business or rendering free services to its guests come under this category.

2. DEPARTMENTS WHICH ARE OPERATED BY OUTSIDERS BUT PRODUCE REVENUE

The hotels commit certain facilities and professional services to guests but sometimes they are not in a position to operate such departments in order to provide committed facilities. Therefore the space is rented out to outsiders to run their business and provide services to the guests. Such persons to whom these shops are given for a specific period are known as concessionaires.

Generally Chemist shop, Handicrafts shop, Beauty Parlour, Hair-dress' shop etc. are given to concessionaires. They either pay specific amount or a certain percentage of their sales to the hotel. In India the first method is more common and a lump-sum is received by the hotel for a specific period. The concessionaires have to run the business according to the terms and conditions of the agreement. Thus the hotel earns revenue from such shops or departments also which are not managed by the hotel but are run by outsiders independently.

CHAPTER XVI

ROOM RATES

The hotel earns major revenue from the sale of rooms. If the assessment of room rates is not made correctly and the rates are kept low then the hotel may run at a loss. On the contrary if the rates are fixed at high level, it may affect adversely the hotel's reputation. It is true that every hotelier wants a fair return but it should be reasonable and based on sound grounds.

FIXING THE ROOM RATES

Fixing the room rates is an important aspect to which a hotelier has to pay a great deal of attention. Once the rates are fixed and announced through tariffs and schedules, they are unlikely to be changed soon. The factors given below may, therefore, be kept in view at the time of deciding the room rates of a small or large hotel in small towns or big cities according to the circumstances in general:—

1. The importance of the city, in which the hotel is situated, may be taken into consideration at the time of fixing the room rent. If other conditions are the same, the room rent of a hotel of large city may be kept higher than the room rent of a small city.
2. The total investment in construction of rooms and its furnishing etc. may be kept in view. The room rent may be fixed in such a way so that the return from the sale of rooms may be comparatively higher than the return of equal investment in a bank on fixed deposit.
3. Availability of non-revenue services—The expenditure incurred on those services be kept in view also, which do not earn direct revenue for a hotel like house laundry, security, maintenance etc. The room charges may be in such a way, so that some part of above expenditure may be covered room rent.
4. The locality in which the hotel is situated gains prominence while

fixing room rates. If the hotel is situated in posh locality where shopping facilities, approach to Railway Station and Airport are worthy, the room rates may be comparatively higher than those situated in backward and far off places.

5. The location of the room also matters a lot. Front rooms, well ventilated rooms and rooms opening to better views may cost more than the dark rooms and rooms opening to indifferent chambers.
6. The room rates may be fixed according to the size of the rooms. If other conditions remain unchanged, the rates of double rooms may be more than the rates of single room.
7. The various amenities that are provided to guests in the hotel—as, air-conditioning, running hot and cold water, attached bath-room, carpet, telephone etc.—are also taken into consideration. If such amenities are more the charges may be more in comparison to those where amenities are less.

   It is correct to say that more the amenities, the higher the grading of, hotel so also the higher the room rates. Rooms of five star hotel would definitely cost more than the rooms in a two star hotel.
8. While fixing the room rates, it is indispensable to keep in view the point of average occupancy, slack season complimentary rates, reduced rates for groups etc. because they affect the revenue of the hotel.

It is an admitted fact that there cannot be any uniformity in the room rates of all the hotels. The reason is that the circumstances of every hotel differ from the other. The Government also cannot fix the room rates because the position and circumstances of all hotels are not similar. Therefore every hotel has to evolve its own procedure for fixing the room rates but above mentioned points may help in fixing the rates to a considerable extent.

HUBBART FORMULA

This is also one of the basis of fixing the room rates. This formula is known as 'Hubbart formula' because Mr. Roy Hubbart was the chairman of the committee which was appointed by American Hotel and Motel Association for developing a formula for computing room rates.

According to this formula an estimate is made of the number of guest rooms to be sold in a normal year. Then a tabulation is made of the cost of operation, to which is added an amount representing the expected fair return on the investment, which total amount is then divided by the number of estimated occupied rooms to obtain average rate that can be charged. The Hubbart formula has been revised by public and private sector according to their requirements for fixing the room rates.

This formula is a common break-even analysis that hotel use to determine their room rates. Under the formula the hotel forecasts estimated revenues and expenses for the next accounting period. It incorporates estimated expenses and desired return on investment with the number of rooms the hotel has available to yield the minimum average room rate the hotel must collect to cover its expenses. The method of calculating rate is as follows :—

Calculation of Average Room Rate By Hubbart Formula

Estimated Operating Expenses	Rs.	* * * *
Add Return on Investment	Rs.	* * *
		* * * *
Less Income from other sources		* * *
		* * *
Divide By Number of Rooms sold		* * *
Result - Average Room Rates		* * *

BASIS OF CHARGING ROOM RATES

Basis of charging room rates means the principle according to which the hotel charges money from the guest for accommodation or a customer is supposed to pay the charges for his stay in the hotel. There cannot be one universal basis of charging room rates applicable to all the hotels in India. The reasons are that the situations, local conditions and the management of hotels are different from each other. In general there are three principal basis of charging room rates and it is at the option of the hotel to adopt any one of the following subject to a minimum charge for one full day. To be more clear it can be said that the guest has to pay for at least one day even if he stays for 2 to 3 hours:

1. Basis of Twenty-four hours
2. Basis of Number of nights spent
3. Basis of Check out time.

1. Basis of Twenty-four Hours

According to this system guest is charged a specific amount for 24 hours from the time of his occupying the room in the hotel. After completing the first 24 hours, he is charged for the next 24 hours or a part of that at full rate, charged continues his stay in the hotel. Under this system the customer is not charged on the basis of days and dates he spends in the hotel. He has to pay full amount either for 24 hours or a part thereof. No charge is taken for the day provided he checks our before the time of his arrival on the day he first occupied the room in the hotel.

Example. A guest arrives and occupies a room in a hotel and 8 a.m. on 18th May on E.P. for Rs. 50 and checks out—

(a) at 2 p.m. on the same day;

(b) at 7 a.m. on 19th May;

(c) at 10 a.m. on 19th May.

Calculate the amount payable by the guest under different circumstances if service charge is taken @ 10%—

(a) The guest will be charged for minimum one day.

Apartment Rs. 50 + Service Charge Rs. 5 = Rs. 55 .

(b) The guest will be charged for one day because he checks out before 8 a.m. on 19th May.

Apartment Rs. 50 + Service Charge Rs. 5 = Rs. 55 .

(c) The guest will be charged for 2 days because he continues his stay after 8 a.m. on 19th May.

Apartment Rs. 100 + Service Charge Rs. 10 = Rs. 110.

2. Basis of Nights Spent

This system is more common in Highway Hotels where the travellers during their journey, like to spend the night in the hotel. The guests are charged for overnight occupancy. A full night's charge is levied for the first night the visitor spends at the hotel. A visitor is supposed to vacate the room so occupied by the dinner time which may be assumed as 7.30 p.m. failing which he is liable to pay the charge for another night.

3. Basis of Check Out Time

Check out time is a time fixed at convenient hours by hotel when the guest can check out from the hotel after paying a reasonable amount. This system is more common toady in India. In some hotels check out and check in time is one and the same but in others they are different. The reason is that the hotel needs a few minutes to clean the room and make it ready for the new guest. The check out time can be different from hotels of one city to hotels of other city according to local conditions and railway or bus timings. In Delhi nearly all hotels have adopted 12 noon as check out time.

The check out time is convenient both for the guests and the hotel employees. It is beneficial for the customers on account of the following reasons—

(a) The customer can get accommodation in the hotel at this time because many guests check out and vacate rooms in the hotel.

(b) If the guests like to pay the reasonable charge for their stay, they may vacate room at this time. If they continue their stay after this time (even for an hour) they have to pay one full day's charge according to the rules.

(c) If check in and check out time happens to be one and the same, the guest, who occupies the room before the check in time, same, the one day's charge from the time he occupies the room till the check out time even if this duration is of an hour or so. At the check out time he is again charged for one full day i.e., up to the check out time of the next day.

In this way it can be said that the check out time helps the guests in getting accommodation and paying reasonable amount for their stay.

The check out time is helpful for the employees of the hotel in many respects—

(a) The hotel gets certain rooms at this time for obliging the new guests by allotting the rooms.

(b) The front office can know room occupancy position at this time easily.

(c) The hotel can charge all the guests staying in the hotel for the next day without bothering the visitors' arrival timings. Thus there are less chances of mistakes.

According to this system a full day's charge is levied for any part of the day on which the visitor arrives and says up to the next check out time or a part thereof.

Hotels generally offer following types of terms to their customers:

(1) European Plan (EP). It includes accommodation only.

(2) Continental Plan (CP). It includes accommodation plus continental break-fast.

(3) ***American Plan (AP).*** It is a combination of room, break-fast, luncheon and dinner. It is also called as Pension or Full Board.

(4) ***Modified American Plan (MAP).*** It has accommodation, breakfast, and one major meal (lunch/dinner) included in the rate.

(5) ***Special Rates.*** These rates are offered to tours, groups, airlines, travel agencies and people attending function in the hotel.

(6) ***Rack Rate.*** It is a normal rate for accommodation.

Example. A guest arrives and occupies a room in a hotel on E.P. for Rs. 50. Calculate the amount payable by the guest under the following circumstances—

Date and time of arrival	Date and time of departure
(a) 18th May at 2 p.m.	19th May at 8 a.m.
(b) 18th May at 8 a.m.	19th May at 8 a.m.
(c) 18th May at 2 p.m.	19th May at 2 p.m.
(d) 18th May at 8 a.m.	19th May at 2 p.m.

Check out time is 12 noon

Service charge @ 10%.

(a) The guest will be charged for one day because he checks out before 12 noon on 19th May.

Apartment Rs. 50 + Service Charge Rs. 5 = Rs. 55.

(b) The guest will be charged for two days because he occupies the room before 12 noon on 18th May. He will be charged at 8 a.m. for one day from 8 a.m. to 12 noon on 18th May. At 12 noon again he will he charged for the next day.

Apartment Rs. 100 + Service Charge Rs. 10 = Rs. 110.

(c) The guest will be charged for 2 days, because he stays after 12 noon on 19th May.

Apartment Rs. 100 + Service Charge Rs. 10 = Rs. 110.

(d) The guest will be charged for three days because he occupies the room before 12 noon on 18th May and stays after 12 noon on 19th May. He will be charged for one day from 8 a.m. to 12 noon on 18th May. At 12 noon again he will be charged for one day up to 12 noon on 19th May. As he continues his stay so he will again be charged at 12 noon on 19th May.

Apartment Rs. 150 + Service Charge Rs. 15 = Rs. 165.

CHAPTER XVII

ACCOUNTING SYSTEM IN HOTELS

A hotel is a business which can be started either in the form of a Sole proprietorship or a Partnership or a Company. In a hotel, like other business concerns, a number of transactions take place during the day. It purchases provisions, soft drinks, alcoholic beverages etc. from suppliers and sells accommodation, meals, drinks and services to its customers. It employs managerial, skilled, clerical and other staff to whom salary is to be paid.

Besides this, a hotel also incurs certain expenses like cartage, wages, taxes and other charges. The proprietor or the management of the hotel likes to know the particulars of all the money, goods and services received and given away because it helps in knowing the correct picture of the financial state of the business.

It is an admitted fact that the employees cannot remember all financial transactions of a hotel, however, sharp their memory may be. Under the circumstances, it is essential to keep a written record of all the transactions in appropriate books which may help in calculating the profit and disclosing the financial position of the hotel. Now-a-days every hotel whether large or small, according to its size and requirement, adopts a special system of accounting and control.

Through these books of accounts and from statistical record, contained therein, one can judge the efficiency and financial success of the hotel. With the help of proper control system one can detect the leakage, extravagant expenses, wastage of material and misuse of fixed assets.

In ordinary commercial houses the Double Entry System of Bookkeeping is used in its traditional form. But the nature of hotel business is different from other commercial houses in many respects. Following are the points distinguishing the two types of businesses:—

In a commercial house the credit is allowed to limited number of customers who are personally known to the trader. One would consider various aspects of a debtor such as his financial stability, goodwill or reputation in the market etc., before allowing credit to him. As the trader knows when the payment will be made by the debtor so he feels no hurry in opening the debtor's account in the ledger immediately. He opens the customer's personal account only at the end of the day after closing the day's business.

On the contrary in hotels the credit is allowed to all guests except a few who appear to be of doubtful nature. Usually the guests are unknown to the hotel. Their departure too is always uncertain, so the personal accounts of the guests are opened immediately as soon as they arrive and occupy rooms in the hotel. The guests' accounts, therefore, are maintained in such a way that it remains complete up to the minute. As their stay is uncertain and they can check out at any moment, their account is kept ready and whenever they to check out, the bill is presented for payment. It is one of the reasons hotel has to maintain the accounts in a different manner.

In an ordinary commercial house the credit transactions with individual customer may be one or two at the most during the day. But the hotel business is such where both cash and credit transactions with an individual guest follow each other pretty rapidly. For example, a guest may arrive at 8 a.m. He takes his break-fast, purchases cigarettes, takes coffee makes local call, takes his lunch etc. all on credit within a short period of 5 hours and checks out at 1 p.m. During the same time all the charges be debited to guest's bill and entered in the hotel's account.

Ordinarily Commercial house does one type of work. Either it is a manufacturing concern or wholesale or retail business for selling the goods. Therefore the problem of control is not difficult. But the hotels on the one hand have to do the job of manufacturer (because they have to prepare dishes) and on the other hand the job of retailer by selling the dishes according to the requirements of the customers.

Sometimes they purchase the finished products and sell it in its original shape like cigarettes, newspapers, magazines etc. Therefore the problem of control in hotels is more complicated. Due to this reason the accounts in hotels are maintained in a different fashion that makes the control easy.

In ordinary commercial house the cash is collected at one point and the credit is allowed by one authority and recorded at only one place. A hotel has many departments. Some departments may deal both with cash and credit but others sell their items and services for credit alone. Thus the cash is collected and credit is allowed at many points. The employees of some departments simply record the charges but other departments collect the cash as record the charges of registered guests and credit card holders. Under such circumstances the internal control of receipts and accounts receivable are most important parts of hotel accounting. The hotel, therefore, adopts a system, with the help of which, self-checking and internal control is possible. In ordinary commercial house the accounts are not maintained with this view hence the system is different.

The hotel purchases different types of articles and merchandise. Either they are sold in their original shape or converted into finished products before sale. They are also supplied at different points either for conversion or for sale. Thus the articles pass through many hands. Therefore the accounts are maintained in a way to ensure that all revenue is accounted for and that all stock and stores in hand are correct and trade expenditure is justified. Not only this but the accounts are maintained in a method which eliminate the wastage and check the misappropriation of goods. All such points are not necessary while maintaining the accounts of a commercial house because the above procedure is not adopted here.

On account of the above mentioned reasons the system of accounting of a hotel is different from that of the commercial house.

It is true that in hotels also, the Double Entry System of Book-keeping is followed but the application of Double Entry System and the way of maintaining the accounts is different. In hotels the tabular or analytical system is used. It is the only successful method to know the analysed and up to date information about cash receipt and payments, goods purchased and sold and services rendered by various departments. This system is also helpful for introducing effective control system.

Hotels having branches or management running chain of hotels like to compare the income, expenditure, profit or loss of one branch with other branches. This comparison is possible only when all the branches may adopt a common system and a common classification of accounting. Therefore today all such large hotels have adopted Uniform System of Accounting. this system provides uniform classification of accounts and standardized method of presenting the financial results.

UNIFORM SYSTEM OF ACCOUNTS IN HOTELS

Uniform System of Accounts in hotels is a manual that provides firstly uniform classification of income, expenditure, assets and liabilities for hotels and secondly standardised, uniform method of presenting financial results of operations. This manual was prepared in order to bring uniformity in accounts in hotels, whether they were large or small. The need of such classification was being felt by hotels since long. In the later half of 1925 the Hotel Association of New York City appointed a Committee of hotel accountants Prepare a manual showing a simple formula for the classification of accounts. This Committee prepared a common manual, both for large and small hotels, showing uniform classification of accounts and instructions for preparing of financial statements. This manual of instructions was called Uniform System of Accounts for hotels.

The American Hotel Association recommended this system of accounting to all hotels of America. Since then this manual has been revised several times. Today it has been adopted by hotels of several countries. In India also this uniform system has been adopted by many good hotels.

The main advantages of Uniform System of Accounts may be summed up as under:

1. This manual of classification has been designed in such a way so that all large and small hotels can adopt. Each hotel can select the head of account according to its requirement and eliminate such items as are not needed by it.
2. The hotels having branches can introduce this Uniform System of Accounts in all the branches. By introduction of this they can easily compare each head of income and expenditure of one branch with other branch or branches.
3. A hotel, having branches, can prepare consolidated Profit & Loss Account and Balance Sheet of all the branches.
4. An employee may not find any difficulty in maintaining the accounts, if he is transferred to some other branch of the hotel or seeks a change in a hotel where also the Uniform System of Accounts is in practice.

For introducing Uniform System of Accounting the activities of a hotel are divided into two main departments. The first is operated or revenue earning departments and the second services or overhead departments. The operated departments are further divided into two parts—Major Revenue Producing Departments and Minor Revenue Producing Departments. Under the head major revenue producing departments we can keep Room and Food and Beverage departments. Telephone, Guest Laundry etc., can be kept under minor revenue producing departments. The Assets and Liabilities are also analysed in detail.

For adoption of Uniform System it is necessary to standardise the terminology and collect all income of one nature under one head of account and all expenses of one nature under the same head of account. In this Chart of Accounts all accounting heads can be identified by numbers. For example Account No. 1 to 10 may represent Assets, Liabilities and Capital; 11 to 20 Income and Revenue and 21 to 30 Expenses.

Further breakdown of major and minor revenue heads, expenses, assets and liabilities can be made by giving sub-numbers.

The hotel or its units may use those accounting heads which are applicable to them only and leave others.

In most of good and large hotels the principles of Double Entry are followed. The accounts are maintained in analytical form and classified according to Uniform System of Accounts.

CHAPTER XVIII

TABULAR SYSTEM OF BOOK-KEEPING

Tabular system of Book-keeping is a system in which items of business transactions are subjected to continuous analysis and classification at the time of recording them in the books of accounts. By Tabular Book-keeping we mean the employment of columns in the books of accounts in order to know the detail of each head of income, expenditure, purchase, sale etc. It is a mere columnar system of Book-keeping where each item is analysed scientifically.

Tabular system of Book-keeping does not differ in any way from the Double Entry System of Book-keeping, but it only implies that the books of account kept are ruled with additional analytical columns for the purpose of collecting together transactions of the same nature, so that the posting of each can be made in totals with a view to avoid waste of time and clerical labour. This system is helpful where transactions of one nature are numerous and regular. In addition to cash book, purchase book and other books of prime entry, the personal ledgers are also ruled with additional columns so as to serve lie purpose of Day Book on the one hand and Ledger on the other, in order to avoid the trouble of opening separate account for each individual. While recording transactions in all such books, however, the principles of Double Entry are strictly followed.

Generally this system is useful for the following industries and establishments:—

1. Hotels.
2. Estate companies for tenants accounts.
3. Insurance companies in respect of keeping the record of premium.
4. Gas, electricity and similar other undertakings for maintaining customer's account.

5. Business with branches and departments.

In hotels the Tabular system is not only desirable but it is essential. In fact, in hotels different types of meals, drinks, articles and services are sold to guests and the management is interested to know the sale of each department. Tabular system is the only system with the help of which details of sales are possible. Secondly, in hotels the amount involved in each individual transaction—cash or credit—follows each other rapidly It is also very essential that the entries should be recorded quickly and guests' accounts be kept to the minute complete and correct so that whenever the customers likes to check out, the bill could be presented for payment. The best and indeed the only method that can be recommended is the Tabular method because the hotel's record and guest's bill are written up instantaneously and simultaneously. This system has the following specialities:—

(1) Tabular system is simple in application, provides continuous dissection and summarises all entries.

(2) The provisions of 'Total' column ensures the arithmetical accuracy of the analysis columns by means of cross casting.

(3) Tabulated results are extremely valuable in affording data for estimating and for comparison.

(4) By using this system the number of ledger accounts can also be reduced.

(5) It helps to watch and control the financial affairs of the hotel. The accurate records of the financial transactions of a hotel can also be produced.

(6) With the help of Tabular system the accounts and statistics are made available to the manager every day which assists him in this managerial work.

(7) This method prevents and detects fraud, pilferage and wastage.

CHAPTER XIX

LEDGER

The book containing the various accounts is called the ledger. Although it is not a book of original entry, it forms an indispensable record in accounting as much as it is in this book that the transactions are ultimately posted into their appropriate accounts in an arranged and classified form. Thus it is the principle book since it affords information for preparing the Profit & Loss Account and Balance Sheet.

TYPES OF LEDGERS

In a small commercial house only one type of ledger is maintained. In that ledger only, all personal, real and nominal accounts are opened. In big concerns, where the transactions become voluminous, the ledger is subdivided and instead of one, several ledgers are maintained. Generally they are three in numbers :—

1. Debtors ledger or Sales ledger—to accommodate the accounts of customers or debtors only.
2. Creditors or Purchase or Suppliers ledger—to contain the accounts of each supplier of goods or creditors.
3. General or Nominal ledger—to accommodate all accounts other than debtors and creditors.

Like big commercial concerns, in hotels also due to voluminous business different types of ledgers are maintained. The number and types of ledgers depend upon the nature of hotel and the policy of the management. In India so far no standard names have been given to the ledgers which can be acceptable to all hotels, therefore there is controversy between the hoteliers regarding the names of ledgers and the accounts opened therein. However, below are given some types of ledgers that can be maintained by large hotels:

Personal Ledger

It is a ledger which is kept in hotels for maintaining the personal accounts of guests or debtors and creditors. For convenience this ledger can further be divided in two groups—one, debtors ledger and the ledger. creditors

Debtors Ledger

It is a ledger in which the accounts of debtors are opened By debtors use mean persons from whom the money is to be recovered by the hotel either for services or for supply of meals, beverages and other articles The debtors ledger can further be divided into two groups. One for the debtors who are still continuing their stay in the hotel and the second who are not staying in the hotel. Either they have checked out without settling the bill or they are responsible for the payment on behalf of the guests who availed the credit facilities of the hotel. For the first group of guests Visitors Tabular Ledger is maintained and for the second City Ledger is maintained.

Visitors Tabular Ledger

It is a ledger maintained for keeping the accounts of the guests staying in the hotel. It is maintained in tabular form so it is known as Visitors' Tabular Ledger (Detailed description of this ledger is given in the related chapter).

City Ledger

City ledger is a ledger in which debtors accounts or accounts receivable other than those maintained in 'Visitors Tabular Ledger, are opened. In India many hotels use city ledger for maintaining the acconts of the following types of debtors :—

(a) Guests who check out without settling the bills.

(b) Credit card holders.

(c) Airlines who are allowed credit facilities.

(d) Travel Agencies who are allowed credit facilities.

(e) Government Departments allowed credit facilities.

In small hotels only one city ledger is maintained for the above types of debtors. But in large hotels for the different category of debtors, individual ledgers are maintained.

CLASSIFICATION OF HOTEL LEDGER

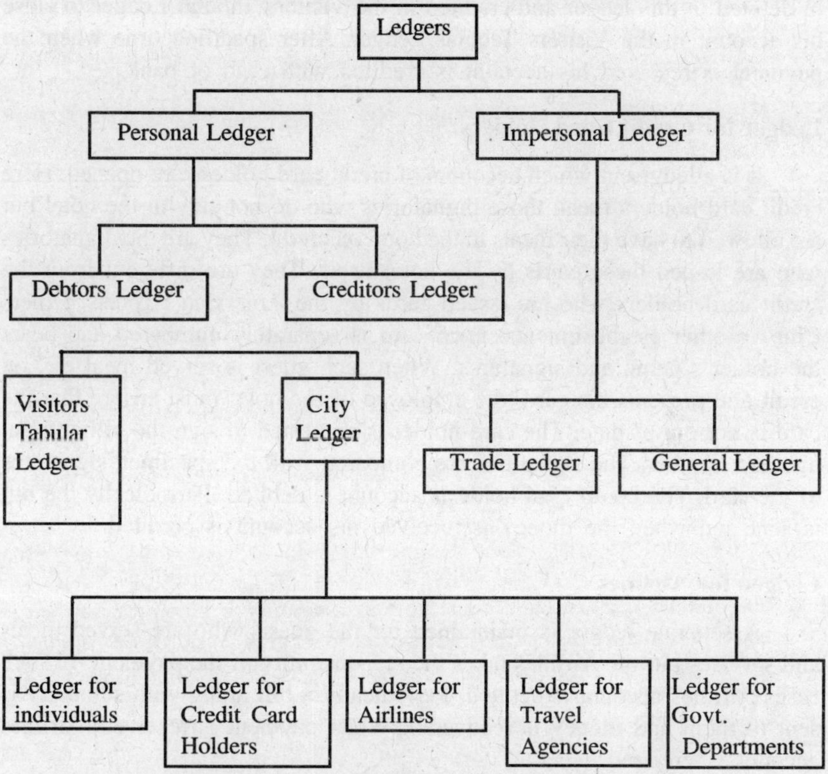

Fig. 3. Classification of Hotel Ledger

Ledger for Individuals

In this ledger the account of those debtors are opened who had been staying in the hotel but checked out without settling their bills. Such guests may be divided into two groups :—

(a) Guests who check out without settling the bill but with the permission of the Manager and with an understanding that the payment be remitted within a specified time.

(b) Guests who check out without settling the bill and without the permission of the Manager of the hotel. They slip away without the bringing their departure to the knowledge of hotel employees.

In some hotels for both types of debtors only one ledger is maintained but some large hotels maintain delinquent ledger for debtors of group (b).

As soon as the guest checks out without settling his bill his account in debited in this ledger and credited in the Visitors Tabular Ledger to close his account in the Visitors Tabular Ledger. After specified time when the payment is received his account is credited with cash or bank.

Ledger for Credit Card Holders

It is a ledger in which accounts of credit card holders are opened. Here credit card holders mean those dignatories who do not stay in the hotel but are allowed to have their meals in the hotel on credit. They are the dignatories who are issued these cards by the hotel itself. They are different from the credit card holders who are issued cards by the American Express, Diners Club or other establishments. Each card is separately numbered and bears the holder's name and signatures. When such guest is served meal etc. on credit and presents his card, the employee of the hotel must ensure that the card is not out of date. The card holder is requested to sign the bill and put his card number. The signatures are compared with the specimen signatures of the card. The credit card holder's account is debited. Periodically the bill is sent and when the money is received his account is credited.

Ledger for Airlines

A separate ledger is maintained for the guests who are served meals and services but the Airlines takes the responsibility of the payment. In such cases Airlines account is debited. Periodically a bill along with summary is sent to them and money is recovered. When payment is received, Airlines account is credited.

Ledger for Travel Agencies

A separate ledger is maintained for the Travel Agencies. Generally it is kept in loose leaf form. If a guest comes through some Travel Agency then Travel Agency takes the responsibility of the payment of the bill according to contract. The bills, after taking the signatures of the guest, are sent to Travel Agency. Periodically a summary is prepared and sent to the Travel Agency. Immediately its account is debited. When the payment is received Travel Agency's account is credited.

Ledger for Government Departments

Government Departments are also allowed credit facilities. Parties and banquets are arranged for them. The Government Deptt. is debited for the charges and the bill is sent to them. When the money is received it is credited in Government Department's account.

MODERN HOTEL LTD

Patel Nagar, New Delhi

City Ledger

Account No. 2 — Folio No. 2

Account of M/s Surjeet Book Depot (Regd.) HKS — Authorised Signatory – Finance Manger

Address–4074, Nai Sarak, Delhi — Paying Authority – M/s Surjeet Book Depot Regd. HKS

Date	Bill No.	Room No.	Authority Ref.	Particulars	Folio	Debit	Credit		Dr.		Remarks
	Cheque	Date	Book			Amount	Commission or Discount	Pament	Cr.	Balance	
1.6.19_	2596	105	Letter No. 26 dated 3.5.19....	S. Harnam Singh Managing Director	62	800	-	-	Dr.	800	
15.6.19_	A E3261	12.6.19_	State Bank of India, Patel Nagar, New Delhi	Receipt No. J 24	77		80	720 (1.6.19)		Nill	

Fig. 4. City Ledger

Creditors Ledger

Creditors Ledger is a part of the personal ledger. It is a ledger in which the accounts of creditors are maintained. By creditors we mean persons or establishments from whom the hotel purchases goods on credit and to whom the hotel has to pay the money. As soon as the Bill and Goods Receipt Voucher is received in accounts department the creditors account is opened in the ledger and credited with the necessary amount. The payment is made on the basis of the purchase sanction. When the payment is made the creditors account is debited. Some hotels call it Suppliers Ledger.

Impersonal Ledger

It means ledger maintained for impersonal accounts. Impersonal ledger can be divided into two groups—one, Trade Ledger and the other, General Ledger.

Trade Ledger

Trade ledger is kept for maintaining all revenue and expenses account. In this ledger all such accounts are opened which have a direct relation to trading like purchase, sales and expenses etc. It is a ledger where double entry of personal ledger is completed. This ledger feeds the data to Profit and Loss Account.

General Ledger

General Ledger is a ledger in which especially the accounts of assets and liabilities are opned. It is often desired to preserve the continuity of Assets and Liabilities accounts for a number of years, therefore for individual asset and individual liability a separate ledger is maintained in loose leaf form. Specimen of Asset Ledger is given in Figure 7.

MODERN HOTEL LTD., NEW DELHI

Endorsed Bills Summary

Month .... **Written by .... on ....**

.... Travel Agency

Date .... **Checked by .... on ....**

Bill No.	Room No.	Name of Guest	Amount		Commission		Net Amount		Account No.	On account of	Initials	Despalch No. & Date	Receipt No. & Date	Remarks
			Dr.	Cr.	Amt.	Credit Note No.	Dr.	Cr.						

Fig. 5. Endorsed Bills Summary

MODERN HOTEL LTD, NEW DELHI

Summary Register

Account of .... **Confirmation letter sent on .... for Dr/Cr**

Address .... **Balance of Rs. .... on ....**

Date	Particulars	Dr. Cr.	Balance	Purchase Sanction		Purchase order			Store Receipt		Remarks
				No.	Date	No.	Date	Amt.	No.	Date	

Fig. 6 Suppliers ledger

X Hotel **Assets Ledger**

Assets Ledger	Month & Date and V. No.	Invoice No.	Particulares	Unit	Rate	Value		Written off Sold or Dep.		Initials	Balance	
						Quit.	Amit.	Quit.	Amit		Qty.	Amt.

Fig.7. Assets Ledger

CHAPTER XX

VISITORS TABULAR LEDGER

A hotel maintains various types of ledgers to keep the record of debtors, creditors, purchases, sales, assets, expenses etc. Visitors Tabular Ledger is one of these ledgers. As its very name shows, it is a ledger meant for keeping the record of registered guests in an analysed form. It serves the purpose of the Day Book on the one hand and registered guests' personal accounts on the other. It is maintained for keeping the record of all transactions relating to sales of goods and services to registered guests in a systematically analysed and chronological order. There are two types of ledgers—one, horizontal Tabular ledger and the other, vertical Tabular ledger. On one side of this ledger, one column is provided to each registered guest and on the other side one column is provided for each item of sale of food, beverages, services etc. As in this ledger several columns are drawn to keep the records of guests on the one hand and the record of sales of different items to guests on the other, therefore, it is known as Visitors Tabular Ledger.

Visitors Tabular Ledger is maintained in loose-leaf form. A separate ledger is maintained for each day. The number of Tabular sheets used for the day depends upon the number of columns in the sheet and the number of rooms available for guests.

The Tabular sheet contains both Debit and Credit sides. Thus Visitors Tabular Ledger records all aspects of both debit and credit transaction either on upper and lower sections or on the left and right section. Such Visitors Tabular Ledger does not confine itself only to sales but it also includes all transactions that concern sales. This implies that amount paid by customer against outstanding debits, allowances and transfer to other ledgers are also recorded. Thus both debit and credit transactions relating to customers are recorded in their respective columns. In such Tabular ledger if one customers are provided for cash sales, then it can give the picture of total sales of the (both cash and credit) of the day.

Tabular Ledger is maintained in the Bill Office. It is written up on the basis of vouchers or checks received by them. As and when the transaction with guest relating to sale or receipt or allowance or transfer etc., takes place the concerned department prepares a check and sends the original copy of check to the bill department. The bill department immediately posts the check in the customers account in the Visitors Tabular Ledger and in his individual bill. Thus the sales record and the customers account are always complete up to the minute.

The customers account, in day's Tabular Ledger, is closed as soon as he checks out either after making the payment or with the permission of the management even without settling the bill. In case of customers, who continue their stay, their accounts for the day are closed at 12 midnight by the bill clerk on night duty. The balance carried forward is calculated and transferred to the respective accounts in the new Tabular Ledger which is opened for the coming day.

When a guest is leaving the hotel and wishes to settle his account, separate lines are drawn diagonally through the room number, the name of the guest and number of sleepers. One should ensure that there are no further charges to be posted to the room being vacated. On complete posting, all day's charges be transferred to the guest weekly bill, the total of the Visitors Tabular Ledger and the guest weekly bill should agree.

The completed Visitors Tabular Ledger gives the following information—

(a) The sale of each department and total sale of the hotel of a particular day. Not only this, the sale of each type of meal, beverages and services.

(b) The total debit balance of a departed guest transferred to ledger account or transferred to other guests account.

(c) Cash paid by guests during the day and allowances given to them.

(d) The details of individual customer's account and the total owing by resident guests at the close of the day.

ADVANTAGES OF VISITORS TABULAR LEDGER

The advantages of Visitors Tabular Ledger can be summed up as under:

(1) All personal accounts of registered guests are opened in daily Visitors Tabular Ledger (sheets), so the names of all registered

customers and the number of rooms and room numbers occupied can be seen at one glance.

(2) All personal accounts of registered guests are opened in daily Visitors Tabular Ledger and transactions relating to them for the day are recorded in their accounts in the Tabular Sheet, therefore, the day's detail of each personal account can be seen without wasting time. It saves the necessity of opening personal accounts of registered guests in the debtors ledger.

(3) Each customer's personal account is debited directly with the help of vouchers known as "checks" without first entering the amount into the Journal or book of prime entry, so there are less chances of mistakes.

(4) The posting is done directly, so it takes less time.

(5) By opening customers' account in the Visitors Tabular Led account of each guest is always complete up to the minute. Therefore, the bill can be prepared easily at the time of checking out of the guest.

(6) Every department sends the original copy of check to the bill for posting, so the original copy of checks are available with the bill clerk. In case of need they can be seen and verified.

(7) In case of controversy, between the hotel guest and bill clerk/ cashier, over certain payments, the Tabular Sheet can prove helpful to the solution of such problems because it indicates the receipt side also.

(8) The tabular sheet is prepared with original copy of the check and each department prepares a statement or summary of its day's sales or service with the help of duplicate copy so that control and checking of accounts can be done efficiently.

(9) In Tabular Ledger the items of sales are recorded in an analysed form. It shows at a glance how much income has been derived from different departments such as Restaurant, Bar, Telephone, Tobacco, Laundry etc., etc.

(10) If one column for chance (cash) sale is added then the management can know the total business of the hotel for the day and the credit position.

(11) It provides to the control a ready guide to check the terms and conditions settled with each and every resident guest, the room

rates agreed upon and whether the rates are inclusive of or without Board.

(12) It serves as a guide for the minute-wise accumulation of debit item under each personal account. Any personal account showing abnormally high debit balance can be referred to the credit department which looks after the interest of the establishment in order to ensure safeguard of credit facilities.

(13) Allowances given to the customers are recorded in Visitors Ledger so it is easy to know the total allowance given to customers and whether it was approved and recorded in correct accounts.

(14) Visitors Tabular Ledger is kept in loose-leaf form using the required number of sheets for each day and carrying forward all the totals from page to page to the final total for the day. Thus the grand totals can be found in the last sheet with the loose leaf method. The entire Visitors Tabular Ledger for one day can be sent to the control department without disturbing the next day's work.

DISADVANTAGES

The main disadvantages of Visitors Tabular Ledger can be mentioned as under:

(1) The tabular Sheets which are used for guests accounts are unwieldy in dimension.

(2) The columns are too many in the Tabular Sheet and they are close to each other. Therefore, there is every possibility of wrong posting.

(3) If any mistake is committed, then it is difficult to locate it till the customer points out. Such error leads to wrong summary and wrong posting in other ledgers.

(4) In the Visitors Tabular Ledger there is no provision for narration like Journal, so it is difficult to know why the customer's account has been debited. So is the case with V.P.O. column. As no explanation is given so it is not known on account of which the money has been paid by front office to an outsider on behalf of the customer.

HINTS FOR WRITING UP THE DAILY VISITORS TABULAR LEDGER

The following points may be useful for a person writing up Daily Visitors Tabular Ledger—

1. Use ink and not pencil.
2. Use Capital letters for writing the names of the guests.
3. The information regarding Room number, Number of persons, Plan, Rate etc. should be written as soon as the account is opened.
4. The writing should be clear and legible.
5. Make small but clear figures, especially when several items are to be charged to the same room number of the same day. Use the top position of the line for the first item and leave space for subsequent items.
6. Do not use noughts in case there is no figures of Rupee/Paisa because it may give scope for manipulating the accounts. Put dashes (—) instead of noughts.
7. A complete Visitors Tabular Ledger has two sides—one, debit and the other, credit. Enter the amount in guests account as per rules given below:—

   (a) If the guest is to be charged for meals/articles/services/sales tax etc., write the amount on the debit side in the customer's account in front of the respective item. For example, if guest is to be charged for laundry service write the amount on the debit side in the guests' account in the laundry column.

   (b) If the guest makes the payment, write it in the guests' account on the credit side in Cash/Deposit column.

   (c) If allowance is given to the guest, write it on the credit side in the Allowance column.

   (d) If the guest checks out without settling the bill and the amount is to be collected either from his office or from travel agency etc., write the amount on the credit side in the ledger column.

   (e) If the guest checks out without settling the bill and other guest is willing to pay his bill, write the amount on the credit side in transfer column in outgoing guest's account. Write it on the debit side in the transfer column of the guest who is willing to pay the bill.

8. Either when the guest checks out or at the end of the day charge sales tax, service charge, surcharge etc. and apartment if it has not been charged so far.

9. After debiting the guests account for all the charges, calculate Daily Total.

10. Add balance b/f (if there is any) in the daily total and find out Grand Total.

11. Find the total of the credit side. It should tally with the Grand Total.

12. Calculate the total of each item of sale and credits on the opposite side. Totals of vertical columns must reconcile with the totals of horizontal columns. This is to check the arithmetical accuracy.

13. Daily Visitors Tabular Ledger is the basic record so it should be neat, clean and free from cuttings, erasures and over-writings.

Illustration 1

The following are the transactions of M/s. Modern Hotel Ltd., 'X' city. On 23rd Sept. 20........ Balances brought forward from the previous day are given below:

Room No.	Name	Time of Arrival	Plan	Rate Rs.	Balance B/F Rs.
101	Mr. Gaurav	2 P.M.	E.P.	60	380
103	Mr. O.P. Lal	7 A.M.	E.P.	60	240
105	Mr. S.N. Talwar	8 A.M.	E.P.	60	200 Cr.

6.30 A.M. Tea was served to all rooms.

7.30. A.M. Mr. Gaurav checked out after settling his bill. He pointed out that he was not served tea on that morning. The manager approved the allowance.

8.00 A.M. Mr. D.S. Mehta arrived and occupied Room No. 102 on E.P. at Rs. 60.

8.30. A.M. Breakfast was served to all rooms except Room No. 103.

9.00 A.M. The following checks were to be entered in the accounts of customers:—

Room No. 102 Laundry Rs. 8

Room No. 105 Newspaper and magazine Rs. 4

11.00 A.M.	Room No. 102 deposited Rs.600 in his account.
1.00 P.M.	Lunch was served to all rooms. Room No. 105 had a guest for lunch.
2.00 P.M.	Mr. S.N. Talwar checked out after settling his account.
3.00 P.M.	Coffee was served to Room No. 102 (Two cups)
3.30 P.M.	Cinema Ticket was purchased for Room No. 102 and front office paid Rs. 6.40 on his behalf.
4 00 P.M.	Mr. & Mrs. M.S. Mehra arrived and occupied Room No. 104 on E.P. at Rs. 100. They deposited Rs. 400 in their account.
5.00 P.M.	Tea was served to all rooms.
6.00 P.M.	Room No. 103 desired to check out. He had no money to pay. Mr. & Mrs. Mehra (R. No. 104) agreed to pay his bill. The manager accepted the proposal and allowed R. No. 103 to check out.
8.00 P.M.	Dinner was served to all rooms. Room No. 102 had a guest for dinner.
8.30 P.M.	Room No. 104 was debited with Rs. 40 for damaging a chair of the room.

Tariff

Tea	Re. 1.00
Coffee	Rs. 1.50
Breakfast	Rs. 6.00
Lunch	Rs. 12.00
Dinner	Rs. 15.00

Calculate service charge @ 10% (on Apartment, Food and Alcoholic Averages) and sales tax on alcoholic beverages @ 10%. No Sales Tax is token on food items.

Check out time 12 Noon.

You are required to prepare Visitors Tabular Ledger for 23rd Sept. 19...........:

Sol. of Illustration 1.

MODERN HOTEL LTD, X CITY

Spet. 23, 20.......

Room No.	101		102		103		104		105		Total	
Name	Mr. Gaurav		Mr. D.S. Mehta		Mr. O.P. Lal		Mr. & Mrs.		Mr. S.N. Talwar			
No of Persons	1		1		1		2		1			
G. R. No.	2040		2043		2041		2044		2042			
Arrival Time	2 P.M.		8 A.M.		7 A.M.		4 P.M.		8 A.M.			
Departure time	7.30 A.M.				6 P.M.				2 P.M.			
Plan	E.P.		E.P.		E.P.		E.P.		E.P.			
Rate Apartment	60	–	60	–	60	–	100	–	60	–		
Rate Board	–	–	–	–	–	–	–	–	–	–		
Apartment	–		60	–	60	–	100	–	60	–	340	–
Board												
Breakfast			6	–					6	–	12	–
Lunch			12	–	12	–			24	–	48	–
Dinner			30	–			30	–			60	–
Tea/Coffe	1		3 +1	–	1 + 1	–	2	–	1	–	10	–
Food Sundries												

Soft Drinks												
Wine/Sprit/Beer			20	–							20	–
Service Charge	–	10	19	20	7	40	13	20	9	10	40	–
Sales			2	20							2	
Room Service												
Local Calls												
Trunk Calls												
Laundry			8	–							8	–
Tobacco												
News Stand									4		4	–
V.P.O.			6	40					95	90	102	30
Miscellancous							40	–			40	–
Transfer							321	40			321	40
Daily Total	1	10	227	80	81	40	506	60	200	–	1016	90
Balance B/F Dr.	380	–			240	–					620	–
Cr.									200	–	200	
Grand Total Dr.	381	10	277	80	321	40	506	60			1436	90
Cr.												

Deposit/Cash	380	–	600	–			400	–			1380	–
Allowances	1	10									1	10
Ledger												
Transfer					321	40					321	40
Balance C/F Dr.											106	60
Cr.			372	20							372	20
Total Dr.	381	10	227	80	321	40		506	60		1436	90
Cr.												

Illustration 2

From the following particulars write up the Visitors Tabular Ledger of Kamal Hotel Ltd., 'Y' City for May 30, 20..... . Following are the balances to be brought forward from the previous day:

Room No.	Name	Time of Arrival	Plan	Rate Rs.	Balance B/F Rs.
101	Mr. H. Datta	7.10 A.M.	E.P.	80	250
104	Mr. M.C. Pant	8.00 P.M.	E.P.	80	340 Cr.
106	Mr. & Mrs. A. Parikh	11.00 A.M.	E.P.	120	360

6.30 A.M. Tea was served to all rooms.

8.00 A.M. Breakfast was served to all rooms except R. No. 101 but R.No. 104 had 2 guests.

8.30 A.M. Mr. A. Roy arrived and occupied R. No. 103 on E.P. at Rs. 80.

9.00 A.M. The following checks were to be entered in the accounts of the following—

R. No.104 Laundry Rs. 6

R. No. 106 Cigarettes Rs. 4

R. No. 103 Telephone 40 P.

10.00 A.M. R.N. 104 checked out after settling his account.

12.00 Noon Lunch was served to all rooms but R. No. 101 had one guest for lunch.

2.00 P.M. Mr. J.P. Sah arrived and occupied R. No. 104 on A.P. at Rs. 120 (Apartment Rs. 80 + Board Rs. 4 0). He deposited Rs. 200 in his account.

3.00 P.M. Guests were to be charged for the following:

R. No. 101 Magazines Rs. 3.00

R. No. 104 Cinema Ticket Rs. 6.40

(money was paid by the front office).

R. No. 103 Telegram Rs. 4.00

(money was paid by the front office).

4.00 P.M.	R.No.101 while checking out pointed that he was wrongly charged for magazines. The hotel gave an allowance Rs. 3 to him. He settled the bill. After investigation it was found that the same bill was to be charged from R.No 103. Necessary entry was passed for it.
5.00 P.M.	Tea was served to all rooms except R.No. 104.
8.00 P.M.	Dinner was served to all rooms.
	Wine was served to R. No. 106 costing Rs. 30.
9.30 P.M.	Mr. & Mrs. A. Parikh checked out without settling the bill. They were allowed by the Manager to check out but remit the payment within a week.
10.00 P.M.	Mr. A. Roy (R. No. 103) wanted to check out but he had no money to pay. Mr. J.P. Sah, however, agreed to pay his bill. The Manager allowed Mr. Roy to check out after making necessary adjustments in the accounts.

Tariff—

	Rs.
Tea	1.00
Breakfast	5.00
Lunch	15.00
Dinner	18.00

Assume that the hotel provides Breakfast, Lunch and Dinner under A.P.

(i) Service Charge @ 10% on food, beverages and apartments;

(ii) Sales Tax @ 5% on food on E.P. only and soft drinks;

(iii) Sales Tax @ 9% on alcoholic beverages;

(iv) Surcharge @ 2% on Sales Tax.

The amount of food and beverages given in the question are exclusive of Service Charge, Sales Tax and Surcharge.

Check out time is 12.00 Noon.

Sol. of Illustration 2.

KAMAL HOTEL LTD, X CITY

May 30, 20........

Room No.	101	102	103	104	105	106	104	Total
Name	Mr. H. Datta		Mr. A. Roy	Mr. M.C. Pant		Mr. & Mrs. A. Parikh	Mr. J.P. Sah	
No of Persons	1		1	1		2	1	
G. R. No.	204		207	205		206	208	
Arrival Time	7.10 A.M.		8.30 A.M.	8.00 P.M.		11.00 A.M.	20.. P.M.	
Departure time	4.00 P.M.		10.00 P.M.	10.00 A.M.		9.30 P.M.		
Plan	E.P.		E.P.	E.P.		E.P.	E.P.	
Rate Apartment	80 –		80 –	80 –		120 --	80 –	
Board	– –		– –	– –		– --	40 –	
Apartment	80 –		80 –	– –		120 --	80 –	440 –
Board							40 –	40 –
Breakfast	– –			15 –		10 --		25 –
Lunch	30		15 –			30 --	– –	75 –
Dinner			18 –			36 --	– –	54 –
Tea/Coffe	1		1 –	1 –		2+2 --	– –	7

Food Sundries														
Soft Drinks														
Wine/Sprit/Beer					—				30	–			30	–
Service Charge	11	10		19	40	1	60		23	–	12	–	67	10
Sales Tex	1	71		1	87	–	8		7	37	–	–	11	83
Surcharge	–	03		–	04	–	02		–	15	–	–	–	24
Room Service														
Local Calls				–	40								–	40
Trunk Calls														
Laundry						6	–						6	–
Tobacco									4	–			4	–
News Stand	3	–											3	–
V.P.O.				4	–	315	50				6	40	325	90
Miscellancous				3	–								3	–
Transfer											222	71	222	71
Daily Total	126	84		222	71	340	–		264	52	361	11	1315	18
Balance B/F Dr.	250	–		–	–	–	–		360	–			610	–
Cr	–	–	–	–	–	340	–						340	–
Grand Total Dr.	376	84		222	71	–	–		624	52	361	11	1585	18

Cr.	–	–		–	--	–	–		–	--				--
Deposit/Cash	373	84									200	–	573	84
Allowances	3	–											3	–
Ledger									624	52			624	52
Transfer				222	71						161	11	161	11
Balance C/F Dr.	–	–				–	–							
Cr.	–	–			–	–								
Total Dr.	376	84		222	71	–	–		624	52	361	11	1585	18
Cr.	–	–		–	–	–	–		–	--	–	–	–	–

Illustration 3

From the following particulars write up the Visitors Tabular Ledger of Blue Bird Hotel, Ltd., 'Z' City for 21st June, 20.............

Balances brought forward from the previous day were as under

R.No.	Name Arrival	Time of	Plan	Rate	Balance B/F Rs.
102	Mr. K. Kumar	7.00 A.M.	E.P.	Apartment Rs. 80/-	100
104	Mrs. P. Dutta	2.00 P.M.	A.P.	Apartment Rs. 80/- Board Rs. 4 0 / -	600 Cr.
105	Mr.R. Sharma	6.00 A.M.	E.P.	Apartment Rs. 100/-	460 cr.

6.30 A.M.	Tea was served to all rooms except R.No. 104.
7.00 A.M.	Newspapers costing 30 paisa was supplied to all rooms.
7.30 A.M.	Mr. S. Mehta arrived and occupied Room No. 101 on EP. @ Rs. 80/- apartment.
8.30 A.M.	Breakfast was served to all rooms except Room No. 102
11.00 A.M.	Front office paid Rs. 10 as taxi charges for Room No. 104.
1.00 P.M.	All rooms had lunch.
2.00 P.M.	The guests were charged for the following—

Room No. 102—Laundry	Rs. 8.00
Room No. 102—Telephone	Re.0.50
Room No. 105—Cinema Ticket	Rs. 4.40

3.00 P.M.	Room No. 102, Mr. K. Kumar checked out without setting the bill, but with the understanding that the payment would be sent within a week.

4.00 P.M.	Room No. 101 was served snacks costing Rs. 10.
5.00 P.M.	Tea was served to all rooms except R. No. 104.
6.00 P.M.	Room No. 104 checked out after adjusting his account
7.00 P.M.	Mr. William arrived and occupied Room No. 102 on E.P. @ Rs. 80 apartment. He deposited Rs. 500 in his account.
8.00 P.M.	Dinner was served to all rooms.

Mr. William had wine in the room costing Rs. 60 . Room No- 101 had a guest for dinner.

Tariff

Tea/Coffee	Re. 1/-
Breakfast	Rs. 8/-
Lunch	Rs. 10/-
Dinner	Rs. 20/-

Assume that only Breakfast, Lunch and Dinner are served on American Plan.

Sales-tax @ 7% on food items on E.P. and A.P. and @ 10% on alcoholic beverages. Check out time is 12 Noon.

Illustration 4

The following are the transactions of M/s. India Hotel Ltd., 'B' City on 10th June, 20 —. You are requested to prepare the Visitors Tabula Ledger for the said date. The following balances were to be brought forward from the previous date:

R. No.	Name	Time of Arrival	Plan	Rate	Balance B/F Rs.
105	Mr. V. Bist	2 P.M.	E.P.	Apt. Rs.60	230
108	Mr. S. Das	5 A.M.	A.P.	Apt.Rs.60, Board Rs.32	380
110	Mrs. & Mr. William	4 P.M.	E.P.	Apt.Rs. 90	425

Sol. of Illustration 3.

BLUE BIRD HOTEL LTD, X CITY

June 21, 20.....

Room No.	101	102	103	104	105	102	Total
Name	Mr. S.Mehta	Mr. K. Kumar		Mr. P.Dutta	Mr. & Mrs. R. Sharma	Mr. Williams	
No of Persons	1	1		1	1	1	
G. R. No.	987	985		986	984	988	
Arrival Time	7.30 A.M.	7 A.M.		2 P.M.	6 A.M.	7 P.M.	
Departure time		3 P.M.		6 P.M.			
Plan	E.P.	E.P.		A.P.	E.P.	E.P.	
Rate Apartment	80 –	80 –		80 –	100 –	80 –	
Board	– –	– –		40 –	– –	– –	
Apartment	80 –	80 –		80 –	100 –	80 –	500 –
Board				40 –	– –	–	40
Breakfast	8 –			– –	8 –		16 –
Lunch	10 –	10 –		– –	10 –		30 –
Dinner	40 –			–	20 –	20 –	80 –

Tea/Coffe	1	–	1	–				1+1	--			4	–
Food Sundries	10	–										10	–
Soft Drinks													
Wine/Sprit/Beer										60	–	60	–
Sales Tex	4	83	–	77		2	80	2	80	7	40	18	60
Room Service													
Local Calls			–	50								–	50
Trunk Calls													
Laundry			8	–								8	–
News Stand			–	30		–	30	–	30			–	90
V.P.O.						10	–						
Miscellancous						446	90	4	40			481	30
Transfer													
Daily Total	233	83	100	57		600	–	147	50	167	40	1249	30
Balance B/F Dr.	–	–	100	–		–	–	–	--			100	–
Cr.	–	–	–	–		600	–	460	--			1060	–
Grand Total Dr.	233	83	200	57		–	–	–	--	167	40	601	80
Cr.	–	–	–	–		–	–	312	50			312	50

Deposit/Cash							–	–	--	500	–	500	–
Allowances													
Ledger			200	57							–	200	57
Transfer													
Balance C/F Dr.	233	83	–	–								233	83
Cr.								312	50	322	60	645	10
Total Dr.	233	83	200	57		–	–	–	–	167	40	601	80
Cr.						–	–	312	50	–	–	312	50

6.30 A.M.	Tea was served to all rooms.
7.00 A.M.	Mr. V. Bist checked out after settling his bill.
7.15 A.M.	Mr. John arrived and occupied R. No. 104 on Apartment Rs. 60/-.
8.00 A.M.	Breakfast was served to all rooms.
9.00 A.M.	The following checks were to be recorded in the accounts of customers:
	R.No. 108 Laundry Rs. 5.50
	R.No. 110 Cigarettes Rs. 4.00
9.30 A.M.	Major Ram Singh arrived and occupied R. No. 105 on apartment Rs.60.
	The front office paid Rs. 6/- taxi charges on his behalf.
10.00 A.M.	R.No. 105 deposited Rs. 400 in his account.
11.00 A.M.	The following checks were entered in the account of the customers:
	R.No.105 Laundry Rs. 7/-
	R.No.110 Cinema Tickets Rs. 10/-
11.50 A.M.	R. No.110 deposited Rs.300/- in their account.
12.00 Noon	Lunch was served to all rooms.
2.00 P.M.	Snacks were supplied to R. No. 110 costing Rs. 4.50
4.00 P.M.	R.No. 104 deposited Rs. 400/- in his account.
4.30 P.M.	Tea was served to all rooms.
6.00 P.M.	Flowers were purchased for R. No. 108 costing Rs. 6/-
6.30 P.M.	R. No. 104 checked out after the settlement of his account.
7.30 P.M.	Dinner was served to all rooms, but R. No. 105 had one guest. Wine was supplied to R. No.

105 costing Rs. 30. Soft Drink was supplied to R. No. 110 costing Rs. 3.00.

Tariff -

Tea	Rs. 1.50
Breakfast	Rs. 6.00
Lunch	Rs.. 12.00
Dinner	Rs.. 14.00

Calculate Sales Tax on food on both E.P. and A.P. and soft drinks @ 7% and on wine @ 10%. No service charge is taken from the guests.

Assume that under American Plan only three meals are served - Bteakfast, Lunch and Dinner.

Check out time 12 Noon.

Sol. of Illustration 4.

INDIA HOTEL LTD, B CITY

10 June, 20.......

Room No. / Name	104 Mr. John		105 Mr. V. Bist		108 Mr. S. Dass		110 Mr. & Mrs. William		105 Major. Ram Singh		Total	
No of Persons	1		1		1		1		1			
G. R. No.	635		633		632		634		636			
Arrival Time	7.15 A.M.		2 P.M.		5 A.M.		4 P.M.		9.30 A.M.			
Departure time	6.30 P.M.		7 A.M.									
Plan	E.P.		E.P.		A.P.		E.P.		E.P.			
Rate Apartment	60	–	60	–	60	–	90	–	60	–		
Board	–	–	–	–	32	–	–	–	–	–		
Apartment	60	–			60	–	90	–	60	–	390	–
Board					32	–	–	–			32	–
Breakfast	6	–					12	–			18	–
Lunch	12	–					24	–	12	–	48	–
Dinner							28	–	28	–	56	–
Tea/Coffe	1	50	1	50	1	50	3+3	–	1	50	13	50
Food Sundries					1	50	4	50			4	50

Soft Drinks							3	–			3	–
Wine/Sprit/Beer									30	–	30	–
Sales Tex	1	37	–	11	2	45	5	43	5	91	15	27
Room Service												
Local Calls												
Trunk Calls												
Laundry					5	50		–	7	–	12	50
Tobacco							4				4	–
News Stand												
V.P.O.	259	13			6	–	10	–	6	–	281	13
Miscellancous												
Transfer												
Daily Total	40	–	1	61	108	95	186	93	210	41	907	90
Balance B/F Dr.	–	–	230	–	380	–	425	–	–	–	1035	–
Cr.	–	–	–	–	–	–	–	–	–	–	–	–
Grand Total Dr.	400	–	231	61	488	95	611	93	210	41	1942	90
Cr.	–		–	–	–	–	–	–	–	–	–	–
Deposit/Cash	400	–	231	61			300	–	400	–	1331	61
Allowances												

Ledger												
Transfer												
Balance C/F Dr.					488	95	311	93	–	–	800	88
Cr.					–	–	–	–	189	59	189	59
Total Dr.	400	–	231	61	488	95	611	93	210	41	1942	90
Cr.	–	–	–	–	–	–	–	–	–	–	–	–

CHAPTER XXI

GUESTS' WEEKLY BILL

The bill is a detailed record of all the business transactions that take place between the individual guest and the hotel. As soon as the guest is registered with the hotel, the bill clerk opens a bill in the name of the guest. In this bill there is provision for recording the charges and deposits for a week therefore it is known as Guests Weekly Bill. The bill contains 7 columns for 7 days record. In addition to the record of charges and deposits the bill also contains other important information regarding the guest, like date and time of his arrival, Room No. where he is staying, Plan, Room Rates and Guest Registration No. etc. Some important informations for guests are also printed at the end of the bill. The bill is written up either manually or with the help of machines.

Thus a guest weekly bill contains:

(1) the guest's name

(2) initials and title

(3) rate to be charged

(4) number of rooms to be occupied

(5) number of sleepers.

The bill should always be kept in room number order on a file or box situated near the visitor's tabular ledger.

A continuation bill is required when a 7 day bill is completed and a guest stays for a longer period. This is often called 'Follow'. New bill should also be headed and attached in front of the first bill, the total of which is carried forward on to the continuation bill.

The bill is divided into two parts—The upper or left part for credit or deposits. At the end of debit amount and the lower or right part for credit or deposits. At the end each day balance due is noted in balance c/f column.

Thus the guest may settle his account by cash/cheque or by means of a credit card. In case the settlement is done by credit cards, the guest account is posted to the ledger account of the credit card company concerned. These folio accounts are subjected to monitoring via credit limits. As long as direct bill accounts maintain an outstanding balance below the house limit posting will continue to be accepted. Once this limit is exceeded, the hotel will seek partial payment against the account or payment in full or raise the house limit at the guest's request.

During the week, if the guest likes to check out, the first copy of the bill is presented for payment. If the guest makes the payment, he is given a stamped receipt by the cashier. The bill department makes a note of this amount in the carbon copy of the bill and the Visitors Tabular Ledger for control purpose. If the guest likes that the payment be made by his office or by Travel Agency then he has to certify the correctness of the amount and has to write the name and address of the person who will make the payment. He has to put his initials also. All this is possible if the hotel permits the guest to do so.

Sometimes the guest continues his stay after a week also. In such a case, the bill clerk closes the bill for the week and the balance is noted in the balance c/f column. At the same time a new bill in the name of the guest for the new week is opened and the balance is transferred to this new bill in the balance b/f column. The original copy of the first week's bill is presented to the guest for payment. When the guest makes payment, it is noted in the new bill.

At the time of presenting the bill it is necessary to insert the date of presentation and the person responsible for presenting the bill must initial it on behalf of the management.

Illustration 5

Mr. Gaurav arrived and occupied Room No. 104 in Modern Hotel Ltd., on 20th Sept. 20....... at 4 p.m. on European Plan at Rs. 50. He desired to check out on 25th Sept. at 9 p.m. You are required to prepare Guest Weekly Bill for presentation on the basis of the transactions given below—

Sept. 20.	**Charge Items**	
	Dinner	
Sept. 21.	**Charge Items**	
	Magazine	Re. 1
	Breakfast	
	Lunch	

	V.P.O.	Rs. 4
	Dinner	
	Deposited Cash	Rs. 150
Sept. 22.	**Charge Items**	
	Breakfast	Rs. 0.80
	Tea on cup	
	Cigarettes	Rs. 6
	Snacks	Rs. 20
	Dinner	
Sept. 23.	**Charge Items**	
	Breakfast	
	Lunch	
	Snacks	Rs 3
	V.P.O. (Telegram)	Rs 4
	Dinner	
	Deposited Cash	Rs. 300
Sept. 24.	**Charge Items**	
	Lunch	
	Cigarettes	Rs. 6
	Laundry	Rs. 5
	Local Call	Rs. 0.80
	Dinner	
Sept. 25. Charge Items		
	Breakfast	
	Laundry	Rs. 8
	Cigarettes	Rs. 6
	Tea (one cup)	
	Dinner	
Tariff–		
	Tea	Rs. 1.00
	Breakfast	Rs. 6.00
	Lunch	Rs. 12.00
	Dinner	Rs. 15.00

Calculate Service Charge on Apartment and Food items @ 10%. Check out time 12 Noon.

Sol. of Illustration 5.

MODERN HOTEL LTD,

Telephonc : 586422		Bill No. 42
Telegram : 'HOTEL'		Date 20-25/9/
	MR. GAURAV	G R. No. 2596

Room No. 104	Plane –. E.P.	Rate– Rs. 50	For one Person
Date of Arrival 20.9.20....	Time of Arrival– 4 P.M.	Date of Dec. 25.9.19–	Time of Dep.– P.M.

	Sept. 20		Sept. 21		Sept. 22		Sept. 23		Sept. 24		Sept. 25	
1	2		3		4		5		6		7	
Apartment	50	–	50	–	50	–	50	–	50	–	50	–
Board												
Breakfast			6	–	6	–	6	–	–	–	6	–
Lunch			12	–	–	–	12	–	12	–		
Dinner	15	–	15	–	15	–	15	–	15	–	15	–
Tea/Coffe					1	–					1	–
Food Sundries					20	–	3	–				
Soft Drinks												
Service Charge	6	50	8	30	9	20	8	60	7	70	7	20

Room Service					–	80			–	80		
Local Calls												
Trunk Calls												
News Stand			1	–								
Laundry									5	–	8	–
Tobacco				–	6	–			6	–	6	–
V.P.O.			4				4	–				
Miscellancous												
Transfer												
Daily Total	71	50	96	30	108	00	98	60	96	50	93	20
Balance B/F Dr.			71	50	17	80	125	80	–	–	20	90
Cr.												
Grand Total Dr.	71	50	167	80	125	80	224	40	20	90	114	10
Cr.												
Deposit/Cash			150	–			300	–				
Allowances												
Ledger												
Transfer												

Balance C/F Dr.	71	50	17	80	125	80			20	90		
Cr.							75	60				

Checked & Found Correct

Please Forward the Bill to .... Amount .... Rs. 114.10

.... Cash Receipt No. ....

.... Allowance Voucher No. ....

E & O. E. (Singnature) Transfer ....

K. Kumar

Signature of Bill Cleak

1. Bill are payable on preesentaion
2. Cheques are not accepted.
3. No Rebate is givenfor meals not taken.
4. Please obtain authorised receipt from the Cashier.

Illustration 6

Mr. and Mrs. K. Kumar arrived and occupied Room No. 205 on European Plan at Rs. 150 in ABC Hotel, 'K' City on 17th June, 20..... at 9 a.m. Their charge and credit items are given below. You are required to prepare weekly bill for presentation. They checked out on 23rd June, 20--- at 6 P.M.

June 17 **Coffee was served.**
Charged for laundry service Rs. 7
Lunch was served.
Telegram charges Rs. 4
Dinner was served with one guest.

June 18 **Tea was served.**
Breakfast was served.
Cigarettes were supplied Rs. 5
Telephone Call 50 p.
Dinner was served.

June 19 **Breakfast was served.**
Lunch was served with one guest.
Flowers were purchased for them costing Rs. 5.
Wine was served costing Rs. 15.
Dinner was served.

June 20 **Tea was served.**
Breakfast was served.
Snacks costing Rs. 10 were served.
Dinner was served.
Total allowance of Rs. 2.80 was given by the Manager for mistake in the bill of snacks.

June 21 **Tea was served.**
Newspaper costing Re. 0.35 was supplied.
Lunch was served.
Magazine costing Rs. 3 was supplied.
Received deposit of Rs. 1689.12 from them.

June 22 Tea was served.
Lunch was served.

Sol. of Illustration 6.

A.B.C. HOTEL LTD., K. CITY

Telephone : 38003 — Bill No. : K/13 1008

Telegram : 'ABCH' — Date : 17-23/19 ......

Mr. & Mrs. K. Kumar

Room No. 205 — Plane –. E.P. — Rate– Rs. 150 — Date of Departure : 23-6-20....

Date of Arrival–17 June, 20....... — Time of Arrival– 9 P.M. — G.R. No. 3818 — Time of Departure– 6 P.M.

	June 17		June 18		June 19		June 20		June 21		June 22		June 23	
	1		2		3		4		5		6		7	
Apartment	150	–	150	–	150	–	150	–	150	–	150	–	150	–
Board	150	–												
Breakfast			16	–	16	–	16	–					16	–
Lunch	30	–			45	–	–	–	30	–	30	–	30	–
Dinner	60	–	40	–	40	–	40	–			40	–		
Tea/Coffee	2	–	2	–			2	–	2	–	2	–	2	–
Food Sundries							10	–						
Soft Drinks													3	–
Wine/Spirit					15	-					20	-		

Beer												
Service Charge												
Sales Tax	6	44	4	06	8	57	4	76	2	24	7	04	3	57
Room Service												
Local Calls			–	50								
Trunk Calls									–	35		
News Stand									3	--		
Laundry												
Tobacco	7	–										
V.P.O.			5	–								
Misc. Transfer												
Daily Total	409	44	217	56	279	57	222	76	187	59	249	04	204	57
Balance B/F Dr.	–	–	409	44	627	–	906	57	1126	53	–	–	–	–
Cr.	–	–	–	–	–	–	–	–	–	--	375	–	125	96
Grand Total Dr.	409	44	627	–	906	57	1129	33	1314	12			78	61
Cr.											125	96		

	June 17		June 18		June 19		June 20		June 21		June 22		June 23	
	1		2		3		4		5		6		7	
Deposit/Cash	–	–	–	–	–	–	–	–	1689	12	–	–	–	–
Allowances	–	–	–	–	–	–	2	80	–	–	–	–	–	–
Transfer	–	–	–	–	–	–	–	–	–	–	–	–	–	–
Balance C/F Dr.	409	44	627	–	906	57	1126	53	–	–	–	–	–	–
Cr.	–	–	–	–	–	–	–	–	375	–	125	96	–	–

Checked & Found Correct.

Please Fowrard the Bills to

....

....

....

(Signature)

1. Bills are payable on persentation.
2. Cheques are not accepted.
3. No rebate is given for meals not taken.
4. Guests are requested to ensure that they obtain authorised receipt from the cashier.

Vikram Singh

(Signature)

Bill Clerk

Wine costing Rs. 20 was served.

Dinner was served.

June 23 Breakfast was served.

Lunch was served.

Soft Drink costing Rs. 3 was supplied.

Tea was served.

Tariff—

Tea	Re.	1.00
Coffee	Re.	1.00
Breakfast	Rs.	8.00
Lunch	Rs.	15.00
Dinner	Rs.	20.00

Charge Sales Tax on food items and soft drinks @ 7% and on wine @ 10%.

Check out time 12 Noon.

CHAPTER XXII

MECHANISED ACCOUNTING – N.C.R. (CLASS 42) POSTING MACHINE

National Cash Registers machines are available in different models. They are used for posting or recording different types of accounts. For example N.C.R. (class 32) posting machine is used for posting city ledger accounts. N.C.R. (class 52) is used in Bar & Restaurant. N.C.R. (class 42) is a machine used in large hotels for posting the transactions into the guests weekly bills and recording the days sales.

This machine is used in hotels where the number of guests is large and many bills are to be prepared every now and then. In such hotels if the posting is done by manual labour then firstly, it takes more time; secondly, there are chances of mistakes; and thirdly more employees are needed. Therefore manual labour is replaced by machines.

N.C.R. (class 42) has following main visible parts:—

1. **Amount Key Board**—containing keys for printing Rupees and Paisa figures.
2. **Room Numbers Keys Board**—containing keys for printing room numbers.
3. **Control Keys**—for printing the names of departments or the head of revenue etc.

   (a) Indoctrination keys—

   Room

   Restaurant

   Bar

Laundry

Local Call

Long distance Call etc.

(b) Debit Balance key

(c) Credit Balance key

(d) Debit Pick up key

(e) Credit Pick up key

(f) Plus and minus key

(g) Debit Transfer key

(h) Credit Transfer key

(i) Allowance key

(j) Paid in full kcy

(k) Paid key

(1) Total key

(m) Sub total key

(n) Miscellaneous key.

4. **Date Changer**—for printing date automatically on voucher and guest bill

5. **Audit Roll Tape**— it is under lock & key and used for copy of entries of the bills.

6. **Left Printer**—for printing guest bill.

7. **Right Printer**—for validating guest checks.

In hotel where N.C.R. (class 42) is used, the customers bills are kept in the form of cards. The guest account is opened in the card in triplicate as soon as he occupies the room in the hotel. The name of the guest, room no., date time of arrival and room rate is written on the bill with hand. After that room charges and other vouchers of meal or beverages served or services rendered to him on credit, are posted in his bill with the help of this machine and his account is debited. Some hotels post room charges in the bill either at the end of the day or at a fixed time or at the time the guest checks out.

OPERATION

When some voucher is to be posted in the guests bill, say Laundry voucher, the following procedure is adopted:

First of all Room No. keys are depressed. After that for printing the amount of the voucher the Rupee and Paisa keys are depressed. The customers bill is feeded into the machine at the left printer and Laundry voucher on the right printer. Then the Departmental Key, say 'Laundry Key' (the sale of which is to be printed) is depressed. The date, name of department, No. of operator will be printed in the Date and Explanation column and the amount in 'charge' column. The impression will come in all the copies of the bill and also in the Audit Roll. At the same time all the above data is printed on the voucher. This is a proof that the voucher has been posted into the bill. If are more than one vouchers to be entered in the same bill, then in the same manner all the vouchers are posted into the bill. After posting all vouchers the 'Balance Key' is depressed. The machine calculates the total of all the items and balance is printed in the 'Balance Due' column in the bill as well as in the Audit Roll.

If new vouchers are to be posted in the old bill where some items are already present then first of all Room No. keys are depressed. After that in order to bring the old balance of the bill in position Rupees and Paisa Keys are depressed. The bill is feeded on the left printer. If the old balance is debit balance then depress Debit Pick up key. If the old balance is credit balance then Credit Pick up key is depressed. The Pick up (balance b/f) key is depressed in order to compose the old balance in the machine. The amount of old balance along with star (*) is printed in the 'Pick up' column. Later on Rupee and Paisa keys are depressed to post the amount of the new voucher, and the voucher is feeded on the right printer. Then Departmental Key is depressed and the data will be printed in Explanation and Charge column.

Finally, Balance key (Dr. or Cr. as the case may be) is depressed. The machine calculates the balance by taking into account the old balance (pick up) and the amount of the newly posted items. If the closing balance comes debit balance but Credit Balance key is depressed then the key will not be pressed. Only when Debit Balance key is depressed then the key will be pressed and the balance will be printed in the Balance Due column. Similarly if according to machine calculation the balance due should be credit then the amount will be printed in the Balance Due column if the Credit Balance key is depressed.

If wrong amount has been posted in the bill by mistake then with the help of correction key it is corrected. Suppose the Restaurant bill was of Rs. 25 but by mistake it was posted as Rs. 35. For correction the bill is feeded on the left Printer. Room No. key, Rupees key (wrong amount), Minus key

(—) or Deduction key and Department (Restaurant) key are depressed. The date etc. will be printed in Date and Explanation column and amount (Rs. 35) in the credit column. Thus the debit of Rs. 35 will be cancelled by the credit of Rs. 35. After that for posting the correct figures (Rs. 25), the usual Procedure will be adopted. Finally, 'Balance' key is depressed and the balance will be printed in the 'Balance Due' column.

During the day when the guest checks out after settling his bill, he is either given the first copy of the bill along with a stamped receipt or the amount received is printed in the bill with the help of in the machine. When the amount paid by the guest is printed with the help of the 'Paid in Full' key in machine. When the amount paid by the guest is printed with the help of the machine, the impression comes in all the copies of the bill and in the Audit Roll. It helps to check the cashier's sheet. For printing it Room No. Keys, Rupees and Paisa keys (for the amount of balance due) are depressed. The bill is feeded on the left printer and 'Pick up' key i s depressed. Finally, "Paid in Full" key and 'Balance' key are depressed. The amount will be printed in the Credit column and in 'Balance Due' column 0.00 will be printed. It means that the balance is nil. In case Part Payment is made, depress Rupee and Paisa keys (for printing the amount received), then instead of 'Paid in Full' 'Paid' key and 'Balance' key are depressed. The amount paid by the guest will be printed in the credit column and the balance in 'Balance Due' column. The impression will come in the Audit Roll also.

Sometimes the amount is charged to wrong accounts. Then the erronous charge is deducted by using 'Allowance'key. Afterwards the amount is charged to the right bill. A Transfer voucher is prepared and explanation is given in the voucher.

At the end of the day or at the check out time or at a specific time (for) example 6 P.M.) all occupied rooms are charged room rent for the day adopting the following procedure :—

The bill of the guest (in which room rent is to be charged) is feeded on the left printer and Room No. keys are depressed.

As the bill contains old balance therefore, first of all Rupee and Paisa keys for the amount of the old balance are depressed to compose the balance in the machine. After that Pick up key (Dr. or Cr. as the case may be) is depressed. Now again Rupee and Paisa keys for the room rent are depressed. After that 'Room' key is depressed. The serial number, number of operator, date and Room (charging head) are printed in Date and Explanation column and the amount of room rent in the charge column.

Finally, Balance key (Dr. opr Cr. as the case may be) is depressed. The N.C.R. machine calculates the balance and prints it in the Balance Due column. The impression also comes on the Audit Roll.

Similarly room rent is charged on all guest bills by repeating the same procedure.

At the end of the day Telephone charges are also posted in the individual bills of guests in the same manner.

At the end of the day the sales summaries of various departments are received by the Bill Section. The Night Auditor is supposed to compare and tally the departmental sales with N.C.R. machine balances. For verification the machine balances are to be recorded on the machine 'D' Card or Statement Card with the following procedure:

First of all the 'Sub Total' key ('X' key) is depressed. The result of this depression is that all the sales of the day are composed in the machine and the machine is ready to print any sale, the key of which is depressed by the operator. The 'D' Card or Statement Card (on which the machine figures sales are to be printed) is put on the left printer. Now Room key, Restaurant key, Bar key, Laundry key, Telephone key etc. all keys of sales are depressed on by one. The result is that the sale of each department of the day is printed on the 'D' Card as well as on the Audit Roll in the same sequence in which the keys are depressed.

In some hotels the Night Auditor also prepares Recapitulation Sheets of every departmental sale. The sale shown by departmental Recapitulation Sheets or the departmental sale summaries are compared with respective balances of sales shown by the N.C.R. machine on the 'D' card or Statement Card.

After the sales have been tallied, the N.C.R. Machine is to be tested before the Trial Balance is prepared to ensure that no previous figures are left in the macine. The following procedure is adopted:

Depress Sub Total key (X key)

Depress Transfer key (Dr.)

Depress Transfer key (Cr.)

Depress Balance key (Dr. or Cr. as the case may be)

The result of the depression should be 0.00.

Now the individual bills of the guests are to be closed for the day with help of the N.C.R. Machine. For this work the following procedure is adopted:

Depress Trial Balance key.

Place individual bill of one guest on the left printer.

Depress Room No. keys of the said guest whose account is to be closed.

Depress Amount keys (as shown in the balance column of the last entry in the said guests bill) for printing the closing balance again.

Depress Pickup key (Dr. or Cr. as the case may be, on the basis of the balance of last entry of the said guests bill).

Depress Space key.

Depress Balance key (Dr. or Cr. as the case may be).

The results of all these depressions is that the last balance of the guests bill is again printed in the bill in the balance column with two stars (**) and in the Pick-up column. The same is printed in the Audit Roll also with two stars. It indicates that the bill of the guest is closed for the day.

Similarly all the individual bills are kept on the left printer one by one and the above procedure is repeated. Thus the closing balances of all the guests are printed in the balance column of the respective bills with two stars. Pick-up column and the Audit Roll.

Release the Trial Balance key.

Now again depress sub Total key.

Place another fresh 'D' Card or Statement Card on the left printer.

Depress Room key, Restaurant key, Bar key, Laundry key, Telephone key, Paid out key and all other Dr. keys one by one.

Depress space key.

Depress Sub Balance key

The result of these depressions is that individually all debit figures and also their total will be printed on 'D' Card as well as on the Audit Roll.

After that the credit items are to be recorded in the following manner:

Depress Sub Total Key.

Depress Allowance key.

Depress Paid key

Depress Space key.

Depress Balance key (Dr. or Cr. as the case may be).

The result of this depression is that all credit figures are printed individually on the 'D' Card Audit Roll. The machine also prints the balance after taking into account the Dr. and Cr. figures on the 'D' Card and the Audit Roll.

Now again,

Depress Sub Total key.

Depress Transfer (Dr.) key;

Depress Transfer (Cr.) key;

Depress Space key;

Depress Balance key (Dr. or Cr. as the case may be).

The result of this depression is that the total of Dr. balances of individual bills of the guests, and the total of Cr. balances of individual bills are printed on the 'D' card as well as on the Audit Roll. Besides this the machine also prints the balance after taking into account the Dr. and Cr. balances of the bills on the 'D' card and the Audit Roll.

Most of the hotels in India maintain City Ledgers manually, therefore, the total of the city ledger cannot be recorded in the 'D' Card with the help of N.C.R. Machine.

Now the Trial Balance is completed with the help of city ledger total current day's balance and the previous day's closing balance. The following formula is adopted—

Previous day closing N.C.R. machine balance	....
Add—Current day's Dr./Cr. N.C.R. machine balance	....
Total	....
Less—Current day's City Ledger balance (Dr./Cr.)	
Balance	....

Now this last balance, shown by the above statement, should agree with the Individual Bills Debit and Credit total balance shown at the end of 'D' Card.

Example—From the given date balance the 'D' Card.

'D' Card Reading (assumed)

Room	....
Restaurant	....
....	....
....	....
Dr. Totals	....
Allowance	....

Paid	....	
Balance (Dr.)	12,593.00	
Transfer (Dr.)	92,696.00	
Transfer (Cr.)	122.00	
Balance (Dr.)	92,574.00	
Assume current day's City Ledger balance (Dr.)		3,582.00
Assume previous day's balance (Dr.)		83,563.00

Solution

Previous day's closing balance (Dr.)	83,563.00
Add - Current day's balance (Dr.)	12,593.00
Total	96,156.00
Less - Current day's City Ledger balance (Dr.)	3,582.00
Balance	92,574.00

Now the balance of this statement Rs. 92,574.00 agrees with the balance of Transfers shown by the 'D' Card.

Thus the Trial Balance is prepared and the arithmetical accuracy is tested.

After the day's sales and Trial Balance are tallied, the N.C.R. machine readings for the day are closed. Adopt the following procedure:

Remove the N.C.R. machine key from left hand side and put it on the right hand side of the machine at appropriate place.

Depress the Total key;

Depress all debit keys—Room, Restaurant, bar etc.;

Depress Space key;

Depress Sub-balance key.

Again Depress Total key;

Depress all credit keys—Allowance, paid etc.;

Depress space key;

Depress Balance key;

Again Depress Total key;

Depress Transfer (Dr.) key.

Depress Transfer (Cr.) key.

Depress Space key;

Depress Balance key (Dr. or Cr. as the case may be).

The result of all these depressions is that all debit amounts, credit amounts, Debit Transfers, and Credit Transfer are printed on the Audit Roll. As the above figures are taken by depressing the total key so in future the above reading will not be repeated by the machine. At the end the following procedure is adopted to test that the machine is clear:

Depress the total key;

Depress all debit and credit keys one by one:

Room, Restaurant, Bar, Allowances etc.

The result of this depression will be that the machine will point OOX. It means, the machine is clear.

After testing the machine the used Audit Roll is taken out and a new Audit Roll is inserted inside the machine. The date is also changed.

On the next day before starting the posting work the N.C.R. machine is again checked by using the following procedure :—

Depress Sub Total key.

Depress All debit and credit keys—Room, Restaurant, Allowance etc.

The result of these depressions will be that the machine will print. OOX. It means no previous figures are left in the machine and it is clear.

Short procedure of operating N.C.R. (class 42) and posting the vouchers-

1. Take out the bill from the Posting Tray,
2. Enter room number;
3. Enter the amount of last balance due;
4. Insert the bill on left printer;
5. Press appropriate Pick up key;
6. Enter the amount of new voucher which is to be posted;
7. Insert the voucher on the right printer;
8. Press the appropriate departmental control key;
9. If more vouchers are to be posted continue the procedure according to No. 6;
10. Press appropriate Balance key;

11. Take out the bill form;
12. Check Pick up;
13. Put the bill back in the Posting Tray.

Advantages

The advantages of N.C.R. (class 42) achine can be summed up as under:

1. The amount is posted into the bill rapidly and in no time the guests bill is prepared. So it is a time saving device.
2. The bills are always neat and clean.
3. The machine does all the calculation work and the balance due is automatically printed on the bills. So there is less chance of error,
4. With the help of this machine simultaneously three prints are taken—one on the customers' bill, second on the voucher which is posted into the bill and third on the Audit Roll. It helps the control department to check that every voucher has been posted in the bill.

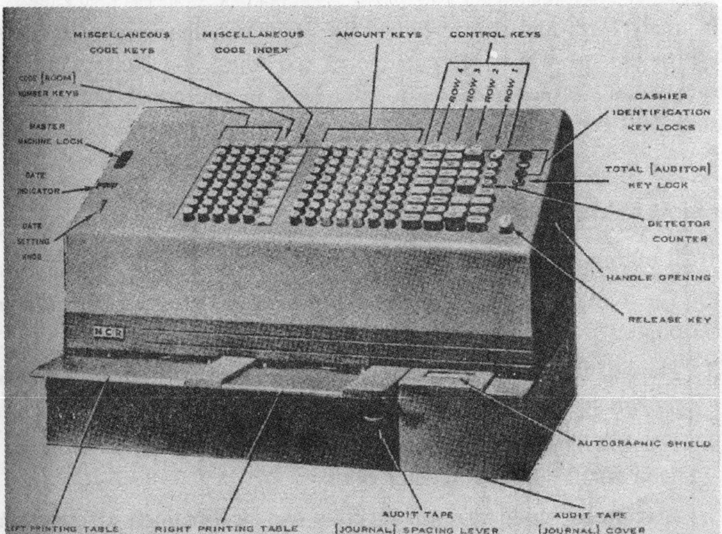

5. The print of each depression of key comes on the Audit Roll. The Audit Roll is locked by the control department, so no operator can manipulate the figures of the Audit Roll.

6. The machine prints the date, name of department, the operators' number, the amount and the balance due. So it helps in telling the date when the amount has been posted into the bill; the name of the department on account of which the customer was charged; the amount debited or credited in the customer's bill; the balance due and the number of operator who has posted the amount. If there is any mistake then the operator can be made responsible for the mistake.
7. The machine stores the total of various departments separately. So with the help of this machine the cumulative total of different departments can be recorded on Night Auditors Machine Balance Card, which is used in place of a Visitors Tabular Ledger,
8. The corrections in the bills are made with the help of the machine and the impression also comes in the Audit Roll so the auditors can know the number of corrections made and allowances given to guests. They can demand the necessary vouchers for allowance and transfer etc.

In many large and deluxe hotels the Tabular ledger has been replaced by these machines, which are capable of recording and storing busy flow of departmental charges and continuous check in and check out traffic and producing bills for presentation to the guests and maintaining daily summary totals.

Advantages of Machine Accounting

1. It eliminates duplication of work.
2. The analysis keys accumulates separate totals in respect of charges posted.
3. The bill is always ready for presentation, providing that no charges remain to be posted.
4. The bill is directly receipted by the machine, thus obviating the need for a separate receipt book.
5. A complete total of cash receipts can be obtained at any time.
6. Records prepared by these machines are more legible.
7. By simultaneous posting operating time and labour can be saved.
8. Machine posting helps to eliminate some of the human errors in calculation.
9. Analysed information for the use of management can easily be Produced.

Specimen of Guest's Weeky Bill

Room No. 104 Rate - Rs. 1100 Name - Mr. KJS No. of Persons - 1 Address - Paschim Vihar, New Delhi Time & Date of Arrival - 25.5.20 ... at 4 P.M. Time & Date of Departure		Telephone : 79334 Telegram : 'MODERN' New Delhi MODERN HOTEL LTD. NEW DELHI Bill No. 0524			0524
Plan - EP/AP/MAP Memo	Date & Explanation	Charge	Credit	Balance due	Pick-up
	647 A 25 May 20.... Room	1110.00		1100.00*	1100.00*
	654A 25 May 20..... Rest.	110.00		1210.00	
Bill due on presentation Check out time – 12 Noon	Guest's sig. .... Charge to .... Address to			Thank you For Visit	Tariff Room. Rs. 1100 S.C. Rs. 110 Total Rs. 1210

Fig. 9. Guest Weekly Bill

CHAPTER XXIII

ALLOWANCE

Credit given to a customers' account, by way of concession, or on the account of other reasons is known as an 'Allowance'. The guest pays to the hotel for lodging, boarding, beverages and sundry services. He may, therefore judge most appropriately, whether the article or service rendered to him was good or bad. As in previous chapters it has been discussed that in the hotel the services or articles that are served to the guests either have no physical property or have the nature of losing its utility. Therefore, the risk is comparatively acute if the guest is not satisfied with the service and refuses the payment. In order to minimise the risk, the hotel has to give patient hearing to the sayings of the guest and has to honour his words to a greater extent than it is in ordinary business enterprise.

When the guest complaints that the service was not satisfactory or claims that a certain charge was made in error, the hotel has to convince his guest either by eliminating entirely the charge in question or by reducing it to a reasonable extent. In this way the credit given to guests account is called an allowance. In hotels the allowance is normally granted on account of the following :—

Lodging or Room Rent

All good hotels charge, for rooms at fixed rates. It is a different issue how much the customer pays for lodging. In case a guest has made a reservation of room for a certain date at a certain rate, if by chance no room remains vacant at such rate on that particular date on his arrival, then the hotel has to accommodate the guest at higher priced room until such room is vacant.

On the availability of the room he is transferred to the desired room. For the convenience of accounting and auditing purposes the guest is charged at the prescribed rates of the room but later on he is given an allowance of the difference between the specified rate of the room and the agreed rate.

In India the hotels are not being governed by a specific body or identic rules, consequently there is no parity in room rates. Like a commercial house there is competition between the hotels. In order to attract the guests some hotels give allowance for lengthy stay. In this case the customer is charged at full rate during the agreed period and is given allowance only after completing the necessary period.

It is customary in India that the hotels give allowance to other hoteliers on apartment if they stay in their hotels.

Telephone Charge

In practice it is found that telephone allowances are more in number that of any other type. It is because the guests are charged wrongly for local telephone calls. The bill department intentionally does not charge from wrong accounts but following reasons are responsible for it—

(i) Sometimes when the guest is ready to check out, he intimates the front office of his departure. The bill department completes his bill after making final enquiry from various departments for pending checks of the said customer. A few minutes before his departure he makes a call from his room. Accidentally if immediately after his departure the room is allotted to a new guest, the bill department will charge the amount in the new guests account.

(ii) Sometimes immediately after the departure of the guest the room is allotted to another guest. During this interval of 5—10 minutes the employee of the hotel makes a call and the new guest is charged for the same because by the time the account is already opened in the name of the incoming guest.

The guest comes to know about this charge either when the bill is presented after a week or before the week when he checks out.

As the charge of local telephone is very low therefore hardly any enquiry is made for such charges and the customer is given an allowance for the call that he says he did not make.

Over Charge

Sometimes a guest is wrongly charged for what he was not availed of or more amount is charged than the required sum.

When the guest points out such over charge, the hotel, after verification, gives an allowance to the guest.

Unsatisfactory Service

The goodwill of a hotel depends upon the service that it renders to its guests. If unsatisfactory service is rendered and the guest is not satisfied, he may refuse to pay for the service.

Hotels are generally very liberal in giving allowance but take drastic action against the person who is found responsible for such unsatisfactory service.

Allowance Voucher and its Approval

In all cases whenever the allowance is given such a proper check or voucher is to be prepared containing the guest's name, room number, name of the department, amount of the allowance demanded, reasons why it is demanded and the signature of the person who prepares it.

MODERN HOTEL LTD.

NEW DELHI

No. 0242

Date ....

Department ....

Name .... Room No ....

Amount Rupees .... Account No ....

Explanation ....

Approved	Guest's	
Sig. of Asstt. Manager	Signature	Signature

Fig. 10. Allowance Voucher

In individual cases, an individual allowance voucher is prepared giving reasons why the guest wants an allowance. Such a voucher is sent to the competent authority—Manager or Assistant Manager for his approval. If he is satisfied with the explanation and reasons, he approves it and the guests account is credited with the necessary amount. It must, however, be noted that no allowance can be granted unless it is approved by the competent authority. Such approved allowance vouchers are examined by the Night Auditor and the Income Auditor.

In case of local telephone call allowance, the bill clerk or the cashier is given the power to give such allowances if he is satisfied with the statement of the guest. However, it is a good rule that he should prepare a combined allowance voucher for the day's allowances and must obtain the approval of the proper authority.

Allowance must be shown in the appropriate column of the Tabular ledger and bill. It is necessary to record allowances in an allowance book showing:

(1) The date on which the allowance was made.

(2) The guest's name.

(3) The amount.

(4) The service concerned.

If the hotel is using a billing machine, the operating of allowance key conjunction with the allowance voucher serves the same purpose. The summary sheet is adjusted from the records of Allowance Book in order to establish the true trading figure for the preparation of final accounts.

CHAPTER XXIV

SERVICE CHARGE AND SALES TAX

Service Charge

In hotels service charge is levied on guests on apartment, food, soft drinks and alcoholic beverages at specified rates. No service charge is levied on the sale of cigarettes, newspapers, laundry service and similar items. On apartment, it is charged by the bill clerk at the time of charging room rent. But in case of food and beverages, it is charged by the concerned department at the time of preparing the departmental bill. In the past, the collection of service charge was distributed amongst the employees. But now the employees are given fixed amount by the hotel and the service charge is treated as revenue of the hotel. In the Visitors Tabular Ledger a column is provided for the service charge and the amount is recorded in that column. Now-a-days some hotels have stopped taking the service charge but have increased the cost of meals, drinks and room rent.

Sales Tax

The problem of Sales Tax was a bit complicated affair till 1972 on account of the controversy between the hotels on the one hand and the Sales-tax authorities on the other. Both parties were in agreement that tax is payable on the sales of food, soft drink and alcoholic beverage but the question was how the gross turnover in respect of such transactions was to be computed. This controversy was over after the Supreme Court's decision on Jan. 4 , 1972. According to Supreme Court's decision on Tuesday the 4th January, 1972, the hotels were required to include the amount of service charge in the price of food served to guests staying on E.P. for the purpose of computing Sales-tax. Regarding the Sales-tax on food-stuffs from the guests staying on

American Plan it was decided that the guest pays a consolidated amount for lodging and boarding. This is indivisible contract of multiple service and not sale of food alone. Moreover, the hotel does not give any rebate if food is not taken by the guest. Therefore the composite contract amount cannot be split-up and Sales-tax but cannot be charged from the guests, staying on American Plan but can be charged on E.P. only. This rule continued till 7th Sept. 1978.

In 1978 this matter again came up before the Supreme Court for its decision when M/s Northern India Caterers (Pvt.) Ltd., appealed judgement of the High Court of Delhi. The Supreme Court decided that service of meal to visitors in a restaurant is not taxable under the Bengal Finance (Sales Tax) Act 1941, as extended to the Union Territory of Delhi and this is so whether a charge is imposed for the meal as a whole or according the dishes separately ordered.

On the basis of above decision the hotels and restaurants stopped charging sales tax on food and soft drinks in Delhi and other states where the said Act was in force from September 1978. But continued to charge sales tax on supply of liquor.

On Feb. 2, 1983 the Constitution (46th Amendment) Bill, 1981 received the assent of the President of India and has therefore become an Act. The Constitution (46th Amendment) Act provides, among other things, for the levying of sales tax on the sales of food-stuffs and beverages by hotels and restaurants, even if service is the dominant feature of the transaction and the customer is not allowed to take the left overs with him. It, therefore, nullifies the effect of the Supreme Court judgement in regard to this matter, but does not cover the period commencing with the Supreme Court judgement in the case of Northern India Caterers i.e., 7th September, 1978 till the date of commencement of the Constitution (46th Amendment) Act. This Act also nullifies The Supreme Court judgement, in the case of Associated Hotels, given on Jan. 4, 1972, whereby it was held that when food is supplied to a guest staying on American Plan, there is no transaction of sale of food and no sales tax can be levied. In this case also, the Constitution (46th Amendment) Act does not cover the period commencing with the date of the judgement and ending with the commencement date of the Constitution (46th Amendment) Act.

After Feb. 2 , 1983 every state is entitled to pass laws levying sales tax on food-stuffs. In Delhi from Feb. 2, 1983 the sales tax is charged on the sale of food items and soft drinks at the rate of 7% and on alcoholic beverages at the rate of 10% as usual.

A guest, who stays on American Plan, has to pay a composite amount for accommodation and food. According to above Amendment Act now food charges are determined by deducting room rent from the composite charge and sales tax is taken at prescribed rate on food items. Some hotels have adopted following practice to calculate the cost of food for charging sales tax—on Continental Plan 1 0% of the composite charge is taken as the cost of food for sales tax. On Modified American Plan 25% of the composite charge is taken as the cost of food for sales tax. On American Plan 40% of the composite charge is taken as the cost of food for sales tax.

Many large hotels calculate the total cost of food on various plans by taking into account the cost of individual meals according to tariff.

CHAPTER XXV

SALES RECORD & CONTROL OF REVENUE PRODUCING DEPARTMENTS

The number of Revenue Producing Departments in a hotel can be a few or more according to the size of the hotel and the policy of the management. For example, in hotel the management may operate Restaurant, News stand and Telephone. The large hotels may operate Bar, Guest Laundry and similar other departments besides the above three.

SALES

Sales of a hotel are of two types—cash sales and credit sales. The products and services of various departments of a hotel are sold to three types of guests—registered guests, credit card holders and unregistered guests from the general public. The sale can be a cash sale or a credit sale depending upon the type of guest involved. If the guest is a registered guest of the hotel and is authorised to avail of the credit facilities or is a credit card holder then he is allowed to charge his purchases to his account. One has to pay in cash if he is not in the above category.

Each department has to keep the record of sales of the department, of the day. It is prepared with the help of carbon copies of checks on the basis of which the products were supplied or services rendered. This record is known as 'Daily Sales Summary' or 'Sales Analysis'. The said record is either compiled on loose sheets or in a bound register. In the later case, it is necessary to have two alternating books. As the internal audit takes place every day and first day's accounts are audited on the following day, therefore, one book may be used for Monday, Wednesday and Friday; the other for Tuesday, Thursday, Saturday and Sunday.

As it has been said above that some departments are involved in cash as well as in credit sales, therefore, the sales record of the individual departments are divided into two groups—one for cash and the other for charge.

The method of maintaining the sales records differ from hotel to hotel. The sales record preforms of some hotels are very elaborate but in others they are very brief according to their requirements. The main purpose of maintaining the sales record is that the management may know the day's total sale and the revenue earned therefrom. In the absence of proper control the true picture of sales cannot be known, therefore, now all good hotel have introduced Internal Control System.

INTERNAL CONTROL OF SALE

Internal Control in hotels is very essential part of the accounting. For internal control it is necessary that no part of accounting should be under absolute and independent control of any one person, but the work of employee should be complementary to that of another. A good internal checking system requires careful planning and coordination of work of each person involved in maintaining the accounting records.

An internal control or internal checking system in a hotel has a threefold purpose. **Firstly**—it must ensure that all charges and allowances to guests and any money received from them have been properly recorded in the guests' account as well as in the hotel's record. It ensures that all revenue is accounted for, that all stocks in hands are correct and the expenditure is justified. **Secondly**—its aim is to prevent fraudulent and negligent practices by hotel employees. **Thirdly**—it should aim to eliminate waste.

It is very difficult to state the manner in which the work of control should be carried out. The system cannot be on and the same for all hotels. The function of control can be performed by an individual clerk in a smaller hotel but by a separate department in larger hotels. The function in both the cases remains the same, of course the scope and the amount of work can differ.

Control in a commercial business is comparatively simple than in a hotel. The commercial business does one type of work and secondly, cash is exchanged for goods sold direct to the public. Hotel differs from a commercial business in several ways—

(1) In hotels the space is rented to guests for a specific period of time, which is intangible and has no physical property.

(2) In hotels the customers either consume goods or avail services of occupy the space first and pay later. They all are of non-refundable nature.

(3) Hotel business involves three things in one location. Purchase of raw material and manufacture of products, sale of products and distribution of goods.

The above factors complicate the control system in hotels.

Toady all large hotels have introduced the check-pad system- It is the best system to control the sales of a hotel. The control is based on checks which are handed by one department to another department. The check pads are retained by the control department and are issued against the signatures of the departmental heads. They are made of different colours to identify the individual department. The departmental heads are responsible to issue them to other employees of their departments after taking their signatures. These check-pads are always kept in sale custody to avoid misuse. In a hotel where this system is in operation it is the rule that on no account should anything be out of service be rendered without a check and whoever receives the must ascertain that it belongs to that particular department and is properly made out.

On the basis of these checks all the departments prepare their sales summaries and send it to the Night Auditor at the end of the day. The Night Auditor verifies these sales summaries with the Transcript sheet or machine balances and other records. Thus at mid-night he audits the sales record of all the departments and prepares a report on the basis of his findings. On the next day all records along with the report are sent to the Income Auditors or control department who after auditing the accounts send all the records to the Accounts department. There the transactions are transferred to different ledgers. The Accounts department with the help of the departmental Sales summaries and Visitors Tabular Ledger, prepares consolidated Day's Sales Summary. Monthly and annual sales summaries are prepared on the same line. This summary helps the preparation of final accounts.

MODERN HOTEL LTD., NEW DELHI
Sales summary of ....Department

V. No.	Particulars	Room No.	Name	Total		Case		Date .... Charge		Remarks
				R.s	P.	R.s	P.	Rs.	P.	

Fig. 11 Departmental Sales Summary

MODERN HOTEL LTD., NEW DELHI
Sales Summary Sheet

Date .... Month ....

Sheet No. ....

Year ....

D.B. (Day Book)	Sheet No.	Amount	Boarding & Lodging		Food	Bervages	Paid Outs	Laundary	Local Call	Trunk Call	Newspaper & Magazines	Total	Brought forward	Grand Total	Allowance	Payments	Carried forward	Outstanding
			Service Charge	Sales Tax														

Fig. 12. Sales Summary Sheet

CHAPTER XXVI

SALES RECORD AND CONTROL OF ROOMS

The hotel earns major revenue from the sale of rooms. Generally two departments are directly involved in keeping a record of the sale or occupancy of hotel rooms. One is Front Office and the other is House-keeping Department. The Front Office keeps a record of sales of rooms and House-keeping Department keeps a record of occupancy of rooms.

The rooms of a hotel are sold either on the basis of advance booking or on the basis of current booking. The reservation for accommodation can be made in four ways—in person, by correspondence, by telephone and by sending telegram. Advance booking can be made either directly by the guest or through the travel agents—with or without a deposit. The advance, so received by the Reservation Department, is sent to the Front Office cashier and an Advance Booking Card is prepared by the Reservation Department.

All Advance Booking Cards for the day are taken out by the Reservation Department and sent to the Front Office in the beginning of every day. As soon as the customer arrives and asks for a room on the basis of his reservation, the Front Office after verification gives a Registration Form to be filled in. This form is prepared in duplicate.

If the customer arrives and ask for accommodation without prior reservation, the Front Office after finding out the position of accommodation fills up Current Booking Card (it is of a distinctive colour). The guest is requested to fill up the Guest Registration form. The Front Office allots room to the customer and writes the Room No. and Guest Registration No. in the Advance Booking Card or Current Booking Card and Guest Registration form.

As soon as the room is allotted s ix copies of Notification Slip are prepared.

Modern Hotel Ltd.

New Delhi

ADVANCE BOOKING CARD

Name . . . . Type of Accom. _____ Rate _____	Arrival ________	Date ____ Flt. No. ___ Time ____
Booked by ________________	Departure	Date ____ Time ____

Address ______________________________________

Tel. No./Letter No. ______________________ Date ____

Phone ☐ Personal Call ☐ Confirmed ☐ W.L. ☐ Ret. advised ☐

Deposit Recd. ______________ M.O./Cheque No. ________

Spl. Remarks ________________________________

Billing Instructions ______________________________

Initials	No.	Arrival G.R. No.	Cancellation	No. Show

Fig. 13. Allowance Booking Card

The first copy of Notification Slip is put in the pocket of the Room Rack (Numerical Index) showing that a particular room is occupied by a particular person.

Room Rack

It is a Rack which presents the visible index of all occupied and guest rooms of a hotel at any given time. It is so placed, in the front office of a hotel, that the room clerk can see it and operate it conveniently without moving away from the counter.

Modern Hotel Ltd. **New Delhi** **NOTIFICATION SLIP**			
	Room. No.	Name	Departure date
Rate	4 16	Rawat Mr. R.S.	May, 25
Rs.250	Nationality	G.R. No.	Arrival date
E.P.	INDIAN	57087	May 22

Fig. 14. Notification Slip

For each room there is a pocket bearing the Room No. on the left hand side. On the centre there is a narrow and small window, where copy of the Notification Slip, containing the coded information, can be inserted. In Notification Slip, the name of the guest, nationality room number, room rent, date of arrival, expected date of departure, G.R. No. etc. are mentioned. The room numbers are printed in the numerical order in which they are situated on the different floors of a hotel. In some hotels the rooms of one floor are printed on one row. Generally the number of different types of rooms are printed with black on different back grounds. It facilitates the desk clerk to spot the different types of rooms. In some hotels the symbols are also made on the pocket, for example—Double bed Green ' D' , room with tub bath—Red ' B' etc. With the help of these symbols, the desk clerk can easily spot the type of room.

In case rooms are under repair or being cleaned or need refurnishing and cannot be sold to guests then a card is inserted in the pocket denoting the word 'N.T.A.' (Not to be allotted) or 'Out of Order' or 'On Change' etc. and the reason of not selling. As soon as the room is ready for sale, the signal card is removed.

The second copy of the Notification Slip is sent to the main Bill Department along with the carbon copy of Guest Registration Form for opening an account in the name of the Guest. The Bill Department on receiving these two documents opens a bill in the name of the guest and charges him for the apartment for the day in the bill as well as in the Visitors Tabular

Ledger. In some of the hotels the Front Office itself opens a bill in the name of the new guest and sends it to the main Bill Department, for charging the apartment, along with Notification Slip and carbon copy of the Guest Registration Form.

The carbon copies of Guest Registration Forms are pasted on the back of the Guest bills. In case of doubt the signatures of the guest on the Registration Forms are compared by the Bill Clerk with the signatures of the respective customers appended by them on vouchers or checks received by the Bill Department in future.

The third copy of Notification Slip is kept in the Information Rack (Alphabetical Index).

Information Rack

It is visible alphabetical index of the guests. It is, therefore, also called Alphabetical Index. It consists of removable pockets. When a guest arrives and a room is allotted to him, one copy of Notification Slip is inserted in the pocket. The pocket is placed in the Information Rack in alphabetical order. Thus all information relating to guest can be obtained at a glance at one place. The Information Rack is helpful for answering the enquiries relating to guest. When the guest checks out the copy of Notification Slip is removed.

The fourth Copy is sent to the House-keeping Department, fifth to Room Service Department and the sixth copy is sent to the Telephone Department for information. The Telephone Department also maintains. Alphabetical Index with the help of Notification Slips.

The Front Office prepares Guest Arrival Sheet with the help of original copies of Guest Registration Forms. The details of Guest Registration Form are entered in the Guest Arrival Sheet as and when the guest arrives and is allotted accommodation. The Arrival Sheet helps in furnishing the data of arrivals of the day.

At the end of the day the Front Office sends back the Advance and Current Booking Cards of the customers (who were allotted accommodation during the day) to the Reservation Department along with those Advance Booking Cards of prospective customers who could not turn up during the day.

They are known as 'No Shows.' The Reservation Department files the played cards serially. It advises the Revenue Department to show the retention of accommodation of one day of all No Shows and to send a bill by charging one day's room rent. If the guest had already paid an advance then the day's room rent is adjusted out of this advance and the balance is refunded.

MODERN HOTEL LTD, NEW DELHI

Arrival Sheet

Registration Card No.	Name of the Guest	Nationality	Room No.	No. of Persons	Rate	Time of Arrival	Arrived From	Expected date of Departure	Address Proceeding to	Purpose of Visit	Date of Arrival in India	Passport No. Date & Place	C. form No.	Signature of Receptionist	Remark

Fig. 15. Arrival Sheet

Departure Sheet

Registration Card No.	Nationality	Room No.	No. of Person	Time of Departuer	Total Night Stayed	Signature of Receptionist	Remarks

Fig. 16. Departure Sheet.

MODERN HOTEL LTD., NEW DELHI
House-keeping Department
Occupancy Report

Date...............
Time...............

Room No.	Guest	Code	Room No.	Guest	Code
101	1	O	111	2	O
102		V	112		X
103	DND	O	113	1	O
104	DL	O	114		V
105		V	115	2	O
106	DND	O	116	1	O
107		V	117		V
108	DL	O	118	1	O
109	2	O	119	2	O
110		V	120		V

CODE

O	Occupied	DND	Do Not Disturb
V	Vacant	DL	Double Lock
X	Room out of Order		

Signature

Fig. 17. Occupancy Report

MODERN HOTEL LTD., NEW DELHI

Nigh Receptionist's Room Sale Report

Night of .... 19 ....

Ground Floor			First Floor			Recapitulation		
Room No	No. of Persons	Rate	Room No.	No. of Persons	Rate	Floor	No. of Persons	Rate
						Total		
							Night Recetionist Night Auditor	

Fig. 18. Night Receptionist's Room Sale Report

It is justified to claim one day's charge as compensation because reservation of accommodation is a contract between a hotel and the guest. The hotel holds a room or rooms at the disposal of the guest for an agreed period. If the guest does not turn up, he must compensate the loss.

It is necessary that the Receptionist, Bill Clerk and Front Office Cashier are thoroughly conversant with the policy of the management in relation to foe room rates. In other words, it can be said that all the concerned persons are supposed to know the rates of different types of rooms, rooms of different facilities, rooms of different floors, charges for extra persons, when concessional or half day rates can be charged, checking in and checking out time etc.

Effort is always made to keep a correct record of room sales. Therefore, besides the record maintained by the Front Office and Bill Department the House-keeping Department also prepares Room Occupancy Report showing room occupancy position. This report is known as House-keeper's Report. This House-keeper's Report is prepared at least twice a day on the basis of Maid's Report. Generally the first report is prepared in the morning soon after cleaning of rooms and the second after the afternoon cleaning. In some hotels a third report is also prepared before the close of the day.

The House-keeping Department uses symbols to give sufficient information regarding the rooms. All hotels do not use one type of symbols. Different hotels use different types of symbols. One set of symbols used hotels is given in the above proforma.

The Front Office and Auditors are supposed to be acquainted with the symbols because they have to compare the House-keepers Occupancy Report with the Room Rack, Night Receptionist Room Sale Report, Arrival Sheet Departure Sheet and other records. The main purpose of this report is to prevent the omission of room sale and find out discrepancy.

At the end of the day the Night Receptionist prepares a report called Night Receptionist's Room Sales Report. This report is prepared on the basis of rooms occupied as shown by the Room Rack and room charges shown by the Guest Bill for the day, whether guests staying from the previous day or arrived on the same day.

In this report the number of rooms occupied along with the number of persons and the rate of each room is recorded. This report is first of all prepared floor-wise. After that a recapitulation is prepared showing the total number of persons occupying rooms and the total room rent earned for the day. This Night Receptionist's Room Sales Report is helpful for the audit of room sales.

When the guest intimates that he intends to check out, the front office closes his bill after finding out his outstanding charges from the departments. The bill is presented for payment. When the guest makes the payment, the cashier prepares a Clearance Card. This card is given to the porter only when he carries the luggage of the guest from the room. After removing the luggage, the porter hands over the cashier's Clearance Card to the Front Office. On receiving the Clearance Card the Front Office removes the Registration Form, charge vouchers and copy of the bill. After this the Front Office enters the particulars of the guest in the Departure Sheet. Copy of the Notification Slip is removed from the pocket of Room Rack and Alphabetical Index.

CONTROL OF ROOM SALE

Control of room sale is actually a reconciliation of the business transacted by the Reception Office with the records of the room sale maintained by the Bill Department during the day. For proper control the Might Auditor must satisfy himself in respect of the following:

(i) Was the room occupied from the previous day?

(ii) If so, has the guest's account been debited with the amount of room charges?

(iii) Did the guest arrive during the day?

(iv) If yes, was the guest charged for the apartment at the time of his arrival?

(v) Was the guest charged for the apartment at the check out time if he continued his stay after check out time?

(vi) Is the rate of the room occupied by the guest correct?

The room sale of a hotel is generally checked with the help of the following documents at different intervals of the day—

(a) Advance Booking Card.

(b) Current Booking Card.

(c) Guest Registration Form.

(d) Guest Arrival Sheet.

(e) Guest Departure Sheet.

(f) House-keeper's Report.

(g) Night-Receptionist Room Sales Report.

(h) Cashier's Clearance Card.

MODERN HOTEL LTD.,

NEW DELHI

CASHIER'S CLEARANCE CARD

ATTENDANT NO. DATE ....

.... TIME ....

Room No. ....

Name ....

Bill No ....

Signature

Fig. 19. Cashier's Clearance Card

First of all the Night Auditor has to see that the guest registration number for the day begins in continuation of the last number of the previous day- This can be checked from the previous day's Arrival Sheet and current day's Arrival Sheet, Advance or Current Booking Card and Copy of Guest Registration Form.

The House-keeper's Report is compared with the Room Rack, Arrival Sheet, Departure Sheet, Receptionist Room Sales Report, Guest's Bill etc. This comparison helps in ascertaining that a room shown occupied by the House-keeper's Report is entered in the Arrival Sheet (if arrived on the current day), a bill is opened and shown occupied by Room Rack and Night Receptionist Room Sales Report. Sometimes Departure Sheet is also to be consulted because it may so happen that the room is shown occupied by House-keeper's Report but the Room Rack may show the room as vacant. It means that the guest checked out after the House-keepers Report was made. It can be ascertained from the Departure Sheet. Sometimes the room is shown vacant by the House-keeper's Report but it is shown occupied by the Room Rack. In such a case Departure Sheet may be seen. If the room number does not appear in the Departure Sheet also, then the guest's bill be located. His Guest Registration Form may be consulted to know his expected departure date, whether he was a walk in or had booked in advance through some Travel Agency or some other establishment. If the guest bill is traced and from other records it is found that he was simply a walk-in and had no prior reservation then it means the guest has checked out without informing the Front Office and without making payment. In such a case the concerned authority may be informed.

Sometimes the House-keeper's Report shows that a room is occupied but the Room Rack shows it vacant. The reason may be a mistake on the part of the Front Office or an unauthorised occupancy. In case of mistake a new Room Rack slip is prepared and put on the pocket of the Room Rack after checking the bill. In case of unauthorised occupancy the concerned authority may be informed. The management makes necessary investigation and takes corrective measures.

The Departure Sheet is also compared with the Cashier's Clearance Card to ascertain their agreement.

The Receptionist's Room Sales Report is compared with House keepers Report in order to know room occupancy position. This comparison helps in knowing correct number of rooms occupied by guests. The total amount of rent shown by the Receptionist's Room Sales Report is compared with room sale column of either Transcript Sheet or Visitors Tabular Ledger or Night-Auditor's Machine Balance Card. They must agree. If they do not agree then it means that there is some discrepancy. The discrepancy is to be detected as early as possible. It is always the duty of Night Auditor to inform the Assistant Manager for investigation. Thus this comparison helps firstly in finding out the rooms were either sold on the same day to the guests or they were occupied by the guests from the previous day have been correctly recorded and secondly that the amount has been charged correctly to the guest's accounts.

CHAPTER XXVII

SALES RECORD AND CONTROL OF FOOD

The hotel earns major revenue from the sale of food and drinks. It offer to the guest various types of food and drink services from its different departments—restaurant, dinning room, dispense bar, cocktail bar etc. It order to achieve the justified maximum return from the sale of food am beverages a proper record of food and beverages sale has to be maintained. Besides this an introduction of a proper control system is essential. In the absence of it the hotel cannot earn the desired maximum returns.

Today all big hotels have introduced the check-pad system. It is the best system to control the sales of a hotel. The control is based on checks which are handed by one department to another department. The food is sold through Restaurant. For maintaining a proper record and its control the Restaurant requires K.O.T. Check pads, Guest bill pads and Summary Sheets. The control department gets them printed and issues to the In-charge of Restaurant against his signatures. The Restaurant In-charge issues the K.O.T. pads to the head waiters/stewards and bill pads and summary sheets to the bill clerk. The checks (K.O.T. or Bill) are prepared in triplicate. All the copies of the check are of different colours. It facilitates the control.

The record of food sale is maintained at two places—One at the kitcher which is the supply point and the second at the Restaurant which is the sales point.

When the guest orders his meal the head waiter or captain records the food items on the waiter's check, which is known as K.O.T. (Kitchen Order Ticket), in triplicate. K.O.T.s are of two types—one is K.O.T. cum-Bill and the other is pure K.O.T.

K.O.T.-cum-Bill is that in which the quantity and the name of food item, the rate and the amount chargeable are recorded. In this case a separate bill is not prepared. This document serves the purpose of the K.O.T. as well as of the bill.

Pure K.O.T. is that in which the quantity and the name of the dish desired by the customer is recorded. In this case later on a separate bill is to be prepared by the bill clerk. This system is better from the control Point of view.

<table>
<tr><td colspan="2" align="center">MODERN HOTEL LTD.
NEW DELHI
KAMAL RESTAURANT
K.O.T.   NO. ....
Table No. ....   No. of Covers....................
Waiter No ....   Date ....</td></tr>
<tr><td>Quantity</td><td>Names of Dishes</td></tr>
<tr><td></td><td>Signature ....</td></tr>
</table>

Fig. 20. Kitchen Order Ticket

In case of pure K.O.T. two copies of the K.O.T. (original and one carbon copy) are given to the waiter. The third copy is retained in the K.O.T. pad.

If any K.O.T. or bill is to be cancelled then it is to be signed by the supervisory staff. Sometimes special K.O.T.'s are also to be prepared. A few circumstances are given below, under which special K.O.T.'s are prepared:

1. In some of the hotels it is a practice that one K.O.T. is made for the main course and for sweets a separate K.O.T. is prepared. In that case the K.O.T. of main course is made first. After the main course is served waiter writes second K.O.T. for the sweets. As only one bill is made for both he K.O.T.'s, therefore, in the second K.O.T. on the top 'following check' is written. It indicates that one

K.O.T. has already been written out for the particular table and for the particular customer.

2. Sometimes, by mistake, the customer is not supplied the required standard portion on the basis of the K.O.T. In that case a separate K.O.T. is written out and on the top of it the word 'Supplement' is written. It is a supplementary K.O.T. of the first K.O.T. Generally the customer is not charged for this supplementary K.O.T. and the word N/C (No charge) is also written on the top of it.
3. Sometimes the waiter meets with an accident and drops some portion of the meal This Portion is to be replaced without any extra charge to the guest. In such a case a special K.O.T. containing the portion required is to be prepared. The words 'Accident' and N/C (No charge) are written on the top of it.
4 Sometimes, by mistake, a wrong K.O.T. is prepared. Now the wrong fish is to be sent back to the kitchen and replaced by the correct dish. In such a case, a special K.O.T. is made showing the correct dish required. Two main leading are used on this K.O.T.—one 'Return' and the name of the dish sent back and the other 'Enplace' or 'in its place' and the name of the new dish to be served.

The waiter, after receiving two copies of K.O.T. from the head waiter, hands over the original copy to the kitchen. The kitchen supplies meals on the basis of the K.O.T. The waiter takes the food from the kitchen to the Restaurant/Dining Room and serves it to the guest.

When the kitchen supplies the food items on the basis of K.O.T., the Kitchen Clerk marks simultaneously the items supplied. When all items of LOT. are supplied, the kitchen clerk enters them in the kitchen summary sheet, which contains columns for the date, K.O.T. No., Waiter No., names of items, the analysis of items etc. This summary is helpful in reconciling the portions the kitchen had prepared and the portion supplied to Restaurant and the balance in hand. This summary is sent to the control department at the end of the day. The control department compares this summary sheet with the Restaurant Summary Sheet to know whether the bills were prepared for the applies made by the kitchen.

After posting the K.O.T. into the Kitchen Summary Sheet, it is put inside the locked box which is cleared by the control department next day in the morning. The waiter, after serving food to the guest, hands over the carbon copy of the K.O.T. to the Restaurant Bill Clerk. The Bill Clerk prepares the bill for presentation. Generally it is prepared in triplicate. The first copy is made for presentation to the guest, the second copy for the control department and the third is retained in the bill book. When the guest indicate that he has finished his meal and wishes to leave, the first copy of the bill is presented to the guest on a side plate and folded half with one corner turned up. If the guest is resident or Credit Card holder and wishes that the amount be debited to his account, he signs the bill and writes his room number or credit card number. The signature of the customer is a proof that he received a particular service. The waiter must ensure that the correct room number or credit card number a placed on the bill, so that the charge may be made from the right account. The amount is debited to the guest's account in the individual bill as well as in the Visitors Tabular Ledger. If the guest is non-resident or if a registered guest likes to make payment in cash, it is received and the amount is recorded in the Restaurant Cash Book. The summary of Cash Book is sent to the control department.

Immediately after the presentation of the bill to the guest, one carbon copy is sent to the control and with the help of the second carbon copy the Restaurant Sales Summary is prepared. Only the Analysis Columns Cash Charge—are filled up at the end of the day with the help of the Restaurant Cash Book. If the amount of the bill appears in the Cash book then the amount is noted in the 'Cash' Column of the Summary Sheet. If it is credit then it is recorded in the 'Charge' Column. At he end of the day this Restaurant Sales summary is sent to the Night Auditors. There it is compared with the Kitchen summary, Machine Balance or Visitors Tabular Ledger.

Illustration—The following food items were served to a group of 5 persons in Kamal Restaurant of Modern Hotel, New Delhi on 3rd Sept. 20......:

2 Cream of Tomato Soup @ Rs. 3.50 each

3 Consomme Royale @ Rs. 4.00 each

2 Vegetable Cutlets @ Rs. 6.50 per portion

3 Poulet Maryland @ Rs. 9.50 per portion

1 Caramel Custard @ Rs. 3.00 per portion

2 Pine apple Conde @ Rs. 3.50 per portion

2 Fresh Fruit Salad @ Rs. 3.50 per portion

5 Coffee @ Rs. 2.00 each

You are required to prepare a Restaurant Bill in proper form for presentation. Service charge is to be calculated @ *8%.* Assume no Sales tax is charged.

MODERN HOTEL LTD., NEW DELHI

(Kitchen Summary Sheet)

Date...............

ANALYSIS

S.No.	K..O.T. NO.	Table No.	Waiter No.	Particulars	Soup.	Fish	

Fig. 21. Kltchen Summary

MODERN HOTEL LTD., NEW DELHI

(Kamal Restaurant)

Date...............

Restaurant Summary Sheet

Bill No.	Waiter No.	Table No.	No of covers	K.O.T. No	Room No.	Name Guest	Total Amount Rs	Cast			Charge		
								Food	S.C.	S.T.	Food	S.C.	S.T

Fig. 22. Restaurant Summary Sheet

Waiter No. 24
Room No. ....

MODERN HOTEL LTD., NEW DELHI
(Kamal Restaurant)

Bill No. 125
K.O.T. No. 8
Date 3-9-20.......

Bill

Quantity	Particulares	Amount Non-taxable Rs	P.	Amount Taxable @ Rs.	P.	Total Rs.	P
2.	Cream of Tomato soup @ Rs. 3.50 each	7	-			7	-
3.	Consomme Royale @ Rs. 4.00 each	12	-			12	-
2.	Vegetable Cutlests @ Rs. 6.50 per portion	13	-			13	-
3.	Poulet Maryland @ Rs. 950 Per portion	28	50			28	50
1	Caramel Custard @ s. 3.00 per porition	3	-			3	-
2	Pineapple Conde @ Rs. 3.50 per portion	7	-			7	-
2	Fresh Fruit Salad @ Rs. 3.50 per portion	7	-			7	-
5	Coffee @ Rs. 2.00 each	10	-			10	-
	Total	87	50				
	Service Charge @ 8%	7	-			7	-
Please do not sign if you have paid	Please pay this amount Grand total	94	50			94	50
	E & O.E.						

Arul Kumar
Bill Clerk

....

Bill No. 125 Waiter N. 24	Waiter's Receipt	Rs.	P.
	Date 3.9.20.........	94	50

Fig. 23. Restaurant Bill

CONTROL

The control of food sale is done with the help of the checks. Generally following documents and checks are helpful in controlling the sale of food:

(a) K.O.T.

(b) Kitchen Summary.

(c) Copy of Restaurant Bill.

(d) Restaurant Summary.

(e) Visitors Tabular Ledger, or Machine Balance Card

(f) Restaurant Cash Book Summary.

Besides the above documents the Night Auditor prepares Transcript with the help of guest weekly bills. It becomes an important tool in the hands of the control for verification.

The control with the help of the above documents and vouchers checks the sales of the day. First of all the control has to ascertain that the details of K.O.T. are appearing in the Kitchen Summary and Restaurant Summary duly analysed and dissected properly so that wrong analysis may not affect the future records and statistics of sales. The control has to ensure that a bill has been prepared for the K.O.T. items and the customers has been charged full amount in accordance with the tariff in the bill. The cash sale is further checked with Restaurant Summary and Cash Book Summary. The credit sale is checked with the help of Restaurant Summary and Visitors Tabular Ledger. The total sale of food shown by Restaurant Summary is also compared with Transcript Sheet or Machine Balance.

The day's sale of food is checked first of all by the Night Auditor. He then sends Kitchen Summary, Restaurant Summary, Transcript Sheet, Visitors Tabular Ledger or Machine Balance Card etc. to the Income Auditor. The Income Auditor after thorough checking, prepares necessary report and other statistics for the information of the manager. At the end he passes all sales records to the accounts department for posting into the respective ledgers.

CHAPTER XXVIII

SALES RECORD AND CONTROL OF ALCOHOLIC BEVERAGES

In hotels all alcoholic beverages are sold through the bar but beverages are kept at two places—One, in the store room known as Wine Cellar and the other, at bar. The account, therefore, is maintained at both the places. In store room a complete record of purchases and issue to bar is maintained. In bar the record of sales is maintained.

The purchases of alcoholic beverages are made either by F. & B. Manager or Purchase Officer through approved agents on the basis of necessary sanction. When alcoholic beverages are purchased the supplier sends an Invoice and Excise Pass along with the consignment of beverages. The store, on receiving the consignment, compares and verifies the number of cases, name of brand, bottle size etc. with the purchase order and the Invoice. Sealed tops of broken bottles are retained and credited for shortage in quantity received.

The method of maintaining the records of purchases and sales of alcoholic beverages is different from hotel to hotel. In some hotels two registers are maintained in the wine store. The first is Daily Material Received Register and the second is Stock Register. In Daily Material Received Register the details of purchases like the name of alcoholic beverage, quantity, manufacturer's name, supplier's name, price, date of purchase etc. are recorded. In Stock Register the quantity in possession during the day, quantity and balance in hand at the end of the day are recorded.

In wine store the alcoholic beverages are stored according to their code classification, temperature and other requirements for preservation. They are kept in the bins. For every kind of beverage one separate bin card is maintained. This bin card is placed in the bin along with the beverage. In bin card the name of the beverage, quantity received, quantity issued to the

MODERN HOTEL, NEW DELHI
Daily Material Received Register

Date	Bill No. Cash Memo No.	R/R No.	Suppliers Name	Description of Material	Quantity	Rate	Amt.	L.F.	Verified Bill No.	Total Amt.	Remarks

Fig. 24. Dally Material Received Register

MODERN HOTEL, NEW DELHI
Stock Register

Voucher No. or Invoice No. & Date	Particulars	Opening Balance	Quantity Received	Total Quantity	Issued	Balance in Hand\	Remarks

Fig, 25. Stock Register

bar and balance left is recorded. Thus every one at a glance can know the quantity of each of beverage left in the stock even without referring to the stock register. The balance shown by the bin card should agree with the actual stock on hand. Maintenance of bin card, in the wine store is useful for checking where internal control system is in operation.

Besides the above two registers and bin card, one Excise Register is also maintained. The maintenance of this register is compulsory for all persons who hold licence for selling alcoholic beverages. If the hotel holds two licences—L-3 and L-5—for the sale of alcoholic beverages in Rooms and Bar respectively then the hotel has to maintain two registers: One for L-3 and the other for L-5. Each page of the register is divided Indian parts. The first part is for the receipts of all types of imported as well as Indian alcoholic beverages, the second part for the issue and the third part for the balance of the beverages. There is also a column for the signatures of the Excise Inspector. The Excise Inspector has the right to inspect the alcoholic beverages and the Excise Register at any time.

MODERN HOTEL LTD., NEW DELHI

BIN CARD

Article No. .... Maximum Stock ....

Codel No. .... Minimum Stock ....

Ordering Level ....

Normal Order ....

Date	Delivery or Issue Note	Quantity or Weight		Balance
		Received	Issued	

Fig. 26. Bin Card

He compares the entries of the receipts of alcoholic beverages with Excise Pass. He then verifies physically the bottles in the wine store and bar, which are not opened with the record maintained by the hotel. After verification he puts his signature in the prescribed column of the Excise Register.

The wine store is locked after the service and key is deposited in a sealed envelope either with the Front Office Cashier or the person Incharge for Keys. Incharge maintains a Key Register where the deposits of keys and recollection of keys are recorded. The signature of the depositor and the signature of the authorised collecting persons are taken into the register.

The alcoholic beverages are sold through the bar. In a hotel there may be one bar or more than one bar according to the size and sales position of a hotel. In large hotels generally there are more than one bar. A person who looks after all the bars is known as Supervisor. The Incharge of individual bar is known as Bar Tender. A number of wine waiters work under, him. The bar prepares requisition, known as Cellar Check, to obtain alcoholic beverages from the wine store. This check contains the quantity, accurate description of beverage including bin number and size. This Check is made in triplicate. The original and one carbon copy are sent to the wine store.

The third copy remains in the check book. The Store Incharge issues beverages according to requisition and takes the signature of the recipient on both the copies of the check. He retains one copy and sends the second copy to the control for audit. As soon as beverages are issued by store, entries are made in the respective bin cards, stock register and excise register.

The Bar maintains a record of the receipts of alcoholic beverages from store and the sale of it in a register known as Bar Consumption Register. There are two types of services rendered by a bar. One is to the guests their rooms and the second in the bar.

If the customer places an order and wants that the alcoholic beverage be served in the room then the wine baiter prepares a check. In some hotels this is called B.O.T. (Bar). It is prepared in duplicate. One copy is handed over to the Cashier, who prepares a bill on the basis of it. In some hotels for serving the alcoholic beverages in the rooms no B.O.T. (Bar) is prepared but a direct bill is made. This bill is similar to Restaurant Bill. In some hotels four copies are prepared—*first* copy of the bill is meant for presentation to the *guest, second* copy for the audit and the *third* copy for bar for supply of beverages. In both the cases, whether the customer wants alcoholic beverage in the room or in the bar, two copies of the bill are given to the wine waiter. He hands over one copy to the Bar Tender. The Bar Tender supplies beverages according to the bill for serving to the customer.

MODEREN HOTEL LTD., NEW DELHI
Excise Register

Page No. ....
Month ....

To be maintained by every person holding licence in Form L-3 to L-30
for the retail vend of Foreign Liquor

Month & Date	DALIY RECEIPTS									ISSUE							BALANCE					
	No. & Date of Pass under which received	Imported Whisky, Rum Gin, Liquor	Indian Whisky, Brandy Gin	Imported Wine	Indian Wine	Imported Beer	Indian Beer Cider	Cider	Sig. and Date of Excise Inspector	Imported Whisky, Rum Gin, Liquor	Indian Whisky, Brandy Gin	Imported Wine	Indian Wine	Imported Beer	Indian Beer	Cider	Imported Whisky, Rum Gin, Liquor	Indian Whisky, Brandy Gin	Imported Wine	Indian Wine	Imported Beer	Cider

Fig. 27. Excise Register

MODERN HOTEL, NEW DELHI

Bar Consumption Register

Date ....

NAME OF ITEMS	FIRST SHIFT					SECOND SHIFT				THIRD SHIFT			
	Opening Balance	Receipt	Total	Consumption	Closing Balance	Receipt	Total	Consumption	Closing Balance	Receipt	Total	Consumption	Closing Balance

Fig. 28 Bar Consumption Register

MODERN HOTEL

NEW DELHI

Allocation sheet

Name of Bar ....

Name of Bar Tender ....

Shift ....

Day & Date ....

Voucher No.	Imported Beverages	Indigenous Beverages	Soft Drinks	Cigarettes & Cigars

Fig. 29. Allocation Sheet

After the service the first copy of the bill is presented to the customer either for payment or for signatures, as the case may be. If the customer makes payment in cash then a receipt is issued to him and entry is passed in the cash book. In case the customer is entitled for credit facility and likes that the amount be debited to his account then he signs the bill. This signed bill is sent to the main bill department for debiting the customer's account.

Generally there are three shifts of the employees in the bar. The bar consumption register is also prepared shifts-wise. Every Bar Tender, at the end of his shift, enters all the bills of his shift into the Allocation Sheet. The total of each type of beverage shown by allocation sheet is then entered into the Bar Consumption Register. The closing balance of the first shift becomes the opening balance of the second shift and closing balance of the second shift becomes the opening balance of the third shift. Thus every shift Incharge prepares the Allocation Sheet of his shift and transfer the total to Bar Consumption Register. At the end of the day all the Allocation Sheets of all the bars and the third copy of the bills are sent to the Control Department.

The control department compares the details of every bill with the allocation sheet and simultaneously prepares a consolidated Allocation Sheet for costing. The cost price and the sales price of each type of beverages are calculated beforehand and printed in the Allocation Sheet of the control department. The control clerk has to count the total sales of each type of beverage and calculate the cost price and the sales price according to the rate printed in the allocation sheet. The total of the sales price column is compared by the audit with the total sale column of Bar Sales Summary Sheet of Cashier.

The bar cashier at the end of the day prepares Bar Sales Summary with the help of second copy of the bill and the Cash Book. The amount of bills are entered in the total column and cash receipt shown by the cash book is entered in the cash column.

The credit sales are entered in the credit column along with Room No. of guest. Thus the total sales is analysed. The total sale shown by this summary should agree with the total sales price of control Allocation Sheet. Thus the sale of alcoholic beverages are controlled.

MODERN HOTEL, NEW DELHI

Allocation Sheet of Control Depatment

Date ....

Items	Total Beverages	Cost Price	Amonut	Seles Price	Amount
Sherry					
11111	5				

Signature

Fig. 30. Allocation Sheet of Control Deptt.

MODERN HOTEL, NEW DELHI

Sales Summary Sheet

Date ....

Cashier ....

(BAR)

Time ....

Check No.	BEVERAGES		Tobacco	Sales Tax	Total	Cash	Credit	Room No.	Remarks
	Soft Drink	Beer, Wine, Spirits							

Signature

Fig. 31. Sales Summary Sheet

CHAPTER XXIX

SALES RECORD OF MINOR REVENUE - PRODUCING DEPARTMENTS

In addition to provide accommodation and meals to the guests, the hotel also provides other facilities to its guests like laundry, telephone, news stand etc. The hotel runs these departments for the convenience of the guests. As the hotel earns comparatively less revenue from such departments, therefore, they are known as Minor Revenue-Producing Departments. In general the sales of such departments can be recorded in the following manner.

These departments make available their articles and services for the guests either for cash or on credit. As soon as the sale takes place the department has to prepare a voucher (check) for the sale. If the guest makes the payment in cash, it is recorded in departmental Cash Book. Once in the day the collection is deposited with the Chief Cashier. If it is a credit sale, the customer has to sign the check. The signed check is sent to the Main Bill Department where it is entered in the guest's individual bill as well as in the Visitors Tabular Ledger.

Thus the original copy of the check either goes to the customer or to the Main Bill Department. With the help of carbon copy the department prepares sales summary of the day. These days it is generally prepared in loose sheets. The proforma of the summary sheet, which can be used by every minor revenue-producing department is given in the related chapter.

SALES RECORD OF TELEPHONE DEPARTMENT

Telephone Department is a minor revenue-producing department of a hotel. It earns revenue by charging from guests for each outgoing call and commission on trunk call at a specific rate. This department provides two types of telephone services—one for communication between the various parts of the hotel and second for outgoing local calls. The hotel does not charge any amount for internal telephone calls but charges for outgoing local calls at a specific rate and for trunk calls as per bill of the telephone department including departmental charges at prescribed rate.

MODERN HOTEL, NEW DELHI

LOCAL CALL

No . ... Date ....

Name .... R.No ....

No. Called ....

Amount ....

Signatures

Fig. 32. Local Call Voucher

MODERN HOTEL, NEW DELHI

TRUNK CALL

No . ... Date ....

Name .... R.No ....

No. Called ....

City Called .... Type of Call ....

Time Connected ... Time Disconnected .....

Time ....

Amount ....

Signatures

Fig. 33. Trunk Call Voucher

The telephone facilities are not only provided to guests but also extended to the employees for hotel's business. The employees are not charged for the local calls if they make it for business. The telephone department keeps a proper record of all the calls either made by the guests or the employees. This practice has three advantages :—

(i) The hotel can check the bill of the telephone department if a proper record of all the calls is maintained in the hotel. In the absence of this it is not possible.

(ii) It helps in charging the correct amount from the guests.

(iii) It can check the practice of misuse of the telephone by employees.

As soon as the call is made by the guest, immediately a telephone check is prepared in duplicate by the telephone department and is sent to the main department for recording the charges into the guests bill. At the end of the day with the help of the carbon copies, an analysis sheet is prepared and is sent to the Night Auditors for audit.

Like Telephone Department all other minor revenue-producing departments maintain their sales record.

CONCESSIONAIRES

Hotel provides many types of services and luxuries to their guests according to its status. Some of the services and facilities are rendered by the departments which are under direct control of the management of the hotel itself and run by its own employees. Other facilities and professional services are offered by the departments that are not operated by the management of the hotel. They are run independently by outsiders in the campus of the hotel. The pace is rented or the lease is granted by the hotel for a specific period. Such person to whom this lease is granted is known as Concessionaire.

There are two methods of granting such lease or giving shops to outsiders—

(i) A fixed amount is given by the concessionaires to the hotel for a specific period.

(ii) A certain percentage of sales is given to the hotel.

The first method is more customary and convenient because it saves the hotel from many botherations. Under this method the hotel is concerned with the agreed amount and satisfactory service to guests according to their terms and conditions. This method is more popular in India.

In the second method the hotel gets only an agreed percentage of the sales of the department. For obtaining justified amount it is necessary for the hotel to control the sales record of the department. In the absence of proper cantrol the leasee can misappropriate the accounts and the hotel may be at a loss. For proper control 'Check Pad System' can be introduced.

Generally the shops and departments are allotted or given on lease on the basis of tenders. After the lease is granted both the parties have to enter into an agreement.

The concessionaires sell their articles or render services to the guests generally for cash. In case, the hotel wants to extend the credit facilities to the guest in these shops, it has to give guarantee to concessionaires for collecting the charges from the guests. When the guest arrives and occupies accommodation, the hotel intimates these shops, like its own departments, the arrival of the est and asking them to extend credit facilities to the new arrivals. The cocessionaires sell their services to registered guests on credit at a reasonable limit. A voucher (check) is prepared and after obtaining the signatures of the guest it is sent to the bill department. The charges are debited in the cutomer's account and collected along with other charges. The accounts department credits the concessionaire's account. The hotel is responsible for collecting charges provided the concessionaire notifies the bill clerk of the charges before the guest checks out. If he fails to intimate the charges to the bill clerk and the guest checks out, then the hotel is not responsible for the loss. When the amount is collected from the guests, it is not immediately sent to the concessionaires but the settlement is made periodically according to the agreement.

It is true that the sale of concessionaries' shop is not the sale of the hotel but a column is provided in the Visitors Tabular Ledger for each such department's sale for the sake of convenience in establishing the total charges to guest's account. Once the charges are recorded in guest's account, the hotel is responsible for collecting it from the guests. The concessionaires also maintain an account of the credit sale on the basis of the carbon copy of the check. They debit the Hotel's account and periodically send a debit note. The hotel according to agreement settles the account. At the time of payment the hotel debits the concessionaires' account and the concessionaires credit the hotel's account. Thus the record of sales is maintained in the concessionaires' departments as well as in the hotel.

CHAPTER XXX

RECORD AND CONTROL OF CASH

The term cash includes coins, currency notes, travellers cheques bank cheques, foreign currency and other credit instruments which are accepted in exchange of valuc. In small hotels only one person handles the cash. He alone receives the cash and makes the payment. In large hotels the cash is received by various departmental cashiers. Once in a day, all the cash so received by be departments, is deposited at one central point, which is known as cash office. It is headed by chief cashier. The major payments are also made by the chief cashier but for petty payments a junior cashier is appointed.

In large hotels there is greater possibility of defalcation or misappropriation of money than in small hotels where the proprietor has a direct control over the receipts and payments of cash. The cash can be misappropriated by cashiers in the following ways—

(a) Omit to enter cash which has been received,

(b) Enter less amount than what actually has been received,

(c) Making fictitious entry on the payment side of the Cash Book, and

(d) Enter more amount on the credit side of Cash Book than what has actually been paid.

In large hotels it is the responsibility of the control department to check the incoming and outgoing cash. In the absence of proper control the money can be embezzled by persons dealing with cash and the hotel is liable to lead a losses.

From the control points of view the cash of a hotel can be divided into groups:

(i) Incoming cash, and

(ii) Outgoing cash.

INCOMING CASH

Incoming cash means the money received in any form, either by the chief cashier or departmental cashiers. The following are the sources of Incoming Cash:

(a) Receipt from the sale of food, beverages and services etc.

(b) Receipt from old debtors or ledger account holders.

(c) Advance from prospective customers.

(d) Rentals from concessionaires.

(e) Sundry receipts, like loan, share capital money etc.

Whatever cash is received either by the Chief Cashier or Departmental cashiers, it is the responsibility of the recipient cashier to keep it in safe custody. For the safety of cash, they are provided with either cash box or other storing facility.

For effective control every cashier is issued a Receipt Book against his signatures. Every receipt bears a consecutive serial number and each folio is in duplicate. The cashiers are supposed to issue receipts out of their receipt books in return of the money they receive either from the staff or from the customers or by post. In case a receipt is issued to an outsider, for the amount above twenty rupees, a revenue stamp is affixed. When the Receipt Book is completed, it is returned back to the control department and a new one is issued. The control department keeps an account of Receipt Books as being issued to different departments, receipt books returned by them and receipt books in their current use. This helps the control department to know whether a particular cashier has issued receipt out of his receipt book, which is in current use. This checks the misuse of receipt books and makes the work of control easy.

The departmental cashiers enter their receipts in their departmental cash books. Every day they have to deposit their days collection with the chief cashier who issues a receipt to the depositors. The chief cashier maintains the main Cash Book. It is kept either in loose leaf form or in bound book form.

Every day (except on bank holidays) the cashier is supposed to deposit the day's collection in the bank and obtain the counter-foil of pay-in-slip as a proof of deposit. He is not authorised to spend any amount out of the day's receipt.

If he requires money he may withdraw from bank. This facilitates the control of cash received. The control may make the following checks on cash received record.

MAIN CASH BOOK

DR. RECEIPT SIDE

Month & Date	Particulars	V. No.	L.F.	Cash	Bank		
					I	II	III

Fig. 34. Cash Book

PAYMENT SIDE

Month & Date	Particulars	V. No.	L.F.	Cash	Bank		
					I	II	III

Fig. 34 (a) Cash Book

(i) Check whether a receipt has been issued out of the appropriate Receipt Book for each amount entered on the debit side of the cash book.

(ii) Whether the original of the cancelled receipt is re-affixed to its copy in the Receipt Book.

(iii) Check the arithmetical accuracy of the receipt side of the cash book with the carbon copy of the receipt and other sources of information - like chance sale columns of departmental summaries, Debtors Ledger, Cash Column of Visitors Tabular Ledger etc.

(iv) Check the accuracy of subsidiary totals and grand totals.

(v) Check whether the amounts are properly dissected in the cash book.

(vi) The day's receipt deposited in the bank be checked with the counter foil of pay-in-slip.

(vii) Check the floating cash without giving prior notice to cashiers. [Generally cashiers need to have on hand a certain amount of ready cash which is known as floating cash. This floating cash is needed by them in connection with money transactions like refunding the balance to the customers, exchanging the foreign currency etc. To some cashiers this float is given every day for their shifts only and at the end of their shifts they have to deposit it back. But some cashiers are given this float for a particular period say one week or one month. All floating cash of a department should be checked simultaneously without giving prior notice.]

(viii) Check the amount of advance received from prospective customers.

Sometimes the prospective customers send advance to secure bookings. There are two practices prevalent. According to the first practice the cashier neither issues any receipt for this cash nor enters it in the cash book. He simply keeps that amount inside closed envelope in the cash box. The control cannot check this amount. The second practice, which is common today in big hotels, is that this cash is treated as normal receipt of the hotel. Proper receipt is issued out of the Receipt Book and the amount is deposited into the bank. In the latter case control is possible. This amount is checked like a normal cash received.

(ix) Verify the cheques whether they are complete in all respect and in acceptable condition.

In hotels the major part of receipts comes in the form of cheques. It is the responsibility of the Cash Office to accept or refuse the cheques according to the situations. The control can make the cashier responsible for wrong type of cheques, therefore, the following points may be kept in view while accepting the cheques—

(a) Cheques may be accepted from the persons who are in the cheque list.

(b) The cheque must be payer's own cheque.

(c) The cheque must be complete in all respect.

(d) The cheque must be in favour of the hotel and not in the personal name of any employee.

(e) Cheque must be crossed and the words 'Payee's Account Only' be written within the parallel lines on the face of the cheque.

(x) Verify the account of foreign currency with the particulars of the exchange vouchers. It is also to be checked that the bank has credited hotel's account with appropriate amount in the form of rupee in place of the foreign currency.

The control makes the cashier responsible for any type of irregularity in connection with foreign currency. Therefore, he should take the following precautions :

(a) The foreign currency that is being received is genuine.

(b) The amount is being received at approved exchange rate.

(c) Signatures must be appended by the guests on the foreign travellers cheques before him.

(d) The signatures of the guests be compared with their specimen signatures already appearing on the travellers cheques.

(e) If needed, the identity of the guest and his signatures be checked with the Passport.

OUTGOING CASH

In small hotels there is only one Cashier. He is responsible for receiving the cash as well as for making the payment. But in large hotels there are many departmental cashiers and a Chief Cashier. Generally the Chief Cashier makes all payment by cheque and the entries are posted in the cash book on the credit side. Only the minor payments are made in cash which, by nature, cannot be paid by cheque. For such petty payments, a junior cashier is appointed. He is given a fixed amount for a specific period. He makes payment out of this money and keeps a record in the Petty Cash Book. At the end of the specific period he submits the account of expenditure along with the vouchers. The chief cashier hands over an amount equal to the amount spent during the period so that petty cashier may begin the next period again with the same fixed amount. The control has to check both Main Cash Book and Petty Cash Book.

For checking the credit side of the main cash book the control has to verify the amount with the counter-foil of the cheque book and a receipt obtained for the payment. It can also be verified with the Invoices, the sanction of payment or bill passed by appropriate authority. The amount of salary can be verified with the salary register and pay bills. The amount of wages can be checked from wages record. Similarly all payments can be verified with related documents.

The control also checks the expenditure shown by the Petty Cash Book. While checking the Petty Cash Book the control will have to keep in view the following points:

(a) whether each item of expenditure is supported by a proper voucher, and whether a receipt has been obtained,

(b) whether the expenditure is justified,

(c) whether the items of expenditure are properly analysed in appropriate columns, and

(d) whether the sub-totals of analysis columns and the grand total are correct.

MODERN HOTEL LTD., NEW DELHI
PETTY CASH BOOK

Dr. Cr.

Receipts Rs.	P.	Date	Particulars	V. No.	Total Amount Rs.	P.	Postage & Telegrams	Printing & Stationary	Carriage & Cartage	?	?	Miscellaneous

Fig. 35. Petty Cash Book

CHAPTER XXXI

NIGHT AUDITOR AND HIS DUTIES

Night Auditor is an official of a hotel who verifies the correctness of the posting to the guest's accounts, checks the entries of the day's sales and verifies whether the cash collected during the day has been duly accounted for with the help of summaries, statements and other documents received from various departments during the night. In large hotels the staff of the control department works as Night Auditor but in most of the hotels the night bill clerk has to perform the duty of Night Auditor also besides his normal duties. He is called Night Auditor because he audits the day's sales at night. During the day guests are arriving and checking out at all hours and the bill clerk is always busy in posting the charges to guests accounts. It is, therefore, done in the night alone when on the one hand there is light work in the bill department and on the other the statements and summaries are received from all the departments after the close of the day. These documents are very essential tools for checking and verification. Without them the audit cannot take place.

The time at which the Night Auditor should start his work of verification of the sales depends on the time when the departmental sales of the day are closed. Generally the day's sales and accounts are closed at 12 midnight. Immediately after that the work of verification starts.

First of all the Night Bill Clerk enters into customers accounts all pending vouchers, left unposted by the previous bill clerk, as well as the vouchers that he received after starting his duty but before the close of the day. After finishing the job of posting he completes each active account by charging the room rates if it has not been charged so far for the day and the accumulated telephone charges to respective guest's account. Now he takes out the balance carry forward of each active account and closes all guests accounts for the day in the Visitors Tabular Ledger as well as in the Guests Weekly Bills. He prepares new sheets of Visitors Tabular Ledger for the coming day and opens all active accounts into them. The balances of active accounts are transferred from the previous day's Visitors Tabular Ledger to the accounts in the new Visitors Tabular Ledger. Similarly in the weekly bills also the balances carry forward of the previous day are written in balance forward columns of the new day. He then totals each debit and credit columns of each sheet of Visitors Tabular Ledger. The total of the first sheet is carried forward to the second sheet. Then the total of each debit and credit items of first and second sheets is done and the grand total of first two sheets is carried forward to the third sheet. The same process is repeated till the last sheet. The last sheet gives the picture of the grand total of each debit and credit items of the day.

Now the Night Auditor tests the arithmetical accuracy of the total of each debit and credit item appearing on the last sheet of the Visitors Tabular Ledger. For testing the arithmetical accuracy the following formula is applied—

(a) Daily Total Vertical figures = Daily Total Horizontal figures.

(b) Daily Total + Balance B/F (Dr.) - Balance B/F (Cr.) = Grand Total (Dr.) - Grand Total (Cr.)

(c) Cash + Allowances + Ledger + Transfer + Balance C/F (Dr.) - Balance C/F (Cr.) = Grand Total (Dr.) - Grand Total (Cr.)

(d) Grand total (Dr.) - Grand Total (Cr.) = Last Total (Dr.) - Last Total (Cr.)

After closing the guests accounts for the day and testing the arithmetical accuracy of the Visitors Tabular Ledger, two transcripts are prepared. One for the active accounts and the second for departed guests accounts. These Transcripts are prepared with the help of Guests bills. In small hotels one sheet is sufficient for transcript but in large hotels more than one sheet are needed. In such a case each sheet of transcript is totalled separately and the total of each sheet is carried forward to the next sheet. On the last sheet of the transcript (active accounts) the total of the transcript of the Departed guests accounts is also entered. Thus it is summarised.

The total individual items shown by Transcript are compared with the respective sale summaries of the departments. Further verification is done in the following way—

(a) The total room sale is compared with the room sale shown by Visitors Tabular Ledger, Room Count Sheet & Night Receptionist's Room Sale Report.

(b) The total of food sale is compared with the Restaurant Sale Summary, Cash Book Summary *and* Visitors Tabular Ledger Food Column.

(c) The total of bar sale is compared with Bar Allocation Sheet of Control and Cashier's Bar Sale Summary and Visitors Tabular Ledger Bar Column.

(d) The total of telephone column is compared with Telephone Traffic Sheet or Telephone Summary and Visitors Tabular Ledger Telephone Columns.

(e) The total of laundry, valet etc. columns are compared with the sales Journals of these departments and Visitors Tabular Ledger respective columns.

(f) The 'Balance B/F' Column is compared with the 'Balance C/F' column of the previous day.

(g) The total of the 'cash receipts' column is compared with the record of the Front Office cash sheet.

(h) The Allowance Vouchers are not listed in the Front Office during the day so the Night Auditor prepares a consolidated statement of all Allowance Vouchers and calculates the total. This total is compared with the allowance Column of Transcript.

In those hotels where N.C.R. Billing Machine is used in the Front Office, the Night Auditor takes reading of amount in each of the accumulating key in the machine. This reading is verified with the total of corresponding summaries of the various departments and other available records. Besides this the Night Auditor also prepares recapitulation separately for each departmental sale. These recapitulation totals are compared with the machine totals. If the amounts tally then it proves that all charges have been posted to guests accounts correctly.

The Night Auditor also prepares a Trial Balance with the help of N.C.R. Machine. The Machine Dr. total is adjusted with the machine total of cash, allowances, Transfer and ledger.

It is also the responsibility of the Night Auditor to remove the bills of those guests who have completed seventh day in the hotel and reopen new bills for them for the new week. The closing balances of the old bills are transferred to the new bills. The old original bills are placed in the mail rack for presentation to the guests. A list of such bills is also prepared. It is sent to the Income Auditor along with the carbon copy of the guests bills. He also prepares a list of those accounts which are left unpaid even after three days of the presentation of the bill. He also prepares a list of those accounts whose balances have exceeded the credit limit allowed to the guests.

After completing his work as Night Auditor, the night bill clerk sends all the Departmental Summaries, Transcript Sheet, Allocation 'Sheet', Visitors Tabular Ledger etc. to the Income Auditor along with his Night Audit Report.In hotels where N.C.R. machine is used the machine balance and Audit Roll is also sent to the Income Auditor.

CHAPTER XXXII

OPERATING RATIOS (OCCUPANCY PERCENTAGES) AND ACCOUNTING RATIOS

The management of a hotel is always interested to know the progress of the hotel, the trend of the business and the effect of their policies. This can be known by measuring the relationship between various quantities like relationship between Rooms available and Rooms sold, between Sale and Net Profit, Investment and Net Profit etc. Such relationship may be expressed by means of Ratio.

ACCOUNTING RATIOS

The Trading and Profit & Loss Account and Balance Sheet is produced annually. Trading Account shows how much profit or loss (Gross Profit/ Loss) is made during a period by transactions concerned directly with trading. The Profit & Loss Account takes into consideration the costs of the overheads and all other expenses. The final balance will show the net profit or net loss made by the hotel.

A summary of the final state of the hotel business as shown by the balances of various assets and liabilities is prepared at the end of the financial year is known as Balance Sheet. All that which is owned by the hotel are called as liabilities and all that which is possessed are called as assets. Liabilities are listed on the left hand side and assets on the right hand side. Capital and net profit are considered liabilities.

A Ratio is a number expressed in terms of another number. For example a hotel has 400 rooms and 1200 employees. The ratio between rooms to em,ployees will be 1:3. The ratio may be expressed as a rational figure or as a Percentage. The following two types of ratios are more common in hotels:

1. Operating Ratio
2. Accounting Ratio.

Operating Ratio

Operating Ratio is calculated with the help of information obtained from summaries, analysis sheets and Statements prepared every day by the various departments of a hotel. It is calculated for a short period say a day or a week.

The control department has to furnish the day's, month's and years' statistics of sales etc. to the management for their information and guidance. Rooms Occupancy Percentage, Bed Occupancy Percentage and Daily Occupancy are perhaps the most important informations that are given to the management by the Internal Auditors every day. The monthly and annual occupancy percentages are also calculated on the same lines and submitted to the management. The Federation of Hotels and Restaurant Association of India nay also require monthly progress in the form of percentages from the member hotels.

The Percentages are worked out as under:

Room Occupancy Percentage

Room Occupancy Percentage is worked out on the basis of number of lettable rooms and the number of rooms occupied by the guests. We have to like into account the total number of rooms in the hotel and from it deduct rooms occupied by the manager or rooms used for operational purposes. The result will be the number of lettable rooms. The percentage is calculated as under:

$$\text{Room Occupancy Percentage} = \frac{\text{No. of rooms occupied}}{\text{No. of lettable rooms}} \times 100$$

Example—A hotel has 170 rooms. Out of these rooms, 2 rooms are used by the manager and 18 rooms are used for operational purpose, 90 rooms occupied by the guests. Find the Room Occupancy Percentage.

Total No. of rooms in a hotel = 170

Rooms occupied for operational purpose and by manager = 18 + 2 = 20

No. of lettable rooms = 170 - 20
= 150

In a hotel out of 150 lettable rooms 90 rooms are occupied

In a hotel out of 100 lettable rooms $\frac{90\times100}{150}$ 60 rooms are occupied.

= 60% rooms occupancy.

Bed Occupancy Percentage

Bed Occupancy Percentage is worked out on the basis of total number beds available for guests and the number of beds occupied by the guests this purpose we have to take into account all the beds of single rooms, double rooms etc. the formula for calculating Bed Occupancy Percentage is as under:

$$\text{Bed Occupancy Percentage} = \frac{\text{No. of beds occupied}}{\text{Total No. of beds}} \times 100$$

Example—A hotel has 100 single lettable rooms and 50 double lettable rooms. Out of these 80 single and 35 double rooms are occupied. Work out Bed Occupancy percentage.

Beds in single rooms = 100
Beds in Double rooms (50 × 2) = 100
Total No. of beds in the hotel = 200
Beds occupied in Single rooms = 80
Beds occupied in Double rooms (35 × 2) = 70
Total No. of beds occupied. = 80 + 70
= 150

Out of 200 beds in the hotel 150 beds are occupied.

Out of 100 beds in the hotel= $\frac{150}{200}\times100$ beds will be occupied

= 75 beds

= 75% beds occupancy.

Double Occupancy Percentage

Double occupancy means rented room occupied twice at different intervals by two different persons during the day. In other words it means a room sold two times during the day. For example on 24th June a room is sold to a guest at 2 p.m. and he is charged for the day assuming 12 Noon is check in and check out time. On the same day he checks out at 5 p.m. after settling his bill. On the same day *i.e.*, 24th June another guest arrives and the same room is sold to him at 6 p.m. He is also charged room rent for one day. This is known as double occupancy of the said room. By percentage of double occupancy we mean the number of rooms occupied by two different persons at different intervals in every 100 rooms. There are two methods of calculating Double Occupancy Percentage. Some hotels calculate Double Occupancy Percentage on the total number of rooms sold but other hotels calculate Double Occupancy Percentage on the availability of total rooms in the hotel. According to the first method the formula to work out Double Occupancy Percentage is as under—

$$\frac{\text{No. of guests - No. of rooms occupied}}{\text{No. of rooms occupied}} \times 100$$

Example—A hotel has 250 lettable rooms. Out of these rooms are occupied by the 230 guests. Find the Double Occupancy Percentage on the total number of rooms sold.

No. of Guests = 230

No. of Rooms Occupied = 200

No. of rooms occupied by two persons = 230 - 200

= 30

In 200 rooms Double Occupancy is in = 30 rooms

In 100 rooms Double Occupancy will be $\frac{30}{200} \times 100$

= 15 rooms

= 15% Double Occupancy

Many hotels take into account the total number of lettable rooms available in a hotel for calculating Double Occupancy Percentage. According to this method the Double Occupancy Percentage of the hotel given in the above example can be calculated as under—

$$\text{Formula} = \frac{\text{No. of guests - No. of rooms occupied}}{\text{Total number of lettable rooms available in hotel}} \times 100$$

$$\frac{230 - 200}{250 \times 100} \times 100$$

$\frac{30}{250}$ 100 or 12 rooms

= 12% Double Occupancy.

Daily Occupancy

Daily Occupancy is calculated on the basis of the following:

(i) No. of guests brought forward in the beginning of the day from previous day,

(ii) No. of guests arrived during the day, and

(iii) No. of guests checked out during the day.

The formula is as under—

Daily Occupancy = No. of guests b/f in the beginning of the day + No. of guests arrived during the day − No. of guests checked out during the day.

Example—On 1st June in a hotel 80 guests were staying in the beginning of the day. During the day 60 guests arrived and 30 guests checked out. Find day's occupancy of 1st June.

Total No. of guests staying in the beginning of the day = 80

No. of guests arrived during the day = 60

No. of guests checked out during the day = 30

Daily Occupancy = 80 + 60 − 30 guests

= 110 guests.

Besides the above statistics some other important information is also given to the management, which is worked out as under:

(i) Average rate per room $= \frac{\text{Total rooms revenue}}{\text{No. of occupied rooms}}$

(ii) Averagerate per guest $= \frac{\text{Total revenue from the rooms}}{\text{Total No. of guests}}$

(iii) Average income per guest for food and beverages

$= \frac{\text{Total income for Food \& Beverage}}{\text{No. of guests}}$

(iv) Percentage of food andbeverage sales to room sale

$$= \frac{\text{F. \& B. sales} \times 100}{\text{Total Room sales}}$$

(v) Percentage of other income to room sales

$$= \frac{\text{All other income (except F. \& B)} \times 100}{\text{Room Sale}}$$

Accounting Ratios

The accounting data, that appears in the book, carries no meaning when it is studied separately. It becomes significant when it is considered along with other figures and converted in the form of ratio. The accounting ratios are much more meaningful when various year's ratios are tabulated and compared with previous year's ratios. Accounting ratios are calculated in respect to longer period say one year.

They are generally of two types:

1. Balance Sheet Ratios
2. Revenue Statement Ratio.

BALANCE SHEET RATIOS

They are the ratios derived from the Balance Sheet. Current Ratio, Acid Test Ratio etc. are the examples of Balance Sheet Ratios.

Current Ratio

It is also known as Working Capital Ratio or Solvency Ratio. It measures the relationship between Current Assets and Current Liabilities. Current assets are those assets which are either cash or may be converted into cash normally within a year. They include cash, stock, debtors, B/R and other liquid resources. Current liabilities are those that are normally payable within a year. Creditors, provision for taxation, B/P outstanding expenses, unclaimed dividend etc. are the examples of current liabilities.

In order to obtain Current Ratio the current assets are divided by current liabilities. Normally the ratio should be 2 : 1.

$$\text{Current Ratio} = \frac{\text{Current Assets}}{\text{Current Liabilities}}$$

Example—The current assets of a hotel are of Rs. 15,00,000 and current liabilities are of Rs. 5,00,000. Find Current Ratio.

$$\text{Current Ratio} = \frac{\text{Current Assets (Rs. 15,00,000)}}{\text{Current Liabilities (Rs. 5,00,000)}}$$

$$= \frac{3}{1} \text{ or } 3:1.$$

This result indicates that for paying a liability of Re. 1 the assets are of Rs. 3 with the hotel. This signifies the hotel's ability to meet the current obligations. This ratio is used for finding out the test of the credit strength of a hotel. The excess of current assets over current liabilities is known as Working Capital. Generally a hotel needs less working capital than a manufacturing concerns. But excess of current assets over current liabilities is essential.

In above example the working capital will be Current Assets (Rs. 15,00,000) - Current Liabilities (Rs. 5,00,000) or Rs. 10,00,000.

Current ratio only indicates the relationship between current assets and current liability. From the liquidity point of view the composition of current asset is more important. It is true that some assets are converted into cash immediately but some assets take weeks or months to be converted into cash.

Therefore it is dangerous to use current ratio alone as index of solvency. In addition to current ratio, it is essential to calculate Liquid or Acid Test Ratio.

Acid Test Ratio

It is also known as Liquid Ratio. It measures the relationship between quick or liquid assets and current liabilities. Quick assets include cash, bills receivable, debtors and other current assets which can be converted into cash immediately without difficulty. Stock is not included in quick assets. Debtors are included after making necessary provision for doubtful debts. Generally from current liabilities Bank Overdraft is excluded. Acid Test Ratio is calculated as under—

$$\text{Acid Test Ratio} = \frac{\text{Quick Assets}}{\text{Current Liabilities}}$$

Example

Current Assets =	Rs. 20,000
less Stock	Rs. 5,000

Quick Assets	15,000
Current Liabilities	7,000
less Bank Overdraft	2,000
Net Current Liabilities	5,000

$$\text{Acid Test Ratio} = \frac{\text{Quick Assets (Rs. 15,000)}}{\text{Current Liabilities (Rs. 5,000)}}$$

$$= 3 : 1$$

This ratio is the true test of solvency of a business. If liquid or quick assets are more than current liabilities, it indicates that the financial position of the hotel is satisfactory. It helps in measuring to what extent liquid assets are available to meet the immediate liabilities without delay.

Proprietary Ratio

It is the ratio of funds belonging to shareholders to the total assets of the hotel company. Funds belonging to shareholders means Share Capital + Reserves + Surplus (both of Capital and Revenue nature) – Losses. External equity of funds payable to outsiders is not taken into account. It is calculated as under—

$$\text{Proprietary Fund} = \frac{\text{Proprietors Funds}}{\text{Total Assets}}$$

$$\text{Or } \frac{\text{Equity Share Capital+ Pref. share Cap. + Gen. Res. + Profit - Loss}}{\text{Total Assets}}$$

Example

	Rs.		Rs.
Equity Share Capital	5,00,000	Gen. Reserve	2,00,000
Pref. Share Capital	4,00,000	Total Assets	18,00,000
P & L Account (Profit)	1,00,000		

Find Proprietary Ratio

$$\text{Proprietary Ratio} = \frac{\text{Rs. } 5,00,000 + 4,00,000 + 2,00,000 + 1,00,000}{18,00,000}$$

$$= \frac{12,00,000}{18,00,000}$$

$$= \frac{2}{3} \text{ or } 0.67 \text{ (nearest)}$$

Thus out of Re. 1 employed in the business shareholders contribution is 0.67 whereas the creditors have contributed the remaining 0 33

Highest the ratio, better it is for the business.

REVENUE STATEMENT RATIOS

They are the ratios which indicate the profitability and efficiency of control over expenses. They are calculated on the basis of the figures of Profit and Loss Account. Some of the Revenue Statement Ratios are given below:

Gross Profit Ratio

This ratio is calculated by comparing the gross profit with net sale. It is also known as 'Turn Over Ratio'. If Gross Profit Ratio of only one department is to be calculated the Gross Profit and net sale of that particular department are taken into account. The formula is as under—

$$\text{Gross Profit Ratio} = \frac{\text{Gross Profit (18,00,000)}}{\text{Net Sale (30,00,000)}} \times 100$$

$$\text{Percentage of Gross Profit on net sale} = \frac{18,00,000}{30,00,000} \times 100$$

$$= 60\ \%$$

Generally the gross profit margin of alcoholic beverages and food is more than the minor revenue producing departments. Higher Gross Profit Ratio is always better.

Net Profit Ratio

It measures the relationship between Net Profit and Net Sale. The formula is given below—

$$\text{Net Profit Ratio} = \frac{\text{Net Profit (3,00,000)}}{\text{Net Sale (12,00,000)}} \times 100$$

$$\text{Percentage of Net Profit on sale} = \frac{3,00,000}{12,00,000} \times 100$$

$$= 25\%$$

This indicates the hotel's performance and its sale promotion.

Stock Turn Over Ratio

It is also known as Inventory Turn Over Ratio. It is calculated to measure the speed with which the stock moves through the business during a Particular period. It is calculated by dividing the cost of the goods sold by average stock.

$$\text{Stock Turn Over Ratio} = \frac{\text{Cost of goods sold}}{\text{Average stock}}$$

The cost of goods sold is calculated as under:

Opening Stock + Purchases - Closing Stock

The average stock is calculated as under:

(Opening Stock + Closing stock) + 2

Example

Cost of goods sold =	Rs. 3,60,000
Average stock =	Rs. 30,000

$$\text{Ratio} = \frac{3,60,000}{30,000} \text{ or 12 times}$$

This ratio reveals the excess of stock and accumulation of damaged or out-dated stock. Too much stock or insufficient stock is always dangerous. It is a wise step to keep only that quantity of stock which may cope up with the sale.

CHAPTER XXXIII

HOTEL CREDIT AND CREDIT SECURITY MEASURES

The term credit means the sale of goods on faith and time given for payment of goods sold on trust. In other words, postponement or payment on good faith is known as credit.

In ordinary business, one would consider various aspects of a debtor such as financial stability and goodwill in the market etc., before selling goods on credit to him. If the trader personally knows the purchaser and is fully satisfied with his financial position then only credit is allowed.

The position of a hotel is entirely different. In hotel the credit is allowed to almost all guests, except a few who seem to be of doubtful nature. Every guest enters the hotel premises without the obligation to pay at the time of his entry. He enjoys the facilities of accommodation, food and other services all on credit. The hotel has to make arrangements for the comfortable stay of its unknown guests. Therefore hotel credit is more risky affair than a commercial house.

In ordinary commercial house the articles, which are sold, have physical property. In case the guest fails to make the payment, the article can be taken back by the trader and can be resold to other customer. While the hotel credit involves the sale of room, services, food and beverages, which once sold either having no physical property or having the nature of loosing the utility, cannot be repossessed or taken back in the event of failure of their guests to pay.

For example in ordinary business if the trader sells a book or a piece of furniture on credit and the purchaser does not make payment within specified time then the trader can take back his article because it has physical property. Of course some depreciation takes place but the loss is not much. It can be resold to other customer. In case of a hotel if the room, food or services are sold on credit and the guest does not make payment, then the articles and services cannot be taken back or repossessed. Either such items have no physical property or they loose their utility.

Not only this, the hotel credit multiplies in various ways. It is not like an ordinary commercial house where the credit of fixed amount is allowed at one or limited times. In hotel the credit to customer is allowed throughout the period of his stay. Therefore, the risk is more and it starts from the time the guest is registered and occupies a room till he checks out after settling his bill.

It is an opinion of some people that there is no risk so long the guest is present in the hotel but it is not true because the guest, whose intention is bad, can depart without informing the hotel after leaving some baggage to give false impression of his stay. On account of such reasons it is important for a hotel to take necessary credit security measures since the time a guest is registered and allowed credit facilities.

The following credit security measures may be adopted by a hotel:—

1. In case where the guest arrives without prior reservation and has light or no luggage with him or seems to be of doubtful nature, he should be asked to pay for his stay in advance.

   No doubt it is very difficult task to welcome a guest warmly in the hotel as soon as he arrives on the one hand and then suddenly asks to pay in advance for what he wants. But the front office has to say politely and tactfully for an advance in order to safeguard the interest of the hotel.

2. There is a credit limit for the guests. If the guests' account shows unusual accumulation of credit amount within a short period then it should be referred to appropriate authority for investigation and recovery where necessary.

3. In safeguarding the hotel's interest the check pad system should be introduced. If the transaction is credit transaction then the check should be signed by the guest in token of his having received the service on credit.

4. If the guest's bill remains unpaid for more than three days after presentation of it, the Credit Security Department should be informed and it should be ascertained that the guest pays the outstanding amount without further delay.

5. A cash advance on behalf of a guest (V.P.O.) should be made only to a limited extent. Preferably it should be given on behalf of those

guests who have a credit balance in their accounts. The hotel should never take the delivery of V.P.P. (value payable post or parcel) on behalf of a guest after making payment unless the front office is advised by the guest to accept the V.P.P. and charge from his credit balance. In no case the V.P.P. should be accepted on behalf of those who have no credit balance.

6. The hotel should take following necessary precautions in connection with cheques that it receives from the guests :—
   (a) The cheques should be accepted from those guests only who are in the cheque list (It is a list of persons and establishments from whom cheques can be accepted. It is prepared on the basis of sound financial position of well known guests).
   (b) The cheques that are accepted should be crossed and the words 'Account Payee only' should be written within two parallel lines to prevent any fraudulent endorsement.
   (c) Third party cheques should not be accepted.
   (d) Post-dated cheques, stale cheques and cheques where words or figures are altered or erased should not be accepted.
   (e) The details of the cheques should be recorded in a Cheques Received Book to supplement sufficient information in the event of the cheque is lost or destroyed.

CHAPTER XXXIV

COMPUTERS IN HOTELS

The use of computers in large hotels is on increase and many luxury hotels have introduced computers for their day-to-day business transactions especially in the areas of finance, accounting, audit and control. Today we find that manual posting procedures advanced to mechanical posting machines to electronic processing procedure based on data relay. The night audit has become a convenient push button operation. It allows the night auditor a chance to audit, not merely post entries for numerous checks/ vouchers.

A computer is a device that can perform very simple operations such as multiplication of two numbers or the comparison of two words. It can store data such as set of words or set of numbers. It can retain information so that sometime in the future the data will be available for processing or printing. They may cause the computer to print any specific part on request. The simple operations that are within the computer's capacity can be performed on the data stored inside, although the sequence of operation that it is to perform must be specified by a person, such a request is called a programme. The sequence will have to be expressed in a form that can be understood by the computer. Such a form is called a computer language.

There are different types of computers is use. They vary according to the size of the hotel. A computer stores information to which additional data can be added or substituted. The operation is done with a high speed. Since computers are capable of storing vast amount of data which can be recalled instantly, it makes the accounting and control work less time consuming and less mentally tiring. All transactions from purchase of perishable and non-Perishable items to the preparation of financial statements, are kept in a computer. When some information is altered for any reason, all the other related records in the computer are at the same time up dated. Computers having visual display units and print out facilities are preferred by hotels.

The computer systems are composed of two basic elements:

(i) Software (programme)

(ii) Hardware.

Software refers to the instructions within a computer system that tells the hardware devices what to do, how to do and when to do it. These instructions are written in a computer language to enable the rapid processing of data.

Computer hardware is visible, movable and easier to distinguish than computer software. It includes:

(i) Central Processing Unit (CPU)

(ii) Input Device

(iii) Output Device.

The central processing is the brain of the system and is responsible for controlling all other system components. The CPU performs all arithmetical computations and logical functions available through computerization.

In a computerised hotel system there are Disk Drives (DD) and Disk Pack Units (DPU). The information is stored in random order and is retrievable also in random fashion. The most common input device that work in the hotel business is the Cathode Ray Tube (CRT). It is a Composer of a television like Video screen and a type-writer like key-board, it is visible on screen. As an operator, you can edit and verify the input information on the screen before transmitting it to the CPU for processing. A line printing terminal (LPT) is needed to print out the information in a hard copy. It produces the printed pages quite rapidly.

Thus, every computer may be regarded as including the following components:

Fig. 36. Models of Computer

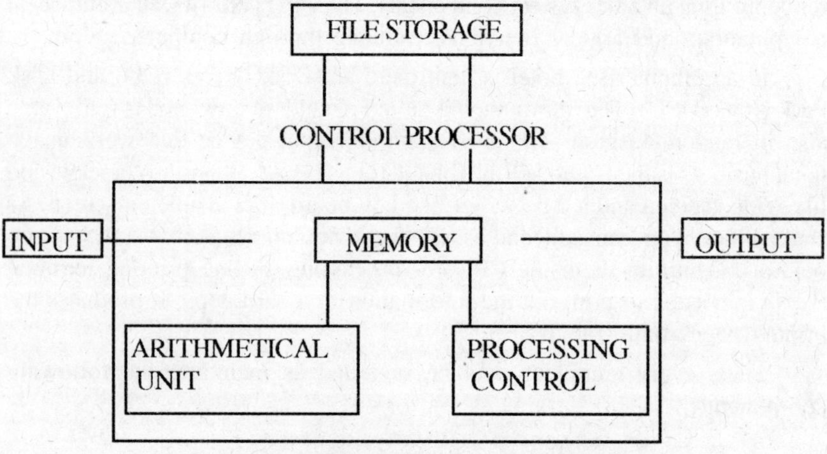

Fig. 37. Basic Elements of a Computer

Input Device

Some means of feeding the information into the system.

Central Processing Unit

The area that information is transferred to be programmed and for calculation to be carried out.

File Storage

Tapes, discs etc. which provide bulk storage area for the users records.

Output Device

Some means of display or printing out results.

These basic elements of a computer are displayed in Fig. 37

Information is fed into the computer by means of a key-board, similar to that of a typewriter. The codes are used for the purpose of simplification. Once these codes are mastered, the storing and recalling of information is relatively simple. For example WB Code will bring forth a list of weekly bills. By using the code you can post all charges to the guest bill which are automatically updated. At a selective time in the evening you can have the computer charge the appropriate room and other predetermined rates to all accounts by using appropriate codes. In computer language technically it is called as 'terming'.

Objects of Data Processing

The main objects of data processing in a hotel are:

(i) transformation of data to information

(ii) a reduction in turn around time

(iii) a reduction in data handling.

BENEFITS OF COMPUTERISED ACCOUNTING

Once the business transactions of a hotel are computerised, following benefits could easily be achieved:

(i) Reduction in communication and posting errors

(ii) Audit procedures are built into the system.

(iii) Reduction in erroneous postings.

(iv) Automatic postings of bank rates and taxes.

(v) Accurate legible guest folios.

(vi) Speedy check out.

(vii) Facilitation of accounts settlement.

(viii) Entire phase of accounting process can easily he monitored at any time by the management.

Guest Accounting

In computerised hotel accounting all postings are done at the point of sale by means of an electronic input of data from the operating department. The audit in hotels is an outgoing process and details can be obtained instantly throughout the day.

Cashier's reconciliation account status and accounts receivable control can be monitored and used by management at any time. The overall guest accounting process is illustrated in Fig. 38.

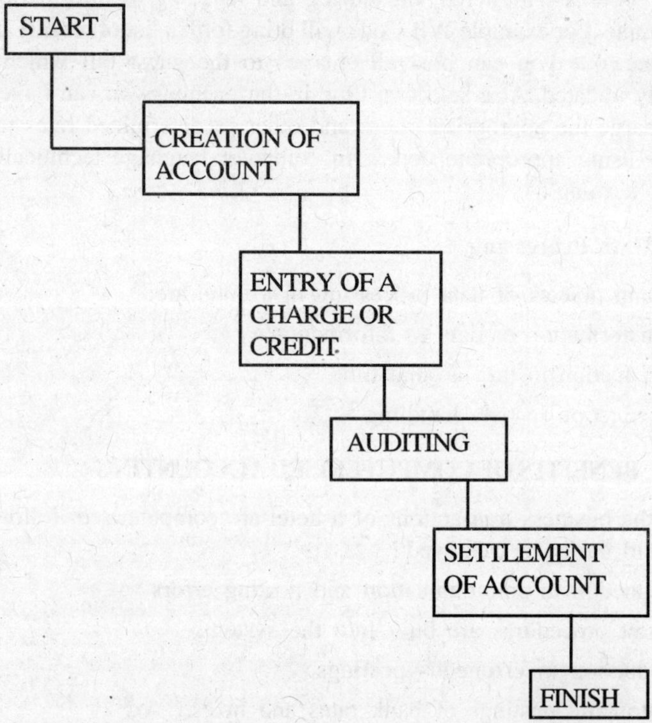

Fig. 38. Computerised Guest Accounting Process

Thus, in a computerised hotel accounting, it is convenient to accomplish guest accounting function through :

(i) the direct guest charge posting

(ii) night auditing

(iii) electronic guest accounting settlement

(iv) folio display and printing

(v) preparation of various reports

(vi) departmental accounting

(vii) Preparation of final statements.

In this system the CRT replaces the posting machine and produces vouchers only after they have reached the front desk.

Basically, it involves the following steps :

(i) *Room Number entry.* You need not sort the voucher by room number because the system works on random entry.

(ii) *Identification.* The first two letters of guest's last name are entered.

(iii) *Posting Code.* Each posting key is assigned a number which must be entered.

(iv) *Reference Code.* The serial number of voucher is entered

(v) *Posting.* The amount of the charge is entered completing the transactions.

On departure, a guest asks for a bill. You may code the appropriate key and the required bill comes out as a print out which can be passed on to the guest for payment. If you like to scrutinize, the copy of the bill can be seen on the VDU.

Telephone Charges

The computer can be linked to the telephone system. This will facilitate automatic recording of all outgoing calls. It is also possible to register the number dialled and the length of the call.

The settlement process is important because it is the guest's final contact with the hotel. The computerised system minimises the check out time and data handling procedures. These goals are achieved through the pre-printing of folios, for guest. There is an automatic transfer function within the operating system. When the guest approaches the desk to check out, on inquiry into the folio package will reveal whether a guest folio must be printed out or not.

Simultaneously the Housekeeping Department is notified of the check out. If there are additional postings, the new folio balance will be displayed and a hard copy printed for settlement. It produces a detailed guest folio with debit (Dr.) and Credit (Cr.) references notations. Thus a computerised pre-checked procedure enhances the check out routine of the hotel guests.

Accounts and Statistics

The computer is so programmed that it can produce all the accounting data, analyse it and present it in the required format. It can produce a volume of statistics such as room sale. Some statistics are confidential and are available only to the management. This is available only if the correct code is keyed in otherwise the computer will not divulge this information. This code may be kept very secret and known only to those entitled to this information. A selected sample of reports generated from computerised system of hotel accounting are:

Guest Bill

It is also called as guest folio and is maintained in a memory system during the guest's entire stay. Charges can be posted from point of sale. This increases the efficiency of the hotel. There is no need to transport voucher physically. The system automatically searches for the complete folio, you have to enter only the name and room number of the guest. These folios are printed at high speed at the time of check out of customer.

Revenue Report

It summarises all guest charges such as room charges, restaurant and bar telephone, laundry, sundry sales, service charges and other services. Guest charges can be attributed to individual areas, so that departmental individual totals are available. This report also contains the various room statistics, traditionally calculated by the night auditor, such as:

- Occupancy percentage
- Average room rate
- Percentage double occupancy.

City Ledger Summary Report

This report contains city ledger accounts indicating credit card summaries.

Revenue Centre Report

This report indicates the following by operating departments: Cash Charge Paid out total.

Guest Account Control Report

This report reflects the net outstanding balances of the guest account ledger and summarises the debts, credit transfers and settlement affecting the guest accounts.

Late Charge Bills

These accounts contain unpaid accounts for guest that have checked out. All such accounts are automatically transferred to the city ledger and bills are printed.

Management Information

Through computerised accounting, a hotel can easily obtain management information relating to reservations, room management and front office accounting. It provides management with up-to-date and projected data, which enables accountants and management to exercise strict control transactions.

The management information system has following benefits management:

(i) better control over revenues.

(ii) control over receivables and payables.

(iii) decision-making.

Therefore, main reports which could be prepared for management's use are:

(i) Revenue Analysis

(ii) Operating Statistics

(iii) Financial Analysis

(iv) High Balance Reports

(v) Sales-mix Reports

(vi) Trial Balance Reports

(vii) Daily Report.

CHAPTER XXXV

PURCHASE PROCEDURE AND RECORD

In hotels the purchases are either made for cash or on credit. The method of purchasing goods in hotels is similar to ordinary commercial houses. If purchases are made for cash, the entry is passed in the Cash Book on the credit side and in the Purchase Account on the debit side. In hotels most of the goods are purchased on credit. In small hotels the credit purchase of goods, which are meant for resale, are recorded in the purchase book and the credit purchases of assets are recorded in the Journal Proper. But in some large hotels one Sub Journal is maintained, known as Purchase Journal. In this Purchase Journal, all credit purchases, including goods for resale, consumable goods, cleaning materials and assets are recorded in a tabular form. At the end of the month one entry is passed in Journal Proper. The totals of different accounting heads like purchase of provisions, beverages, cleaning material, different assets are debited and sundry creditors account (Accounts Payable) is credited. The Purchase Journal is maintained in a tabular form.

In hotels all purchases are made by the Purchase Department on the basis of requisition duly sanctioned by the appropriate authority. Two types of articles are purchased by the Purchase Department. One is either raw material or consumable articles and the second is the assets.

Purchase of Raw Material or Consumable Articles

The purchases of raw material or consumable articles are made on the basis of Standard Purchase Specifications like description of quality, size, weigh etc. from the purchasing agents or suppliers. Every good hotel employs Purchasing agents generally for a year, specially for the supply of perishable goods like vegetables, fruits, chicken, mutton, eggs etc. Purchases which are meant for sale are of two types. One is the purchase of raw material like groceries, provisions etc. which are converted into other shape for sale and the second, items like drinks, cigarettes etc. that are sold in their original form.

The purchase policy adopted by the management will depend on the size, type and style of the hotel and the quantities and commodities involved Generally, following methods are used by hotels:

(1) contract purchasing
(2) quotations and tenders
(3) periodical purchasing
(4) requirement purchasing
(5) marketing purchasing.

In case of those articles for which purchasing agents are not employed quotations are obtained at least from three sellers. This does not apply where the value of an item is very small and it is required urgently. In such a case the Purchase Manager is authorised to place an order without inviting quotations. In case the articles are purchased from the Central Government or State Government or Government undertaking or Autonomous bodies of Government, it is not necessary to call for quotations.

In case of quotations the purchase department ensures that the quotations received correspond to the required specifications including quality, make, quantity required, the date of supply, mode of delivery etc. In case of provisions and food-stuffs the samples may be tested by the medical officer before accepting the quotations. If the quotations are accepted, the purchase department issues purchase order. Four copies of the purchase order are made by the purchase department according to the practice of most of the hotels. The original copy is sent to the supplier. One copy is sent to the Stores. One copy is sent to the Accounts department along with the sanction order of purchase of goods and the last copy is retained in the order book.

Receipt of Consumable Goods

Consumable goods, purchased by a hotel, are of two types. The first type of consumable goods are provisions, groceries, merchandise etc. which are not perishable. They go to the stores from the gate and afterwards they are supplied to the respective departments. The second type of consumable goods fresh vegetables, fresh fruits, chicken, dairy products etc. They are sent to the respective departments from the gate directly.

On receiving the purchase order the goods are collected and packed by the supplier. He prepares an Invoice/Challan. The goods are sent to the hotel along with the Invoice/Challan. As soon as the first type of consumable goods like groceries, merchandise etc. reach the gate of the hotel along with the copy of Challan or Invoice the Time-keeper checks the goods. He certifies that the goods are in order by affixing the stamp on the Invoice. The Time-keeper also makes 4 copies of Goods Received Voucher (G.R.V.). Three copies of G.R.V. are sent to the stores along with the goods and Invoice. Last copy is retained by the Time-keeper in the G.R.V. Book. As soon as the goods are received along with Invoice they are checked and verified by the Store-keeper with the purchase order to ensure that the goods received are correct in quantity and quality specifications. The goods are also physically verified by the store-keeper with the purchase order to ensure that the goods received are correct in quantity and quality specifications. The goods are also physically verified with the Invoice and purchase order. Sometimes he himself checks the quality of goods. But when he is not competent to check the quality himself then he takes the help of a competent person from the department concerned or other experts. After verifying the goods they are entered into the Stock Register. The Store-keeper has to give a certificate on the Invoice that the goods have been received, the quantity is correct, the quality has been tested and they have been entered in the Stock Register on a particular page. The store-keeper has to sign and affix the stamp on the Invoice and G.R.V. Then the Invoice is passed on to Accounts Office for payment. The Invoice is accompanied by a copy of G.R.V.

The Accounts Department will see whether the G.R.V. and Invoice contain the stamp of Time Office as well as Stores and the signature of Time-keeper, Store-keeper and the person who has verified the goods according to specifications. The invoice and challan are compared with the copy of purchase order.

The second type of consumable goods, that are purchased by a hotel, are of perishable nature. Such perishable goods like vegetables, fresh fruits, butter, cream etc. are received by the time office. They are compared and checked with the challan or invoice by the time office at the entrance gate. The time office maintains a Fresh Supplies Register and enters the supplies in this register. Such fresh supplies are not sent to the stores but they are sent directly to the kitchen or concerned department along with challan. The kitchen or the concerned departments compare the items with the challan and ensure that the goods are correct in quantity, quality and specifications. Such departments maintain Consumption Register. The entry is passed in this register. The In-charge of the department signs the challan and sends it to the accounts department. After a few days, a consolidated bill of the challans of fixed duration is received by the Accounts Department. It compares the date-wise entries of each challan with the bill.

Purchase of Assets

For the purchase of assets like machinery, furniture, silver ware, crockery, cutlery, line etc., an asset purchase requisition is made. Along with this purchase requisition, justification for the purchase of the said asset is to be given. It is also to be stated whether purchase of the said asset exists in the budget. The proper sanctioning authority has to approve it. After that it is sent to the purchase department. The purchase department invites tenders. When the tender is approved then the order is placed. On receiving the asset along with the invoice and the delivery challan, the asset is properly checked. It is entered in the property register. For each type of asset individual register is maintained. In invoice similar type of certificate along with page number of property register is given. The invoice, delivery challan etc. are sent to the accounts department.

Purchase Journal

The Accounts Department maintains a Purchase Journal. It is a book of original record in which all credit purchases are entered. As said above some hotels, for convenience, asset purchased on credit are also entered in this purchase journal. It is maintained in a columnar form. The Invoice, copy of G.R.V. etc. are verified according to the method stated above. After verification, the entry is passed in the Purchase Journal (Suppliers Journal).

The amount of Invoice is entered in the column of sundry creditors for supplies (credit column.). The L.F., G.R.V. No., date and name of suppliers etc. are filled in at the same time with the help of Invoice and G.R.V. The amount is entered in the respective analysis columns.

Suppose sugar worth Rs. 1,000 is purchased from M/s Raman Bros. on Jan. 2, on credit. The amount shown by Invoice *i.e.,* Rs. 1,000 will be entered in the credit column of Sundry Creditors for supplies. G.R.V. No., date etc. will be written in respective columns. In particular column the name of supplier *i.e.,* M/s Raman Bros, will be written and in analysis column the amount i.*e.,* Rs. 1,000 will be debited by writing it in provision (sugar) column. Thus Suppliers account is credited and sugar (an item of provision) is debited. Similarly the purchase of furniture of Rs. 8,000 from M/s Rawan Bros. and purchase of rice of Rs. 2,000 from M/s Mehra Bros. will be entered in the columns on Jan. 2.

As soon as the above entries are passed in the Purchase Journal, it means purchase of sugar, furniture and rice have been debited and sundry creditors for supplies (M/s Raman Bros. M/s Rawat Bros. and M/s Mehra Bros.) individual accounts have been credited. At this time Dr. Column of Sundry creditors for suppliers, Payment Voucher No. Column, Paid *vide* cheque No.

Columns are left blank if these columns are made in the Purchase Journal (all hotels do not adopt this pattern of Purchase Journal).

At the end of the month each analysis column is totalled and one entry is passed in the General Journal in a consolidated form as under:

GENERAL JOURNAL

Date	Particulars	L.F.	Dr. Rs.	Cr. Rs.
20....	Dr.		3,000	
Jan..31	Provision A/c			
	(Sugar Rs. 1,000)			
	(Rice Rs. 2,000)			
	Furniture (Asset) A/c Dr.		8,000	
	To Sundry Creditors A/c			11,000

A hotel maintains two types of ledgers—Personal ledger and Impersonal Ledger. The personal ledgers are of two types in large hotels. One is Debtors ledger and the other Creditors Ledger. In the above example Creditors personal accounts (M/s Raman Bros A/c, M/s Rawat Bros A/c and M/s Mehra Bros A/c) are opened in the Creditors ledger. The second type of ledger is Impersonal ledger. In large hotels two types of impersonal ledgers are maintained—One is Trade ledger (in this ledger accounts relating to purchases, sales, income and expenses are opened) and the other General ledger (in this ledger accounts relating to assets and liabilities are maintained).

In the above example provision account (total purchase of sugar, rice etc. under the analysis column of provision) will be opened in Trade ledger. Furniture (asset) account will be opened in the General ledger.

In some hotels later on control account (Sundry creditors for supplies account) is opened with the total credit purchases. But in other hotels a

MODERN HOTEL LTD., NEW DELHI

STOCK REGISTER

Date...............

Name of Article–Sugar

Month & Date	Particulars	Invoice No.	Receipt			Issue		Balance	Remarks
			Quantity	Rate	Amount	Quantity	Deptt.		
20........	To Bal. b/f							30 kg	
Jan. 1	To Purchase	115	40 kg	Rs.10/kg	400	–	–	70 kg	Daurala suger pur-chased
" 1									

Fig.39. Stock Register

MODERN HOTEL LIMITED, NEW DELHI

PURCHASE (SUPPLIERS) JOURNAL

Sundry Creditors for suppliers Dr. Rs.	Cr. Rs.	Payment Voucher	L.F.	G.R.V.	Date	Particulars	Paid	Analysis: Provisions Rice	Sugar	Flour	Cleaning matcrials	Furniure	Remarks
					20 –								
	1,000		5	125	Jan. 2	M/s Raman Bros.			1,000				
	8,000		6	126	Jan. 2	M/s Rawat Bros.						8,000	
	2,000		7	127	Jan. 2	M/s Mehra Bros.		2,000					

Fig. 40 Purchase (Suppliers) Journal

Sundry creditors list is prepared to find out total amount of creditors for Balance Sheet.

CREDITORS LEDGER

M/S RAMAN BROS A/C

Date	Particulars	J.F.	Dr. Rs.	Cr. Rs.	Dr/Cr. Rs.	Balance Rs.
Jan. 2	By Purchases as per Purchase Journal (Sugar)			1,000	Cr.	1,000

M/S RAWAT BOOKS A/C

Date	Particulars	J.F.	Dr.	Cr. Rs.	Dr/Cr. Rs.	Balance Rs. Rs.
Jan. 2	By Purchase of Furniture			8,000	Cr.	8,000

M/s Mehra Bros A/C

Date	Particulars	J.F.	Dr. Rs.	Cr. Rs.	Dr/Cr. Rs.	Balance
Jan. 2	By Purchase as per Purchase Journal (Rice)		2,000		Cr.	2,000

TRADE LEDGER

Provision A/C

Date	Particulars	J.F.	Dr. (Rs)	Cr. (Rs.)	Dr./Cr.	Balance
Jan. 2	To Sundries as per Purchase Journal		3,000		Dr.	3,000

Furniture A/C

Date	Particulars	J.F.	Dr. Rs.	Cr. Rs.	Dr/Cr. Rs.	Balance Rs.
Jan. 2	To Sundries as per Purchase Journal		8,000		Dr.	8,000

After passing entries in the respective ledger accounts, the payment is made. For making the payment, the Accountant has to prepare a payment voucher or pay order, which is to be approved by the Accounts Officer or Accounts Manager. After approval a cheque is prepared which is signed by the Account Manager/Officer, and one or more authorised signatories. The Cashier prepares a Journal Voucher. In Journal Voucher the Accounts Payable A/c (individual account in Subsidiary ledger) is debit Bank A/c is credited.

Journal Voucher

Date ....

Particulars	Dr.	Cr.
	Rs.	Rs.
Debit—Accounts Payable A/c	1,000	
(M/s Raman & Bros.)		
Credit—Bank A/c		1,000
	1,000	1,000
Cashier Accountant	Finance	Manager

The cheques is sent to the creditor and entry is passed in the cash book on the credit side, in the bank column.

Cash Book

Dr. Cr.

Date	Particular	Cash	Bank	Date	Particulars	Cash	Bank
	To Bal. b/d	10,000	75,000	......	By Accounts Payable	......	1,000

Procedure for payment is the same for all items of purchases, supplies and assets.

In some cases for the items of fresh supplies, an advance is deposited by the hotel with the supplier. Suppose a hotel likes to purchase 50 litres of milk every day from the 'Fresh Milk Supply Agency'. The agreed rate is Rs. 4 per litre. The said 'Milk Supply Agency' wants that the hotel should deposit Rs. 6,200 with them as an advance for Jan. The hotel will send a cheque of Rs. 6,200 to Fresh Milk Supply Agency. As soon as the said advance is sent the entry will be passed in the Cash Book on the credit side.

Cash Book

Dr.

Date	Particulars	V.N.	L.F.	Cash	Bank
20– Jan.	To Bal. b/d			25,000	80,000

Cr.

Date	Particulars	V.N.	L.F.	Cash	Bank
20— Jan.	By Advance to Fresh Milk Supply Agency (Jan. 1 to Jan. 31)				6,200

During the month when the milk is received by the hotel, the entries are passed in the books of account like other fresh supplies. At the end of the month one adjusting entry is passed by debiting the particular head say F. & B. Fresh Supply of Milk A/c and crediting Advance to Fresh Milk Supply Agency A/c.

F & B Fresh Milk Supply A/c Dr.	6,200
To Advance to Fresh Milk Supply Agency A/c	6,200

Similar type of record is maintained for other fresh supplies also where advance is paid by a hotel to the respective suppliers.

In the previous example, if sugar is purchased from Raman & Bros for Rs. 1000, furniture is purchased for Rs. 8000 from Rawat Bros and Rice is purchased for Rs. 2000 from Mehra Bros all on Credit, the Ledger posting

CHAPTER XXXVI

RECORD OF INCOME

A hotel is a commercial enterprise and gets its revenues from various services which basically comprise:

(1) accommodation sale or room sales

(2) food sales

(3) beverage sales

(4) sale of laundry services

(5) telephone services

(6) miscellaneous incomes.

Apart from the income derived from above items, the hotel enjoys additional revenues from leasing or renting shops or show cases arranged or within the establishments and also investment in other concerns, thus often receiving various incomes. All such incomes are received from the guests either in cash or on credit. If it is a cash sale, the entry is passed in the Cash Book of the respective department on the receipt side. On the other hand if it is a credit sale to a guest, the entry is passed in the respective Guest Weekly Bill and Visitors Tabular Ledger with the help of check or voucher. The department enters the sale in the departmental sale summary.

In some hotels both Guest Weekly Bills and Visitors Tabular Ledger are maintained by the front office Bill Department. As soon as any transaction takes place, the entry is passed in the Guest Weekly Bill as well as in the customer's account in the Visitors Tabular Ledger. At the end of the day Recapitulation of Guest Ledger Transcript is prepared. Besides this a record of transfer is also prepared. In most of the hotels today only Guest Weekly Bills are maintained. In that case at the end of the day Guest Transcript is done as given in previous pages. Before making the payment to any of them the Trial Balance may be prepared as given below:

Trial Balance

as on 31st Jan. 20—

Ledger Accounts/Particulars	L.F.	Dr. Rs.	Cr. Rs.
Sundry Creditors Account			11,000
Raman Bros. Rs. 1,000			
Rawat Bros. Rs. 8,000			
Mehra Bros. Rs. 2,000			
Provision Account		3,000	
Furniture Account		8,000	
		11,000	11,000

Sheet is prepared with the help of Guest Bills. This resembles with Recapitulation of Guest Ledger Transcript. The total column discloses the individual sale of each department and the total sale of the hotel of the day.

The Transcript is sent to the Accounts Department after completing the night Audit. Accounts Department maintains one Income Journal on monthly basis. It contains horizontal columns for each head of income like Room sale, Food sale, Laundry sale, Telephone sale etc. Vertically it contain column for each day of the month and one column for the total. For example if it is the month of January, then this monthly Income Journal will have 31 vertical columns for 31 days of January and one for total. The daily departmental income from sale shown by Transcript is transferred to this Income Journal in the respective column of the day. For example the income of various departmental sale shown by the Transcript of 1st Jan. 20— will be transferred to the column of 1st Jan. 20—. Similarly the sale of each day transferred to this Income Journal. At the end of the month the total of each debit and credit column is done. Thus the total column of Income Journal reveals the total sale of the month, the total of city ledger (Account receivable) and cash received during the month.

This monthly income from various departments is posted in the individual accounts like—Room sale A/c, Food sale A/c etc. as shown in the illustration in following pages. But before posting to ledger accounts one consolidated Journal entry is passed in the following way—

Cash A/c	Dr.	
City Ledger A/c	Dr.	
Allowance A/c	Dr.	
To Room Sale A/c		....
To Food Sale A/c		....
To Laundry Sale A/c		....

Since Cash Book is maintained in a hotel, there is no need of preparing Cash A/c. During the year the cash sale, receipt from the City Ledger account holders or receipt from other sources are recorded in the Cash Book. The payment of various expenses and Sales Tax paid to the Government are also recorded in this Cash Book. Therefore, the balance shown by Cash Book at the end of the year or when required is transferred to the Trial Balance.

In City Ledger the individual accounts of Debtors are opened. The posting is done everyday in the individual accounts on the debit side. During the year, whenever money is received from the City Ledger Account holders, the entry is passed in the Cash Book on the debit side and in the individual debtors account on the credit side. If some account holders do not pay part of their debts, then their accounts show a debit balance at the end of year. With the help of these debit balances a Debtors List is prepared. The total of Debtors List is transferred to the Trial Balance under the head Sundry Debtors.

Allowance means credit given to customers accounts either by way of some concession or for any other reason. It is given to the customers at the time of settlement of their bills. Suppose a guest has to pay a bill of Rs. 2000 including Rs. 1000 for apartment. If he is being given an allowance of Rs. 100 on apartment, then Rs. 1900 only will be received in cash and will be entered in the Cash Book or Cash Column. In Allowance Column Rs. 100 will be shown. In the Guest Ledger Transcript the sale of apartment will be shown at full value i.e., Rs. 1000 and sale of other items Rs. 1000 but Rs. 100 will be shown in Allowance Column and Rs. 1900 in the Cash Column. The same will be copied in the Income Journal of the day. If during the month there is no other item of allowance, then at the end of the month the total column will show an allowance of Rs. 100. The Cash will be less by Rs. 100 than the total sale. Allowance Account is opened in the ledger like Allowance on Apartment A/c, Allowance on Food A/c, Allowance on Laundry services A/c etc. These Allowance Accounts are shown in the Trial Balance. At the time of preparing Final Accounts, these allowances are not shown as loss on the debit side of Profit & Loss Account but are deducted from the respective sales heads (Apartment sale, Food sale, Laundry service sale etc.). In the above example the Ledger Account balance of Apartment sale was Rs. 1000 and Allowance on Apartment was Rs. 100. It will be shown in Trading and Profit & Loss Account on the credit side as under:

By Room Sale	1000	
Less Allowance	100	900

According to this method a hotel can know the total figure of Allowance as well as the individual figures of allowances of all heads. These figures can be preserved and can be compared with the figures of the past years.

Individual departmental sales accounts are opened in the trade ledger like Room Sale Account, Food Sale Account, Laundry Sale A/c etc. The posting is done on monthly basis from the income Journal as under:

Room Sale A/c

Date	Particulars	V.No.	J.F.	Dr.	Cr.	Dr./Cr.	Balance
20—					Rs.		Rs.
Jan\31	By amount as per Income Journal				40,000	Cr.	35,000
Feb. 28	By Amount as per Income Journal				40,000	Cr.	75,000

The income of each month of the department is posted to the respective departmental sales account. At the end of the year the amount shown by Balance column on the last day of the year will disclose the total sale of the particular department. This total income is transferred to the Trial Balance. The method of recording income has been given in the following example:

JOURNAL

Date	*Particulars*	*L.F.*	*Dr.*	*Cr.*
20 –			Rs.	Rs.
Jan. 31	Balance (b/f and c/f)		8,000	1,800
	Cash A/c Dr.		45,600	
	City Ledger A/c Dr.		1,000	
	To Room, Sale A/c			30,000
	To Food Sale A/c			20,000
	To Sales Tax A/c			14,00
	To Local Call A/c			500
	To Laundry			900
			54,600	54,600

MODERN HOTEL LIMITED, NEW DELHI

Recapitulation of Guest Ledger

INCOME

Number Rooms	Number Persons	Sheet No.	Room	Food	Sales Tax	Local Tel. Call	Laundary	Daily Total	Bal. B/F.	Total Dr.	Cash	Allowance	Transfer to city Ledger	Bal. C/F	Total Cr.
3	3	1	300	220	15	4	10	549	111	660	200	--	100	360	660
2	4	2	1100	180	13	5	20	1318	98	1416	116	--	900	400	1416
2	2	3	200	100	7	1	--	308	12	320	120	--	--	200	320
Total			1600	500	35	10	30	2175	221	2396	436	--	1000	960	2396

Record of Transfer

Guest Ledger Page No.	Endorser Name	Endorser G.R. No.	Endorsee	City Ledger Amount Rs.	City Ledger Room No.	Authority letter No.	Remarks
1	Mr. Gaurav (Manager)	115 Bill No. 25	M/s Surject Book Depot (Regd.) HKS Publication	100	102	R/P 205 dt...	
2	Mr.M.Mehra	126 Bill No. 35	M/s Mehra Bros.	900	116	M/B 192 dt...	
				1000			

MODERN HOTEL LIMITED, NEW DELHI

Income Journal for the month of Jan. 20 ...

Date	Room Rent	Food Sale	Soft drink	Sales Tax	Local Call	Laundry Total	Daily Total	Balance b/f	Total Debit	Cash	Allowance	Transfer	Balance c/f	Total Credit	Short	Excess
Jan.																
1	1600	500	--	35	10	30	2175	2396	436		1000		960	2396	--	--
2																
3																
31																
Total	30,000	20,000	--	1400	500	900	52,800		1800	54,600	--	1000	8000	54,600		----

Cash Book

Dr. Analysis

Date	Particulars	L.F.	Front Office	Restau.	Misc.	Cash	Bank	Memo. Drs./ Crs.
Jan.								
31	To Front Office		45,000			45,600		
31	To Cash	C					45,600	
31	To Rahul						100	
	(Receipt No. 806)							
						45,600	45,600	

Cash Book

Cr.

Date	Particulars	L.F.				Cash	Bank	Memo. Drs./ Crs.
Jan.								
31	By Bank	C				45,600		
31	By Sales Tax (Cheque No.)........						14,00	
31	By Balance c/d						44,300	
						45,600	45,700	

CITY LEDGER

Account of Mr. Gaurav
Address–BI–48 Paschim Vihar
New Delhi

Authorised Signatory–General Manager letter No. R/P 205
Paying Authority–M/s Surjeet Book Depot (Regd.) HKS

1	2	3	4	5	6	7	8	9	10	11	12
Date	Bill No. Cheque No.	Room No. Date	Authority Ref.	Particulars	L.F.	Dr. Rs.	Com-mission	Dr. Rs.	Dr. Cr.	Bal	Remarks
Jan.											
31	25	102	R/P 205 dt...	Mr. Gaurav, Manager		100					Received
31	A/2115	Jan. 31	State Bank	Receipt No.....				100		Nil	Cheque

Account of Mr. M. Mehra
Address–Kamla Ashram, Naini Tal

Authorised Signatory–Finance Manager M/B 102 dt...
Paying Authority–M/s. Mehra Bros.

1	2	3	4	5	6	7	8	9	10	11	12
Jan. 31	35	116	M/B 192	Mr. M. Mehra, Manager		900			Dr.	900	

TRADE LEDGER

Room Sales Account

Date	Particulars	V.No.	J.F.	Dr.	Cr.	Dr./Cr.	Blance
20–				Rs.	Rs.		Rs.
Jan.31	By Amt. as per Income Journal				30,000	Cr.	30,000

Food Sales Account

1	2	3	4	5	6	7	8
Jan. 31	By Amt.as per Income Journal				Rs.		Rs.
					20,000	Cr.	20,000

Sales Tax Account

1	2	3	4	5	6	7	8
Jan. 31	By Amt. as per Income Journal				1400		
Jan. 31	To Bank (Cheque No. ...)			1400			Nil

Local Telephone Call Account

1	2	3	4	5	6	7	8
Jan. 31	By Amt. as per Income Journal				500	Cr.	500

Laundry Sale Account

1	2	3	4	5	6	7	8
Jan. 31 Income	By Amt. as per Journal				900	Cr.	900

Guest Ledger Account

1	2	3	4	5	6	7	8
Ian. 31	Income Journal Jan. 31			8,000	1800	Dr.	6,200

CHAPTER XXXVII

FOREIGN EXCHANGE AND HOTELS*

Foreign Exchange means foreign currency. This foreign currency includes all coins, currency notes, bank drafts, travellers cheques etc. of foreign countries. The Foreign Exchange Regulation Act, 1973 provides the statutory basis for exchange control which is operated by Reserve Bank of India through Banks, Travel Agencies, Hotels etc., which are allowed to deal in Foreign Exchange. It came into force from January 1, 1974 repealing the Act of 1947. This Act applies to whole of India as well as to all citizens of India residing abroad and branches/agencies outside India of those companies which are registered or incorporated in India. Any Bank or Travel Agency or Hotel, whosoever, likes to deal in Foreign Exchange, has to obtain a licence from the Reserve Bank of India. The Reserve Bank of India under-section 7 of Foreign Exchange Regulation Act, 1973 issues licence to the applicant to purchase the Foreign Exchange. The licences are of two categories:

1. Authorised Dealers in Foreign Exchange.
2. Restricted Money Changers.

Banks are issued the first category licence. They are the Authorised dealers in Foreign Exchange. They can buy and sell the foreign currency at the current rate.

Hotels are issued Restricted Money Changers Licence. It is known as R.L.M. The hotels, which obtain Restricted Money Changer Licence, can Purchase Foreign Exchange from the customers and sell it to only those who are Authorised Dealers in Foreign Exchange ***i.e.,*** banks. Such approved hotels are entitled to use certain percentage of the Foreign Exchange earned by

---

* Readers' are advised to refer latest rules and regulations regarding foreign exchange.

them for the purpose of their publicity abroad, promotional tours of their officers/ agents abroad and import of goods or equipment subject to the approval of the Apartment of Tourism.

Every money changer has a minimum limit of dealing of Foreign Exchange. If the dealing is less than the minimum limit, then its licence is cancelled.

As said above, hotels get Restricted Money Changers Licence and can receive the payment of their bills in Foreign Exchange from foreign guests The hotels which are licence holders, have to fulfil the following conditions—

1. Foreign Exchange is to be accepted from foreign customers on account of the payment of their hotel bills.
2. When the foreigners pay their bills in foreign currency, the balance can be returned to them in Indian currency. In case the foreign guest requests the hotel that the balance be refunded to him in foreign currency on account of some special circumstances, then the hotel may advise the guest that he can use this refunded Indian currency for meeting his petty expenses like paying the taxi charges etc. and the balance of Indian Currency left with him can be converted into foreign currency at the time of leaving India at the Airport.
3. The rates of purchase of foreign currency notes, coins, travellers cheques etc. should be displayed at a prominent place or near the cash counter at which money changing business is conducted.
4. The foreign currency has to be sold to Authorised dealers in Foreign Exchange (banks) on the next working day.
5. Foreign currency should be accepted at the rate not lower than the rates offered by their bank.
6. All purchase or sale of foreign currency will be at the risk of the hotel.
7. Monthly statements of foreign currency, purchased from the guests and sold to Authorised dealers, should be submitted to the Reserve Bank of India not later than 10th, of the following month in a prescribed proforma.

There is no legal restriction on the amount of foreign currency or travellers cheques etc. that a tourist may bring into India, provided he makes declaration in the Currency Declaration Form given to him on arrival in India by the Custom Authorities. This will enable the foreigner not only to exchange the foreign currency brought in by him but also to take back the unspent currency, out of India on departure. Cash, Bank Cheques and Travellers

Cheque up to US $ 1000 or equivalent need not be entered in the Currency Declaration Form at the time of entry in India.

The foreign guests are required to pay hotel bills in Foreign Exchange. But some foreign customers are exempted to pay in foreign currency. Therefore foreign customers can be divided into two categories: (1) Exempted customers and (2) Non-exempted customers.

Exempted Customers

Following customers are exempted to pay their hotel bills in Foreign Exchange. They can pay their bills in Indian currency :—

(a) Foreign nationals employed in India and getting salary in Indian currency.

(b) Diplomats and official guests of diplomatic mission in India including officers of United Nations and other International organisations.

(c) National of those countries with whom India has Rupee Agreement. Rupee Agreement means we can pay or receive the money from those countries or people of those countries in the form of Rupee. The names of these countries are—U.S.S.R., Poland, Romania, Czechoslovakia, German Democratic Republic. Besides the above, customers from Nepal and Bhutan can also pay in Indian currency.

(d) Employees of shipping companies and airlines and their flying crew.

(e) Foreign national on a visit to India at the invitation of the Central Government and State Government.

(f) Foreign students studying in India on Government of India scholarship.

(g) Foreign guests of exporters enjoying blanket permit facility granted by Reserve Bank.

(h) Foreign national on a visit to India at the invitation of any person resident in India, if payment is made on behalf of foreign national by Indian host provided he has obtained general or special permission from the Reserve Bank of India.

Non-Exempted Customers

All foreign guests, except the customers of exempted categories, have to make payment of their hotel bills in Foreign Exchange.

Payment may be accepted from foreign guests in any of the undermentioned permitted currencies:

1. Australian dollars
2. Austraian schillings
3. Bahrein dinars
4. Belgian francs
5. Canadian dollars
6. Danish kroners
7. Deutsche mark
8. French franc
9. Hongkong dollars
10. Italian lira
11. Japanese yen.
12. Kuwaiti dinars
13. Malaysian dollars
14. Netherlands guildars
15. Norwegian kroners
16. U.K. Pound sterling
17. Singapore dollars
18. Swedish kroners
19. Swiss francs
20. U.S. dollars
21. ________
22. ________

When a foreign guest comes to a hotel for stay, he is required to pay his hotel bill in Foreign Exchange if he is not in an exempted category. It is necessary to make this point clear that a foreign guest has to make the payment of apartment (accommodation) charges in Foreign Exchange, which appear in a hotel bill (Guest Weekly Bill). If he takes meal in a Restaurant of a hotel and makes the payment in the Restaurant then he is at liberty to make the payment either in foreign currency or in Indian currency which is derived from the foreign currency. But if he signs the Restaurant Bill and the amount is debited in his weekly bill then he has to make the payment of the whole amount (including food charges etc.) appearing in the weekly bill in foreign currency.

It is the responsibility of the hotel to make foreign guest aware that according to Government of India Rule the foreigners are required to pay their hotel bills in Foreign Exchange. They can be made aware of it by mentioning this rule in Guest Registration Form, Welcome Slip, Tariff Card etc.

When a foreign guest makes payment in Foreign Exchange, the hotel has to give an Encashment Certificate to the payer whether he asks for it or not. In case where the balance amount after adjustment towards bills for goods supplied/services rendered, is refunded in Indians currency, item 'C' of form ECR (Encashment Certificate) should be filled in with a remark indicating refund in Indian currency. This certificate should be serially numbered and issued on the official printed letter head of the hotel holding Restricted Money changer licence. A duplicate copy of such certificate of encashment should be kept with the money changer (Hotel) in book form for production to Reserve Bank, as and when called for.

ENCASHMENT CERTIFICATE

Serial No.......... Date ....

We hereby certify that we have purchased today foreign currency from..........holder of Passport No...........Nationality..... and paid net amount in rupees after adjusting the amount towards settlement of bills for goods supplied/services rendered as per details given below:

A. Details of Foreign Currency notes/coins/travellers cheques purchased.

Currency purchased (indicating clearly notes and travellers cheques separately)	Amount	Rate	Rupee equivalent
1	2	3	4

Total.........

B. Details of adjustment made towards settlement of bill for goods supplied/services rendered.

Bill Nos.	Date(s)	Amount
1	2	3

Total.........

C. Net amount paid in rupees..........Amount in words..........(Total under A minus Total under B)

(Stamp and Signature of Authorised Money Changer)

Note: This certificate should be preserved by the holder to facilitate reconversion of the rupee balance (out of the amount stated at C) if any, into foreign currency at the time of departure from India and/or for payment of passage/freight cost in rupee, if necessary.

This certificate is preserved by the hotel to facilitate reconversion of the Rupee balance (amount stated in the encashment certificate under the heading 'C') into foreign currency at the time of departure from India or payment of passage or freight cost in Rupee.

A hotel has to maintain RLM-1, RLM-2, RLM-3, RLM-4, RLM-5, RLM-6, RLM-7 in respect of their money changing business.

RLM 1—It is a Daily Summary and Balance Book of foreign currency notes and coins.

RLM 2—It is a Daily Summary and Balance Book of Foreign Travellers Cheques.

RLM 3—It is a Register of Purchases of Foreign Currency from the public. At the end of the day the posting of purchases of Foreign Exchange is made in RLM 3 register. It contains individual columns for the currency of each country which is acceptable. It also contains the column for each day of a month. Every day posting is done in the respective column of that date and currency. During the month if one sheet is completed then the total of each amount column is done and carried forward to the next page or sheet. Thus up to the last day of the month posting is done. On the last day, the grand total of each amount column is done. On the last sheet, at the bottom, summary is prepared. The total of Rupee equivalent column should be equal to the summary of Indian currency total column. One copy of RLM 3 is detached from the register and forwarded to the Reserve Bank of India at the end of each month.

RLM 4—It is a Register of sale of foreign currency notes and coins to Authorised dealers. In simple language we can say that it is a copy of Bank Pay-in-slip. The duplicate copy of Pay-in-slip is detached and forwarded to the Reserve Bank of India at the end of each month.

RLM 5—It is a Register of foreign travellers cheques surrendered to Authorised dealers (banks).

RLM 6—It is a monthly statement of purchases and sales of foreign currency notes and coins. It indicates the balance of different currencies in the beginning of the month, purchases of foreign currency notes and coins during the month, payment of balance amount to customers during the month, sale to Authorised dealers (banks) during the month and Balance at the end of the month. This statement must reach the Reserve Bank not later than 10th of the following month.

ECR

Name and address of the money changer	(To be issued by Restricted Money Changer) RBI Lincence No..........

RLM 7—It is a monthly statement of Travellers Cheques purchased from the guests and surrendered to Authorised dealers. It also shows the opening balance of Travellers Cheques of each country in the beginning of the month, purchases during the month, amount surrendered to Authorised Dealers during the month and closing balance at the end of the month. This monthly statement must reach the Reserve Bank not later than 10th of the following month.

Reserve Bank is authorised to send an Inspecting Officer to inspect the books of accounts and other documents of money changers. The hotels which are Restricted Money Changers should assist and extend cooperation to the Inspecting Officer to carry out inspection smoothly. The hotel must show all books of accounts, registers, documents and furnish all information or answer questions relating to money changing business to the Inspecting Officer.

Restricted Money Changers are not permitted to sell the foreign currency notes, coins etc. to the public. They have to surrender their collections of foreign currency notes and coins etc. to the Authorised dealers in foreign exchange immediately not later than the next working day.

Restricted money changers are authorised to transact the money changing business only at the location indicated in the licence granted to them by Reserve Bank of India.